Christian Philosophy

Christian Philosophy

Bouvert Regulas

2013

CHRISTIAN PHILOSOPHY

Christian Philosophy – Published by the Rev. Dr. Ashish Amos of the Indian Society for Promoting Christian Knowledge (ISPCK), Post Box 1585, 1654 Madarsa Road, Kashmere Gate, Delhi-110006.

© Author, 2013

All rights reserved. No part of this book may be reproduced or transmitted in any form or by any means, electronic, mechanical, photocopying, recording, or by any information storage and retrieval system, without the prior permission in writing from the publisher.

The views expressed in the book are those of the author and the publisher takes no responsibility for any of the statements.

ISBN : 978-81-8465-299-4

Laser typeset by
ISPCK, Post Box 1585, 1654, Madarsa Road, Kashmere Gate, Delhi-110006.
Tel: 23866322/23
e-mail: *ashish@ispck.org.in   ella@ispck.org.in*
website: *www.ispck.org.in*

Contents

Preface .... *vii*

Introduction .... *ix*

PART 1
History of Philosophy

1.	Definitions	...	3
2.	Nature of Philosophy	...	36
3.	Origin of Western Philosophy	...	48

PART 2
History of Christian Philosophy

4.	Early Christian Philosophy	...	73
5.	Medieval Christian Philosophy	...	95
6.	Reformational Christian Philosophy	...	123
7.	Modern Christian Philosophy	...	140
8.	Postmodern Christian Philosophy	...	159
9.	Contemporary Christian Philosophy	...	224
10.	Christian Philosophy	...	241

Conclusion	...	286
Endnotes	...	291
Bibliography	...	299

encouraged me during my student days to write articles for Christian journals. Dr. Thannickal, who corrected me when I was wrong and rebuked me when I was negligent, is an ideal Christian and a role model for me. I cannot forget the influence and leadership input of Dr. Ken R. Gnanakan, my philosophy professor, who helped me in studying Religion and Philosophy at Acts Academy at the post-graduate and doctoral levels. Also, I am thankful to my wife, Maheswari Regulas, for her support for this project. Above all, I thank God for enabling me to write this book. I dedicate this book to my Master, Lord Jesus Christ.

Bouvert Regulas
Andaman, India

Preface

There is an inner longing in man for something deeper; our hearts' desire must come into line with the will of God. This book is a call to that kind of mental realignment. It gives the reader the ability to understand Christian Philosophy and false philosophies. This is the primary purpose of the book.

The main objectives of this book are listed below.

- Help the reader understand the origin and growth of Christian philosophy

- Help the reader understand the relation between theology and philosophy

- Help the reader study the nature of reality, theistic belief and validity of Christian faith and experience

- Help the reader do a comparative study of religion and philosophy.

- Help the reader understand Christian Philosophy.

This book can be used as a textbook in Bible colleges and seminaries at the post-graduate level. Pastors and teachers of the Word will also find this book highly useful.

I am grateful to my friends and colleagues for their encouragement and appreciation. I am also grateful to all those who encouraged me and made helpful suggestions. I am thankful to Dr. Rev. Ashish Amos, Ella Sonawarne, Rajesh Williams and the entire staff of ISPCK, Delhi, for publishing this book. Also, I am indebted to Dr. John S. Thannickal, who first taught me philosophy at Bethel Bible College, Punalur, and

Introduction

Philosophy has crowded out the truth of Christian faith. Reason has its legitimate place in science and everyday affairs. It has its true function in grasping and evaluating what is set before it. But it is not the sole criterion of truth. As the ruler of social sciences, philosophy has become a necessary condition for survival in our times of biblical religion and morality. God did not create man without reason, or without making it obligatory upon him to obey reason in all those matters with respect to which reason can be a sufficient guide. Philosophy, in so far as it is the perfection of human reason, is the perfection of a God-given gift. Only the function of philosophy is differently conceived, depending upon whether that function is understood as ultimately ministerial to teachings of divine revelation, or as identical with an intrinsic rationality that itself is the most divine thing in human life.

The most fruitful and fateful product of Greek thought is its amalgamation with Jewish and oriental ideas in the great cosmopolitan centres of the Greek world. There are evidences that this process was going on in the cities of Asia, Syria and Egypt, but the only extensive account of it is found in the works of Philo, the Jewish philosopher of Alexandria. He tried to graft Plato's idealism upon Hebrew monotheism. He started with Plato's two principles, pure being or God and pre-existing matter. In his endeavour to bridge the gulf between them, he interposed between God and the world the powers of God, goodness and justice; and to gather these into a final unity. In the formation of this conception, he merged the Platonic idea of the good, the Stoic world-reason and a number of Jewish ideas, the glory, the word, the name of God, the heavenly man and the great high priest, and personified the whole as the one mediator between God and the world. Christian thought laid hold of this idea and employed it as its master-category for the interpretation of the person.

The history of philosophy is the study of philosophical ideas and concepts through time. Western, religious or secular ideas have had their own unique schools of philosophy, arrived at through both inheritance and through independent discovery. Such theories have grown from different premises and approaches; examples of which include rationalism. The history of philosophy seeks to catalogue and classify such developments, and therefore, understand the development of philosophical ideas through time. Although the word 'philosophy' originates in the Western tradition, many figures in the history of other cultures have addressed similar topics in similar ways. The usefulness of dividing philosophy into Western Philosophy and Asian philosophy, in contrast to the notion that there can be one philosophy, not many, is open to challenge. To say this is not to deny that there are important traditions in philosophy that are intimately bound up with historical and geographical circumstances. At the same time, there are examples of philosophers who are persecuted by the majority in their geographical circumstances and stand against the common opinions and practices of their time and place. Many claim that geographical and time notions of Western and Asian philosophy are rather vague and imprecise, thereby committing the fallacy of over-generalisation.

Different schoolmen have different approaches. There is no one generally-accepted system. The term "scholasticism" refers to those medieval schools of thought that were concerned with defining and systematising the Christian understanding of reality. The Realists followed Plato in holding that universals were real. The things that we see and touch are really copies of an eternal archetype, which in some way has brought them into being. The Nominalists took the opposite view. They rejected the idea of universals altogether. They believed that there was no such thing as goodness or greenness apart from particular good or green things, and that all such general, abstract words were merely a manner of speaking. The conceptualists steered a middle course. They took the view of Aristotle as universals do, in fact, being to the realm of thought; but they also stand for something that is actually there that gives unity to the diversity of the world of our experience. Idealism seemed to present a spiritual bulwark against the rising tides of materialism and secularism. It seemed to offer a rational basis for Christianity. With Hegel, the history of the World, which is the autobiography of the Absolute Spirit, is an integral part of philosophical reflection. Rejecting idealism, other philosophers, many working from outside the university, initiated lines of thought that would occupy academic philosophy in the early and mid-

20th century: In the late nineteenth century and early twentieth century, several forms of pragmatic philosophy arose. Husserl initiated the school of phenomenology. Kierkegaard and Nietzsche laid the groundwork for existentialism.

The early church was as divided as we are today over the issue of accepting or rejecting philosophy. Tertullian (160-220 AD) was against philosophy and made the famous statement that 'Jerusalem has nothing to do with Athens.' At the same time, Justin Martyr (100-165 AD), Clement of Alexandria (150-203 AD) and Origen (185-254 AD) echo the opposite extreme, whereby philosophy was seen as preparatory for Christian teaching, especially through the logos doctrine. Religion insists more on behaviour than on belief. Orthodoxy is not confined to the defining of faith. It includes the living of it. No religion has claim to our allegiance if it does not produce a tradition of humanity and social responsibility. Philosopher of religion is the religious philosopher. Christian theology is religious philosophy. So, we can say that Christian theologian is the religious philosopher. All these philosophic lines of thought lead us into the formation of a Christian philosophy.

Part 1

History of Philosophy

The first part of the book focuses on the origin and definitions of Philosophy. Philosophy with its general outlook is briefly sketched in this part, which will help us in understanding what philosophy is and how it is related to other disciplines. The introduction of terms such as 'philosopher' and 'philosophy' has been ascribed to the Greek thinker Pythagoras. The term 'philosophy' was made famous by Plato's and Aristotle's volume of written works that survived for over two thousand years. 'Philosopher' replaced the word 'sophist' (*sophoi*), which was used to describe 'wise men', teachers of rhetoric, who were important in Athenian democracy.

Socrates had used the word 'philosopher' for himself in order to distinguish himself from others. Plato's dialogues often used the two terms to contrast the sophists—who are devoted to seeking wisdom from those who arrogantly and falsely claim to have it, from the philosopher—really wise men or great thinkers. Socrates frequently characterised the sophists as incompetents or charlatans, who hid their ignorance behind word play and flattery, and so convinced others of what was baseless or untrue. In the beginning, the word was used to express the love for knowledge. Philosophers in Greece were known as such because of their love for knowledge. Different philosophers have expressed different opinions about the origin of philosophy. According to Plato, philosophy finds its origin in the wonder or curiosity created in the mind of man.

All schools of philosophy arrived at through independent discovery. Such theories have grown from different premises and approaches; examples of which include rationalism, such as supernaturalistic philosophies and religions. Philosophy in its true nature had never been purely abstract theoretical inquiry and, positively speaking, has been always concerned with human problems like suffering and freedom. This part of the book will help us understand what philosophy is and how it is related to other disciplines.

Chapter 1
Definitions

This chapter focuses on various definitions and branches of philosophy. It also deals with how philosophy is related to other disciplines.

It is rather difficult to give a proper definition of a term, as scholars have different opinions and definitions of the term. An attempt has been made in this part of the book to put down the definitions as concisely and as simply as possible.

A Christian philosopher must go through the terms defined below as he or she faces the current issues of the modern world. In order to have a Christian philosophy that has biblical foundations, a Christian philosopher must spend his or her time and energy on gaining insights into the necessary and current terminologies of the Christian philosophical world.

In the ancient world, the most influential division of philosophy was the Stoics' division of philosophy into logic, ethics, and physics, including both natural science and metaphysics. In contemporary philosophy, specialties within the field are more commonly divided into metaphysics, epistemology, ethics and aesthetics. Logic is sometimes included as another main branch of philosophy, sometimes as a separate science that philosophers often happen to work on and sometimes just as a characteristically philosophical method applying to all branches of philosophy.

Basic Terminologies

Philosophy

The word "philosophy" itself is of Greek origin; *philosophia* is a compound of *philos* (friend or lover) and *sophia* (wisdom). The ancient Greek word *philosophia* literally means 'the love of wisdom.' Thus philosophy means 'love for knowledge' or 'wisdom', or 'passion for learning.' When the term "philosophy" is used in an academic context, it typically refers to the philosophical tradition that began with ancient Greeks. Philosophy is an enquiry into reality as a whole. This has important implications. Philosophy is an intellectual discipline that is concerned with the nature of reality and the investigation of the general principles of knowledge and existence. Philosophy is not a science, like chemistry or biology but tests or experiments of possibilities that indicate whether certain hypotheses are true or false, tenable or untenable. Dr. Radhakrishnan said that *sophia* or wisdom is not mere knowledge. It is knowledge lived. It is the way of life where valid knowledge is the condition of just action.[1] Others state that philosophy examines the process of inquiry itself. Still others argue that philosophy is continuous with the best practices in every intellectual field. In the beginning, the word was used to express the love of a particular person or group for knowledge. The inhabitants of Athens (Greece) were called philosophers for their love for knowledge.

Though a single definition of philosophy is controversial and the field has historically expanded and changed depending upon what kinds of questions were interesting or relevant in a given era, it is generally agreed that philosophy is a method rather than a set of claims, propositions or theories. Its investigations are based upon reason, striving to make no unexamined assumptions and no leaps based on faith or pure analogy. Philosophy means 'to think about a subject in a reasonable way with the aim of developing between philosophical reflection and other types of working scientifically on technology and culture.'[2] In its technical sense, the term 'philosophy' is now used for the conscious endeavour of thought, by the speculative process, to interpret the whole of human experience as a consistent and systematic unity, which would be the ultimate truth of all that may be known. The term is also used, in a wider sense, for all interpretations of experience, or parts of experience, however obtained, whether by revelation, intuition or unconscious speculation. Some of the ruling conceptions of speculation, such as God, spirit, order, causation, true and false and good and evil, were not discovered by reason, but given in experience.

Philosophy is reflection on experience in order to apprehend its ultimate meaning. It is a rational examination of reality as a whole, aiming at a systematic set of maxims, principles or beliefs. Philosophy is the rational discussion of ultimate questions. Even a superficial discussion of this definition involves us in actually doing philosophy. Philosophy is an enquiry into reality as a whole. This has important implications. Philosophy tries to look at that reality which includes but transcends such spheres.[3] To Bertrand Russell, philosophy is a logical knowledge of basic principles of different sciences. Some encyclopedias have described philosophy in terms of intellectual inquiry and the use of critical analysis and reasoning, as well as dialogue or introspection, to solve intractable and fundamental problems. Still others argue that philosophy is continuous with the best practices in every intellectual field. Although the word "philosophy" originates in the Western tradition, many figures in the history of the East have addressed similar topics in similar ways. When the term "philosophy" is used in an academic context, it typically refers to the philosophical tradition began with the ancient Greeks that provided us with an abundance of manuscripts and archeological sites to study and research.

According to Ludwig Wittgenstein, the object of philosophy is the logical clarification of thoughts. Philosophy is not a theory but an activity. A philosophical work consists essentially of elucidations. The result of philosophy is not a number of philosophical propositions, but to make propositions clear. Philosophy should make clear and delimit sharply the thoughts that otherwise are, as it were, opaque and blurred. *Friedrich Nietzsche said that grasping* the limits of reason is truly philosophy. *To George Berkley,* Philosophy is nothing but the study of wisdom and truth. *According to John D. Barrowarrow,* "the point of philosophy is to start with something so simple as to seem not worth stating, and to end with something so paradoxical that no one will believe it." Francis Bacon said that Philosophy is nothing but a copy and a reflection of nature, and adds nothing of its own, but is merely a repetition and echo. According to Arthur Schopenhauer, "to repeat abstractly, universally, and distinctly in concept the whole inner nature of the world, and thus to deposit it as a reflected image in permanent concepts always ready for the faculty of reason, this and nothing else is philosophy." Philosophy is reflection on experience in order to apprehend the ultimate meaning.[4] Here is a longer definition: Philosophy is a racial examination of reality as a whole, aiming at a systematic set of universal maxims, principles or beliefs. The definition of the word "philosophy" in English has changed over the centuries; in medieval times, any research outside the fields of theology or medicine was called "philosophy."

Although the word "philosophy" originated in the Western tradition, many figures in the history of other cultures have addressed similar topics in similar ways. The philosophers of the Far East are discussed in Eastern Philosophy, while the philosophers of North Africa and the Near East, because of their strong interactions with Europe, are usually considered as part of Western Philosophy. Philosophy in Sanskrit or Hindi is known as *Darshan*, which means knowledge of the truth. *Darshan* has been derived from the Sanskrit root, *drish*, which means to see. It has also been called metaphysics (*Tatvajnan*), which means the knowledge of the real or truth. So, both the combined will mean "true knowledge" or "reliable knowledge", which is generally gained by seeing. Western philosophers have recognised *Darshan* as a science. So the word "philosophy" has been used as science or *Darshan*. Various western philosophers have defined philosophy differently. According to Aristotle, Philosophy is the science that discovers the real nature of supernatural things. Indian philosophers have viewed philosophy from a different angle. Manu has called it *Samkhyak Darshan* and knowledge leading to salvation and in the absence of which man cannot free himself from earthly bondage. Modern Indian philosophers considering enquiry, logic and critical exposition as necessary components of philosophy, i.e., *Darshan* have made its definition even more comprehensive. The famous philosopher of this age, Dr. Radhakrishnan, has defined philosophy as a critical exposition of reality. It is not merely bookish knowledge, but the result of logical thinking and contemplation. For him, philosophy has for its function the ordinary life and guidance of action. It sits at the helm and directs our course through the chances of the world. The ideas of thinkers are evolved in the process of their history. We must learn not only to reverence them, but to acquire their spirit.[5]

Theology

Theology is the combination of two Greek words: *theos* (God) and *logos* (word or science). Theology is the science of God. It is the study of God in relation to His universe. Theology is considered as the queen of the science, and Systematic Theology is the crown of the queen. In other word, in theology, a man organises his thoughts concerning God and His universe. Theology rests upon a solid objective basis. Theology is commonly divided into four parts:

(1) *Exegetical Theology*: It directly occupies the study of the sacred text. It includes the study of biblical languages, Biblical Anthropology, Biblical Hermeneutics and Biblical Theology.

(2) *Historical Theology*: It traces the history of God's people in the Bible and of the Church. It embraces Biblical History; Church History, History of Missions and History of doctrines and of creeds.

(3) *Systematic Theology*: It takes the materials furnished by exegetical and Historical Theology and arranges them in a logical order, the ten great heads of theological study.

(4) *Practical Theology*: It treats of the application of theology in the regeneration, sanctification, edification, education and service of man. It embraces Homiletics, Church Organisation, Christian Education and Missions.

Theology is the study that deals with the logical coherence of beliefs about God, God's attributes and God's work in creation, redemption and providence. Koyama redefines theology as a "reflection on history in the light of the Word of God." This is a definition in reverse that relativises theology. Consequently, the focus of theology tends to move from God and His infallible and immutable Word to depraved man's religion, art, poetry and ideologies. The study of theology is a complex task. It seems best to see the unity of the Bible. Theology should see the unfolding of God's revelation; it should be based on a study of the Bible; and it should draw the study together around the developing focus of the theocratic kingdom. There is no evidence of an organised study of biblical theology in the Bible. The earliest evidence is found with Irenaeus (A. D. 130-200) who recognised the progressive revelation of God. Later, Augustine (A. D. 354-430) suggested five historical periods of divine revelation. During the Reformation, the issues were basically soteriological, and thus biblical theology as a science did not develop during that time.

The Bible should be the primary source book for our theology. A proper understanding of God's Word as it relates to our socio-cultural context is imperative. The Bible is the divine norm for both our God-ward and man-ward relationships. The answers we give to persons in any religious context must be scripturally based. Another important aspect that needs the attention of the theologian is the question of social responsibility of the Church. A clear theology needs to be developed that sets forth a practical plan of action for eradicating the ills of society. This theology must be both macro-structural and micro-ethical when speaking of issues involving inequality and injustice.

Religion

Every community builds up its own religion. Most religions include the following elements:

- Beliefs of the community about God.
- Beliefs of the community about God's relationship with the world.
- Ways in which people worship God and pray to him.
- Rules that the community follows because of its beliefs about God.
- The community believes that places and people are holy.

The English word "religion" derives from the Latin *religio*. Servius said that this word came from *lig*, which means "to bind." It signifies the binding relationship between man and God. Cicero suggested that it was derived from *leg*, which means 'to take up, gather, count, or observe.' It suggests the observation of the signs of divine communication.[6]

We should remember this whenever we discuss the religious practices of another person, especially when that person belongs to a religion different from our own. The relationship between God and every particular thing or living creature is unique, with an individual quality of its own. Each individual has his own experience of God, but he or she can share it with others and practice it with others in the community. Religion is both an individual and social activity. The religious attitude to life can be summed up as follows[7]: (i) People worship God as transcendent; (ii) People feel dependent upon God; (iii) People feel that they owe a duty to God; (iv) people pray with confidence; (v) people think of God in personal terms; (vi) people see the universe as a whole and as related to the will of God; and (vii) people believe that God is the One who acts first in His relationship with them.

According to Martineau, "religion is a belief in an ever-living God, which is a Divine Mind and Will, ruling the universe and holding Moral relations with mankind." Galloway defined religion as a "man's faith in a power beyond himself, whereby he seeks to satisfy emotional needs and gains stability of life, and which he expresses in acts of worship and service.'[8] God himself is unchanging, always the same eternal Being who is beyond human power to describe His fullness. It is not surprising that people have a different idea of Him. Writing the word *God* in italics will help us to remember that "God" is a special word, which describes the Eternal Creator whom we can never fully understand or speak about carelessly. God is the living, eternal being in whose presence all creatures "live, and move, and have their being" (Acts 17.28). He has revealed Himself in many different ways, and human beings in particular have always felt His presence and responded to Him in worship. This living relationship between God and men is the basis of all religions.

In describing the relationship between God and the world, people say that God is transcendent and that He is "immanent." "Immanent" means "dwelling within." Immanence can, however, be a misleading word if we suppose that it means that God lives only within the created world. Some people think that it is better to say that God in relationship with the word. These are two important words about God. They belong to each other as the two sides of a coin. "Transcendent" means that something is beyond what is natural and normal, and different from it. When people say that God is transcendent, they intend to make statements like the following:

- God is not limited to particular places and times as human beings are.
- God lives outside the natural world in which human beings live.
- Human beings can never fully know the will or thoughts of *God*. He is beyond their understanding.
- God is always there first: He is the creator of all things and initiator of all events.

Human beings feel awe when they remember the presence of God. He is good and trustworthy in a way that they are not.

Western Philosophy

Western philosophy (also known as "European Philosophy") is a term that refers to philosophical thinking in the western or occidental world, as opposed to the various kinds of Eastern or Oriental Philosophy and in distinction to varieties of indigenous philosophies. Historically, the term "Western Philosophy" refers to the philosophical thinking of western civilisation beginning in ancient Greece. The word "philosophy" originated in the West. Western philosophy has had a tremendous influence on and has been greatly influenced by Western religion, science and politics. In the West, philosophy is an expansive and ambiguous concept. Today, however, what generally distinguishes philosophy from other Western disciplines is the notion that philosophy is a deeper and more rational, fundamental, classical and universal form of thought.

Western philosophies typically either disavow the existence of God or else hold that God or the gods are something separate and distinct from the universe. The obvious exception here is the Greek and Roman pantheon of gods and goddesses during ancient times, which is very distinct from the influence of Abrahamic religions, which teach that this universe was created by a single, all-powerful God who existed before and only partially separately from this universe. Some aspects of the true nature and properties of this God would be incomprehensible to us as creations than other disciplines. Western philosophies have formulated questions about the nature of God and His relationship to the universe based on a Monotheistic framework within which it emerged. Many Western philosophers generally assume that the individual is something distinct from the entire universe, and they attempt to describe and categorise the universe from a detached, objective viewpoint.

Asian Philosophy
In the West, the term "Asian Philosophy" (also known as Eastern Philosophy) refers very broadly to the various philosophies of the East, namely Asia, including India, China, Japan, Persia and the general area. One must take into account that this term ignores that these countries do not belong to a single culture. Asian philosophy refers very broadly to the various philosophies of China, Japan, Korea, India and Iran. Asian philosophic traditions generally tend to be less concerned with the existence or non-existence of God or gods. Although some Asian traditions have supernatural spiritual beings and even powerful gods, these are generally not seen as separate from the universe, but rather as a part of the universe, just as Greek and Roman supernatural beings. Conversely, most Eastern religions teach that ordinary actions can affect the supernatural realm. Asian philosophy is the belief regarding the relationship between God or gods and the universe.

Asian Philosophy will examine the Chinese philosophies of Taoism and Confucianism, Islamic philosophy of the Middle-East and the Indian philosophies of Hinduism, Jainism and Buddhism. The main goal is to provide students with an understanding of the significance of these philosophies in their own right as well as a comparative understanding of them. This comparison will involve an analysis of the similarities and differences between these Asian philosophies, as well as an analysis of how they stand in relation to Western Philosophy. The method for accomplishing this goal is *philosophical*—achieved through the rational analysis of the main principles of these philosophies: (1) in themselves, (2) in contrast with each other and (3) in contrast with some mainstream Western philosophical and religious traditions. The subject requires students to understand various views on this matter in Indian, Chinese and Japanese thought. Students will study texts on Confucius and Indian philosophy. On completion of the subject, students should develop good knowledge and understanding of the process of thinking, reasoning and reflecting in Asian intellectual cultures, as well as an ability to articulate and evaluate these views. The long history of Asian peoples and the significance of their cultures should be highly esteemed in the field of philosophical thought. We should move from the history of Israel or the history of Christianity in the West to the history of Asia in order to gain insights into God's ways with the nations and to discover what place history beyond the Jewish-Christian tradition plays in God's saving purposes in the world.[9] Asian philosophies have not been as concerned by questions relating to the nature of a single God as the universe's sole creator and ruler. The distinction between the religious and the secular tends to be much less sharp in Asian philosophy, and the same philosophical school often contains both religious and philosophical elements.

Christian Philosophy

Christian Philosophy is a term that describes the fusion of various fields of philosophy, historically derived from the philosophical traditions of Western thinkers such as Plato and Aristotle, with the theological doctrines of Christianity. Christian philosophy originated during the Middle Ages as medieval theologians attempted to demonstrate to the religious authorities that Greek philosophy and Christian faith were, in fact, compatible methods for arriving at divine truth. Augustine developed classical Christian philosophy, largely by synthesising Hebrew and Greek thought. He drew particularly from the Greek pagan thinker Plato, Neo-Platonism and stoicism, which he altered and refined in light of divine revelation of Christian teaching and the Bible.

Christian philosophers are under two constraints: first is the belief that basic conceptual questions must have answers. The other is that the Scripture often appears to be undermined on such questions.[10] Christian philosophy is that which supports biblical teaching and stands contradictory to the unsound teachings of the heretics and secular philosophy. Christian philosophy is a philosophical study of the Christian faith and doctrines. The secular philosophy or philosophy in general cannot be accepted as it is. It is the role of the Christian philosopher to reveal pure Christianity and stand against the un-Christian teachings of philosophy. A Christian philosopher has the responsibility to distinguish between Christ-centered philosophy and the other. Christian philosophy is the philosophical implications of pure Christian theology, which is based on the Holy Bible. Christian philosophy is the philosophy that reveals pure Christianity to the non-Christian world.

Philosophical Theology
Philosophical Theology pursues such an examination of the ideas of a theology associated with a particular religion. Christian philosophical theology takes the Christian faith as its starting point and examines it philosophically.[11] There are typically two different categories in philosophical theology: The first category includes attempts to demonstrate the truth of religious claims by appeal to evidence available apart from purported divine revelations. The second category includes attempts to demonstrate the consistency and plausibility of theological claims using philosophical techniques. This first category uses what is called natural theology to understand Christian claims. The second appeals to philosophy to understand theological convictions derived from divine revelation.

Philosophical Anthropology
The study of the subject "philosophical anthropology" is a subject that we must consider independently, even without reference to other elements of the Christian doctrine. The biblical reference to the nature of humanity must be recognised as it occurs within the overall context of our place within creation and our standing before God. Philosophical anthropology is the study of man with the philosophical perspective.[12] *Anthropo* is the Greek word for man. Anthropology is the science of man or the study of man. Here we have an outlook on man in a way of philosophical thinking. Philosophical anthropology mainly deals with man and his relation to God and his universe. Man's depravity, his sinful nature, salvation, his destiny, etc., are the important topics in this discipline. As philosophical theology deals with God and God-related matters, philosophical anthropology covers the area of man.

Metaphysics
Metaphysics addresses questions that have existed for as long as the human race. A central branch of metaphysics is ontology, the investigation into what types of things there are in the world and what relations these things bear to one another. The metaphysician also attempts to clarify the notions by which people understand the world, including existence, objecthood, property, space, time, casualty and possibility. Metaphysical thinking produces a government dominated by doctrines of abstract rights and these rights are considered as inalienable rights. Thus natural rights are substituted for divine rights. Social organisation becomes legalistic, formal and structural without adequate content. Metaphysics was first studied systematically by Aristotle, though he did not use that term. He calls it 'first philosophy' and says it is the subject that deals with the "first causes and the principles of things."

Metaphysics is a branch of philosophy concerned with explaining the ultimate nature of reality, being, and the world. Its name derives from the Greek words *meta* (after) and *physika* (those on nature). In metaphysics, ontology is the inquiry into the meaning of existence itself, sometimes seeking to specify what general types of things exist. The philosophy of mind is a part of metaphysics. More recently, the term "metaphysics" has also been used more loosely to refer to the "subjects that are beyond the physical world." In Christian philosophy, *metaphysics* deals with the things of the other world, such as heaven, hell, angels, soul, spirit and the life after death of mankind. Metaphysics is the study of the unseen world and its relation to human beings.

Within these broad branches there are now numerous sub-disciplines of philosophy. At the broadest level, there is the division between Analytic philosophy and Continental philosophy. For Continental philosophy subdividing philosophy between 'experts' is problematic for the very nature of the unifying task of philosophy itself; however, for most of Analytic philosophy further divisions simplify the task for philosophers in each area. The interest in particular sub-disciplines waxes and wanes over time, and sub-disciplines become particularly hot topics and can occupy so much space in the literature that they almost seem like major branches in their own right.

Branches of Philosophy
The traditional branches of philosophy are metaphysics, epistemology and philosophy of mind, philosophy of language, philosophy of logic, political

philosophy, ethics and aesthetics. Applied philosophy, the philosophical critique of various social activities and intellectual pursuits, is a more recent addition to Philosophy. Philosopher Mortimer Adler excludes logic and includes all second-order problems. Second-order problems are often found arranged under various branches of philosophy. He divides these second-order philosophical problems into two branches. The first branch addresses the objects of thought, such as Being, Cause, Change, Infinity, Fate and Love. The second branch addresses the subjects, or procedural domains, of thought, e.g. philosophy of religion, philosophy of history, philosophy of language, philosophy of science, etc. Meta-philosophy also attempts to understand both branches of second-order thought aided by the other major branches, e.g. metaphysical knowledge in religion, epistemology in religion and axiology in religion. In any case, one problem in meta-philosophy is to provide such taxonomy.

Religious Philosophy
Religious philosophy is the study of the philosophy of Religion. Philosophy of religion is the study of the meaning of the concept of God and of the rationality or otherwise of belief in the existence of God. Philosophy of religion has classically been regarded as a part of metaphysics. In *Metaphysics*, Aristotle described *first causes* as one of the subjects of his investigation. For Aristotle, the 'first cause' was the unmoved mover, which has been read as God, particularly when Aristotle's work became prevalent again in the Medieval West. Philosophical religion is the critical examination of religious ideas in general. Religious philosophy is concerned with religion as a pervasive feature of human culture.

The aim of the philosopher is to understand and evaluate religion from a philosophical standpoint rather than to defend religion by philosophical argument.[13] One way to understand the tasks at hand for philosophers of religion is to contrast them with theologians. Theologians predominantly consider the existence of God as axiomatic or self-evident. Most theological treatises seek to justify or support religious claims by two primary epistemic means: rationalisation or intuitive metaphors. A philosopher of religion examines and critiques the epistemological, logical, aesthetic and ethical foundations inherent in the claims of a religion. Whereas a theologian could elaborate metaphysically on the nature of God either rationally or experientially, a philosopher of religion is more interested in asking what may be knowable and opinable with regards to religions' claims. A philosopher of religion does not ask what is God, for such a question assumes the existence of God and that God has a knowable nature. Instead, a philosopher of religion asks whether there are sound reasons to think that God does or does not exist.

Social Philosophy
Philosophy of social sciences is the philosophical study of some basic concepts, methods and presuppositions of social sciences such as sociology and economics. It is the study of society with philosophical approach. It deals with the study of man as a social animal. Philosophical approach shall be contributed to the study of sociology in order to develop a new branch of philosophical study and research called Social philosophy. Social philosophy deals mainly with the study of society with the philosophical approach. The field of sociology will be much benefitted through this newly emergent philosophical thought. If men could follow the uniform course of progressive intellectual development of knowledge that the natural and physical scientists employed, their understanding of the social world would be rapidly advanced and most of the problems of society could be quickly eliminated. It gives us training to have a rational approach concerning ourselves, our religion, culture, institutions, values, etc. It makes us become objective and rational. Such qualities make us more broad-minded. Then we can overcome our prejudices, misconceptions, caste and religious hatreds. It makes our life richer and fuller.

Political Philosophy
Political philosophy helps us to understand the relation between philosophy and politics. Political philosophy is the study of basic topics concerning government, including the purpose of the state, political justice, political freedom, the nature of law, the administration of justice and paternalism. Some universities offer this course as Political Science. Both are same only. It mainly deals with political issues from the philosophical perspective. So many political philosophers have discussed matters of people and their relation with the state. Plato and Aristotle were pioneers in this filed. Then Karl Marx, Immanuel Kant, Bertrand Russell and many others contributed a lot to this particular filed of philosophy. The current analytic political philosophy owes much to John Rawls, who, in a series of papers from the 1950s onward (*Two Concepts of Rules* and *Justice as Fairness*) and his book *A Theory of* Justice (1971), produced a sophisticated and closely argued defense of a liberal welfare state.

Educational Philosophy

It is Philosophy of education. Educational philosophy is the study of the purpose and most basic methods of education or learning. Educational philosophy has a set of rules and guidelines for learners in the field of education. Philosophy itself is a term that originated for the purpose of wisdom. It is the study of learning and obtaining wisdom. Philosophy demands learning and the systematic enquiry in touch with the world and man's relation to this world. Educational philosophy is the important branch of philosophy, because of its very nature, which supports and encourages learners and educators in order to promote wisdom and knowledge with the method of systematic enquiry. Educational philosophers have widely contributed to the field of education with the philosophical perspective.

Moral Philosophy

In philosophy, moral relativism, moral absolutism, moral objectivism, moral realism and moral naturalism, which all maintain the existence of moral facts: facts that entities can both know and judge, whether through some process of verification or through intuition. Moral relativism is the position that moral propositions do not reflect objective or universal moral truths, but make claims relative to social, cultural, historical or personal circumstances. Moral relativists hold that no universal standard exists by which to assess an ethical proposition's truth. Relativistic positions often see moral values as applicable only within certain cultural boundaries or in the context of individual preferences. An extreme relativist position might suggest that judging the moral or ethical judgments or acts of another person or group has no meaning, though most relativists propound a more limited version of the theory. Some moral relativists hold that a personal and subjective moral care lies or ought to lie at the base of individuals' moral acts. Moral objectivism or moderate moral realism is the position that certain acts are objectively right or wrong, independent of human opinion. Some moral objectivists believe that humankind can derive moral knowledge from external sources such as a deity or revealed doctrines. Some hold that moral facts inhere in nature or reality. In each case, however, moral facts remain invariant, though the circumstances to which they apply may differ. Moreover, each of these schools of thought sees moral facts as objective and determinable.

Moral pluralism or value pluralism is the idea that there are several values that may be equally correct and fundamental, and yet in conflict with each other. Moral pluralism is a theory in meta-ethics or a set of values in itself. Moral pluralism acknowledges the co-existence of opposing ideas and practices, but accepts limits to differences, such as when vital human needs get violated. Moral realism is the view in philosophy that there are objective moral values. Moral realists argue that moral judgments describe moral facts. This combines a cognitive view about moral judgments, a view about the existence of moral facts, and a view about the nature of moral facts. Moral realism asserts that moral statements express propositions about the actual state of reality, that a statement such as 'murder is wrong' is in fact true or false in the same way that the statement 'it is raining' or 'the Earth revolves around the Sun' is true or false. Moral relativism rejects the idea of an objective morality, but its proponents do not agree as to the nature of morality. Moral absolutism is the belief that there are absolute standards against which moral questions can be judged, and that certain actions are right or wrong, devoid of the context of the act.

Mystic Philosophy

Mysticism represents the belief that direct knowledge of God and of spiritual truth or ultimate reality is attainable through immediate intuition or insight and in a way differing from ordinary sense perception or the use of logical reasoning.[14] Mysticism as a transformative philosophy and religion understands ultimate truth in a way that is distinctively different from that of conventional philosophy and religion. Mysticism points out to a paradoxical situation of a third way that sees the absolute in the relative, the absolute contemplative in sensual and rational life. Mysticism demands, on the one hand, the opening up of a new dimension that unites life beyond the different concepts and beyond belief and, on the other hand, this leap also represents the deepening of each and every individual philosophy and religion. Mysticism as transformative philosophy and religion shows the path from the prevalent form of experience, thinking, and life to the restoration of original awareness. Anibha Gupta writes:[15]

> Western mysticism can be termed as an effort to be one with the divinity who is more or less conceived as a person and is called by different names, i.e. the Father, the Lord, the King of Kings, etc. This oneness with the person belongs more to feeling than to reason, more to affection than to cognition. The mystical union is like a spiritual marriage where the mystic must feel the closeness of his God as a bride feels closeness or nearness when she meets her spouse. This feeling is not amenable to reason or intellect nor is it an object of philosophical dialects. Only love can help a person to experience it, because love beareth all things, believeth all things, hopeth all things, and endureth all things.

Mystic philosophy simply means a man's personal experience of God. A mystic is concerned only with the inner life of the soul. A more restricted usage of the term confines to the higher stages of mystical prayer, which are given to the individuals by God. The term *mystical* has suggested confusion with the Greeceo-Roman mystery religions, identification with the Neo-Platonism of the mystical theology of Dionysius. Mysticism flourished in Germany and other European countries in the Middle Ages.

Philosophy of History
Philosophy of History is the study of the methods by which history is derived and accepted. It mainly deals with the philosophical perspective of the study of history and the history of philosophy is the study of the historical survey down through the centuries, mainly dealing with philosophy. Those who make the survey of the history of philosophy are known as the historical philosophers. There have been whole ages in whose minds the so-called questions about reality as a whole have been assigned. Whatever may be fully of a historian of a philosophy, there already have been philosophers who have thought themselves to have solved their problems to their utmost satisfaction.[16]

Philosophy is not possible without time, which is a historical element. History has been understood as the developing, self-articulation of reality and in this sense, it has been regarded as identical with philosophy. For a philosopher, the very relation between history and philosophy would become a problem, not in the realm of history but that of philosophy. History is different from science and it has its own distinctive methods of investigations. Philosophy of history will examine their validity. History is concerned with the doings of men as human beings. We cannot study it without some view of the nature of man. The study of history is more than writing and remembering a chronicle of events. The study of history takes into account of what is distinctively human. Therefore, it cannot proceed with the rigorous logic of science.[17] There have been both a history of philosophy and philosophy of history. History sees philosophy as merely an occurrence among other occurrences. But philosophy claims to judge the very validity, meaning and reality of history.

Philosophy of Science
This is an active discipline pursued by both trained philosophers and scientists. Philosophers often refer to and interpret experimental work of various kinds. But this is not surprising. Such branches of philosophy aim at philosophical understanding of experimental work. It is not the

philosophers in their capacity as philosophers who perform the experiments and formulate the scientific theories under study. Philosophy of science should not be confused with the science it studies any more than biology should be confused with plants and animals. Philosophy of physics is the philosophical study of some basic concepts of physics, including space, time and force. Philosophy of science includes not only, as Sub-disciplines, the philosophies of the special sciences, but also questions about induction, scientific method, scientific progress, etc. Science does not deny change but merely asserts that the change is according to a law that is in itself unvarying and which, if known, would give us the knowledge of what the change would develop into. Science is concerned with the law as essentially self-existent in nature while our knowledge of the law has elements of both truth and falsehood.[18] Philosophy of Science is an active discipline pursued by both trained philosophers and scientists.

It is for identifying and assessing five elements either related to or implications of a Christian philosophy of science. The philosophy of science deals with the general philosophical issues associated with natural sciences such as philosophy of nature. The nature and status of the Bible with respect to a Christian philosophy of science will be discussed. The way one views the nature of the Bible profoundly influences how one understands the relation between the Bible and philosophy of science. Conversely, one's understanding of the philosophy of science deeply impacts one's articulation of its relation to the Bible.

Analytic Philosophy
During the 1960s and 1970s, there also arose increased communication between the 'analytic' and 'continental' disciplines, although these meetings were generally antagonistic in nature. Nonetheless, it seemed for a time that the distinction between analytic and continental philosophy would eventually collapse. However, after the death of Sartre and rise of postmodernism in the 1980's, analytic philosophers became more overtly opposed to the methods and conclusions of continental philosophers. Derrida, in particular, was the target of much criticism and ridicule.

Analytic philosophers are mainly the English philosophers, and the Continental philosophers are the philosophers from the European Continent. From the early 20th century until the 1960s, continental philosophers were rarely discussed in British and American universities. The few mentions of continental philosophy were generally dismissive and hostile. However, due to student demand, philosophy departments began offering courses in continental philosophy in the late 1960s and 1970s. The vast majority of academic periodicals in philosophy today only accept papers written in a broadly analytic style. The term *analytic philosophy* designates a group of philosophical methods that stress clarity of meaning above all other criteria. The term 'analytic philosophy' may mark merely a family resemblance across disparate philosophical views, or historical lines of influence. The broad generalisation can be made as analytic philosophy is characterised by its emphasis on clarity and argument, typically achieved through modern formal logic and analysis of language, and a respect for the natural sciences. Analytic philosophy tends to treat philosophy in terms of discrete problems, capable of being analysed apart from their historical origins. It is just like scientists consider the history of science inessential to scientific inquiry. Husserl is also a respected subject of study in the analytic tradition. Husserl's notion of a *noema* (a non-psychological content of thought), his correspondence with Gottlob Frege and his investigations into the nature of logic continue to generate interest among analytic philosophers.

Continental Philosophy
Continental philosophy is a term that originated among European philosophers to describe various philosophical traditions strongly influenced by certain 19th and 20th century philosophers from mainland Europe. The term is typically used in contrast with analytical philosophy. The term continental philosophy was first widely used to describe university courses in the 1970s, emerging as a collective name for the philosophies then widespread in France and Germany, such as phenomenology, existentialism, structuralism and post-structuralism. The traditions comprising continental philosophy include German Idealism, phenomenology, existentialism, structuralism, post-structuralism, French Feminism and some other branches of western Marxism. Some scholars have suggested that the term may be more pejorative than descriptive, functioning as a label for types of philosophy rejected or disliked by analytic philosophers. Nonetheless, some scholars have ventured to identify common themes that typically characterise continental philosophy:

- Continental philosophers generally reject scientism, the view that natural sciences are the best or most accurate way of understanding all phenomena.

- Continental philosophy usually considers these conditions of possible experience as variable: determined at least partly by factors such as context, space and time, language, culture and history. Thus continental philosophy tends towards historicism.

- Continental philosophy typically holds that conscious human agency can change these conditions of possible experience. Thus, continental philosophers tend to take a strong interest in the unity of theory and practice and tend to see their philosophical inquiries as closely related to personal, moral or political transformation.

- A final characteristic trait of continental philosophy is an emphasis on meta-philosophy. In the wake of the development and success of natural sciences, continental philosophers have often sought to redefine the method and nature of philosophy.

Linguistic Philosophy

Philosophy of language or linguistic philosophy is the study of the concepts of meaning and truth within human languages. As the term indicates, Linguistic Philosophy does not deal with reality, the world of man, but with the language with which we speak about reality, the world and man. Linguistic philosophy was born of a reaction against this naive view of language. It brought to light that language is not a neutral tool that serves to depict a ready-made reality. In fact, it plays an active role in the very understanding of reality. Language is primarily instrumental in character. It is an attempt to communicate a state of affairs that is generally, not perceptually, or rather experientially, present.[19] Philosophy presupposes more specifically philosophy of language as a theory of meaning. It is being increasingly realised today that the understanding of a particular theory of meaning or philosophy of language is very basic to our understanding of a philosophical theory.

Linguistic philosophers examine the philosophy of language. Philosophers of language search for the grammatical principles and tendencies that all human languages share. Among the concerns of linguistic philosophers is the range of possible word order combinations throughout the world. Questions about the meaning and truth of religious statements have gained an overall popularity. According to Wittgenstein's Fideism, the criteria of the meaning and truth of religious statements are to be found wholly within the religion itself.[20] Language has therefore a determining influence on the way we experience and understand reality, the language he uses influences man's thought. Thus the philosophical task is now to shift from an interest in 'knowing the truth' about the world to a concern to determine the 'meaning' of the language we use to describe it. Philosophy now deals with 'meaning' rather than with 'truth.' Language has an important bearing on how we understand the world; more specifically, how we use language is the central part of philosophy.

Philosophy of Mind

Philosophy of psychology is the study of some fundamental questions about the methods and concepts of psychology and psychiatry. Philosophy of mind is the philosophical study of the nature of the mind and its relation to the body and the rest of the world. Philosophy of perception is the philosophical study of topics related to perception; the question *what the immediate objects of perception are* has been especially important. Philosophy of mind is the philosophical perspective of the study of psychology. Philosophy always gives priority to thinking and imagination. It is the work of the mind. So it is related to psychology. Especially mystical philosophy is closely related to the mind realm.

Philosophers use the characteristics of inward accessibility, subjectivity, intentionality, goal-directedness, creativity and freedom and consciousness to distinguish mental phenomena from physical phenomena. Many fields other than philosophy share an interest in the nature of mind. In religion, the nature of mind is connected with various conceptions of the soul and the possibility of life after death. In many abstract theories of mind, there is considerable overlap between philosophy and the science of psychology. Once being part of philosophy, psychology split off and formed a separate branch of knowledge in the 19th century. While psychology uses scientific experiments to study mental states and events, philosophy uses reasoned arguments and thought experiments in seeking to understand the concepts that underlie mental phenomena.

Meta-philosophy

Meta-philosophy (Greek, "meta" and "philosophy") is the study of the subject, matter, methods and aims of philosophy. It is the philosophy of philosophy. Meta-philosophy is the study of philosophical method and the nature and purpose of philosophy. Meta-ethics is the study of whether ethical value judgments can be objective at all. The recursive study of philosophy is an integral part of the philosophical enterprise because it is intertwined with all branches of philosophy as is logic or epistemology. Most meta-philosophy is part of either the formation or criticism of a philosophical school, but some philosophers devote their time almost exclusively to meta-philosophy, such as Stephen Toulmin, Richard Rorty and some continental philosophers.

An important question for meta-philosophy is "What is philosophy?" and because different philosophers have offered different answers, it is the task of meta-philosophy to adjudicate. Prior to adjudication, however, the meta-philosopher must identify, clarify and understand the alternative conceptions of the nature of philosophy as well as his or her available reasoning tools and their limits.

Natural Philosophy
Natural Philosophy or the philosophy of nature, known in Latin as *philosophia naturalis*, is a term applied to the objective study of nature and the physical universe that was regnant before the development of modern science. Any method of inquiry or investigation or any procedure for gaining knowledge that limits itself to natural, physical and material approaches and explanations can be described as naturalistic. Forms of science historically developed out of philosophy or more specifically natural philosophy. Modern notions of science and scientists date only to the nineteenth century. Before then, the word "science" simply meant knowledge and the label of scientist did not exist. Isaac Newton's 1687 scientific treatise is known as "The Mathematical Principles of Natural Philosophy." John Questebrune wrote *A Short Introduction to Natural Philosophy* in a period between1718 and1720.

Naturalism is any of several philosophical stances, typically those descended from materialism and pragmatism that do not distinguish the supernatural from the natural. Many modern philosophers use the terms *methodological naturalism* or *scientific naturalism* to refer to the long-standing convention in the scientific method, which makes the methodological assumption that observable effects in nature are best explainable only by natural causes. They contrast this with the approach known as *ontological naturalism* or metaphysical naturalism, which refers to the metaphysical belief that the natural world is all that exists, and therefore, nothing supernatural exists. The historical support of methodological naturalism by Christians is noted by Numbers. Despite the occasional efforts of unbelievers to use scientific naturalism to construct a world without God, it has retained strong Christian support down to the present. And well it might, for scientific naturalism, was largely made in Christendom by pious Christians.

Popular Philosophy
Alfred Korzybski has written about Popular Philosophy. The works of Albert Camus have been enlisted as Popular Philosophy. In particular, Jean Paul Sartre claimed that it was philosophy for students at the high school level. Camus' works are generally considered as literature and not as philosophy, although they definitely posed some philosophical questions. It can be considered as popular philosophy. Popular philosophy contains philosophic matters that are easy for the public to understand. As it is understandable to the general public, it does not keep up the higher level of philosophical thinking.

The classical intellectual uses the influence gained in their field for moral or political purposes and thus goes from their scientific field to the public space. New philosophers invert this to derive their scientific legitimacy. They are not studied by philosophy students. The so-called integral thought is an example of new-age ideology, written for a popular audience that at least strives for the appearance of philosophical rigour.

Non-philosophy
Non-philosophy is a concept developed by the French philosopher Francios Laruelle. Laruelle published on non-philosophy throughout the 1980s and 1990s. He currently directs an international organisation dedicated to furthering the cause of non-philosophy, the organisation "Non-Philosophical Internationale." It stands in particular opposition to philosophical heirs of Jacques Lacan, such as Alain Badiou. Non-philosophy has made little impact outside France. Laruelle claims that all forms of philosophy, from ancient philosophy to analytic philosophy, are structured around a prior decision, but that all forms of philosophy remain constitutively blind to this decision.

Laruelle's concept of the subject here is not the same as the subject-matter, nor does it have anything to do with the traditional philosophical notion of subjectivity. It is, instead, a function along the same lines as a mathematical function. The concept of perfomativity (speech act theory) is central to the idea of the subject of non-philosophy. In this sense, non-philosophy is radically performative because the theorems deployed in accordance with its method constitute fully-fledged scientific actions. Thus Non-philosophy is conceived as a rigorous and scholarly discipline. Brassier also defines Non-philosophy as the theoretical practice of philosophy proceeding by way of transcendental axioms and producing theorems that are philosophically uninterpretable.

Epistemology
Epistemology is the study of knowledge and its nature, possibility and justification. Epistemology or theory of knowledge is the branch of philosophy that studies the nature and scope of knowledge and belief. The term "epistemology" is based on the Greek words *episteme* (knowledge or science) and *logos* (word or explanation). It was introduced into English by the Scottish philosopher James F. Ferrier (1808-1864). Much of the debate in this field has focused on analysing the nature of knowledge and how it relates to similar notions, such as truth, belief and justification.

Epistemology also deals with the means of production of knowledge as well as skepticism about different knowledge claims. In other words, epistemology primarily addresses the following questions: 'What is knowledge? How is knowledge acquired? What do people know? In philosophy, generally, empiricism is a theory of knowledge emphasising the role of experience, especially experience based on perceptual observations by the five senses. Certain forms treat all knowledge as empirical, while some regard disciplines such as mathematics and logic as exceptions. Rationalists believe that knowledge is primarily acquired by a priori processes or is innate.

Constructivism is a view in philosophy according to which all knowledge is constructed in as much as it is contingent on convention, human perception and social experience. It originated in sociology under the term Social Constructionism and has been given the name constructivism when referring to philosophical epistemology. Contextualism in epistemology is the claim that knowledge varies with the context in which it is attributed. The motivation behind contextualism is the idea that, in the context of discussion with an extreme skeptic about knowledge, there is a very high standard for the accurate ascription of knowledge, while in ordinary usage, there is a lower standard.

Philosophy of Arts
It is also known as 'aesthetics', which is the study of general features of the arts, taste and beauty. The arts include drama, music, painting, poetry and many other fields. Aesthetics has been a branch of philosophy by the period of A. Baumgarten (1714-62). But the important contributions came from other academic disciplines, as well as from artists and arts critics. Contemporary aesthetics include the study of the theory of aesthetics, philosophy of arts and philosophy of arts criticism. The most significant issues concerning this area with regard to Christians are aesthetic

responsibility, approached to art, social frameworks and relationship between theology and philosophy. Islalotionist Christians tend to ward off contemporary art as something dangerous to their faith. Synthetic and accommodating Christians are inclined to use Christian teachings to justify contemporary art, either as a liturgical means of worship or as something good in itself.[21] Transformational Christians usually expect Christians to promote renewal within contemporary arts. Christian criticism of arts and involvement in them might make little redemptive difference unless we address the economic basis for social frameworks of contemporary arts.

Experimental Philosophy

Experimental philosophy is a form of philosophical inquiry that makes at least partial use of quantitative research—especially *opinion polling*—in order to address philosophical questions. This is in contrast with more traditional methods found in philosophy, whereby a philosopher will frequently begin by appealing to his or her personal intuitions on an issue and then form an argument with those intuitions as premises. The philosophy of science discusses the underpinnings of the scientific method and has affected the nature of scientific investigation and argumentation. Deep ecology examines the moral situation of humans as occupants of a world that has non-human occupants to consider as well.

Applied Philosophy

Though often seen as a wholly abstract field, philosophy is not without practical applications. The most obvious applications are those in ethics and political philosophy. The political and economic philosophies of Machiavelli, John Locke, Rousseau, Karl Marx, J. S. Mill, Gandhi, and others —all of these have been used to shape and justify governments and their actions. In the field of philosophy of education, progressive education, as championed by John Dewey, has had a profound impact on educational practices. Logic has become crucially important in mathematics, linguistics, psychology, computer science and computer engineering. If philosophy has no bearing on action, it can hardly be knowledge. It cannot provide even hope, unless hopes were to mean a mere fancied wish-fulfill heart. At best it would be an intellectual pastime and at worst an intellectual escape; and really such be the case, Milton would be right in consigning both the philosophers and their problems to hell.[22]

Making a distinction between pure philosophy and applied philosophy, we can say that some of the problems, i.e., questions about God, the knowledge of the external world, the knowledge of other minds, questions about good and bad, right and wrong fall in the area of pure philosophy; and some others such as abortion, euthanasia, sexual immorality, world hunger, civil disobedience and capital punishment are dealt within applied philosophy.[23] Other important applications can be found in epistemology, which aid in understanding the requisites for knowledge, sound evidence and justified belief. Aesthetics can help to interpret discussions of music, literature, the plastic arts and the whole artistic dimension of life. In general, the various philosophies strive to provide workers in their respective fields with a deeper understanding of the theoretical or conceptual underpinnings of their fields.

Philosophy and Other Disciplines
Philosophy cannot predict reality. This is the task of several other sciences dealing with special problems. The orientation proposed by the sciences remains hypothetical, even if it is a result of interdisciplinary work. Philosophy could be regarded as orientation about science.[24] Orientation is a pre-scientific phenomenon and precedes philosophic reflection. Philosophy alone should not try to solve or manage the problems but rather seek the help of other disciplines, having thought of its meaning. We can easily understand that philosophy and other sciences are interrelated and function together with the help of one with another.

Philosophy and Education
Education is concerned with the three functions of mind: knowing, willing and doing. Philosophy has some relation with these three aspects of mind. Education and Philosophy are close to each other and both may be regarded as an art. Art and Philosophy and Art and Education have sufficient similarity. The main aim of art is realisation of truth or reality. Philosophy provides suitable background for this realisation. Education makes children competent for this realisation.

In education, the main aim of study is to determine as to what should be the nature of education. With this viewpoint, education is nearer to Philosophy. In Philosophy and education, the emphasis is on synthesis rather than on analysis. In education, so much importance is attached to the mental development of the child and on this basis, curriculum and other activities are determined. From this point of view, education is nearer to Philosophy.

Philosophy and Religion

Philosophy is a remote and abstract subject. Such is the popular opinion. Philosophy is nobody's handmaiden. In the past, philosophers wrote on these subjects with the express intention that practical results of this kind should indeed follow. In particular, this has not been infrequently the aim of writers on the philosophy of religion. At the same time, the concepts and arguments of religion are such that practical results are likely still to follow on philosophical inquiry into them. In treating human nature and dignity, philosophy differs from religion in a purely rational way.

The object of philosophy and that of religion are the same. A typically philosophical examination of religion is bound to consider before anything else the question whether religion itself is to be described as rational or non-rational. Certainly, this question can have no simple answer of the form 'Religion is rational' or 'Religion is non-rational.' Any account of religion must recognise a number of elements in it—emotional, belief, moral, ritual and possibly institutional. Philosophy is largely concerned with language, for it is closely related to the sentences and arguments for a clarificatory activity. Philosophy is theory of reality and religion is the total response of the whole personality towards this same reality.[25] Therefore, the philosopher will find more to say about the belief element in religion than about the others. The philosopher will find particular possibilities for his own activity if he studies a religion like Christianity, in which the element of verbalisation is extremely strong. The philosopher will naturally turn to the religion that he knows best. This is how it comes about that the philosophy of religion means in practice the philosophy of the Christian religion. The interesting part in philosophy is the activity of getting things clear. It is to be concluded that the comparative study of religions may itself throw up problems calling for a philosophical treatment.

Philosophy in its wider sense 'the science of all' comes very close to religion. The relation of the more narrow to the wider sense of philosophy is similar to the relation of philosophy to religion.[26] Education emerged as part of religion. Religious institutions were centres of education with the development of civilisation. Education was separated from religion. Religion and Philosophy support each other. Both accept the existence of the invisible, but Philosophy does not believe in rituals and ostentation. Both education and Philosophy support religion so far as search for knowledge and its achievement are concerned. But religion gives more importance to mysterious knowledge.

Philosophy and Theology

Philosophy is a remote and abstract subject. It is nobody's handmaiden. Theology is opposite to it. It is formed by religious thinkers. It is to be noted that the modern Protestants view that religion is radically irrational and that religion is beyond rationality and non-rationality because it is unscientific or non-empirical or it deals in unverifiable supernatural causes. However, it should never be forgotten that theology was formed and reshaped on the event of philosophy. Ronald B. Mayers says that philosophy and theology are interdependent for the Christian thinker. Theology and philosophy are concentric circles as the latter attempts to work out in detail and systematise a Christian worldview based on and within the parameters of divine revelation and theological doctrine.[27] Philosophy functions differently than theology. However, philosophy is never independent of God and His revelation. Philosophy is the handmaiden of theology in dealing with the ontological and epistemological assumptions of the theologian.

Emmanuel Kant, as professor of philosophy at Kongsberg, lectured each winter semester on Metaphysics. Alexander Gottlieb Baumgartner wrote a standard textbook on Wolffian rationalism, which comprised also a treatise on natural theology. He delivered a series of lectures expressly on philosophical theology. A consistent attempt has been made to show the strength of theological rationalism and thereby the concept of philosophical theology emerged. The lectures set out Kant's views on much of the content of the traditional metaphysical theology, namely the nature and attributes of God, his relation to the world, creation and providence. He also reconsiders at some length, the speculative proofs of divine existence under the headings 'onto-theology', 'Cosmo-theology' and 'physico-theology' respectively.

Philosophy and Science

Originally, the term "philosophy" was applied to all intellectual endeavours. Aristotle studied what would now be called biology, meteorology, physics and cosmology, alongside his metaphysics and ethics. Even in the eighteenth century, physics and chemistry were still classified as natural philosophy, that is, the philosophical study of nature. Today, these latter subjects are popularly referred to as sciences, and as separate from philosophy. More recently, psychology, economics, sociology and linguistics were once the domain of philosophers in so far as they were studied at all, but now have only a weaker connection with the field. We can discuss science philosophically just as we discuss religion philosophically. The scientific account is based on experiment and observation. The only valid scientific evidence is that of the senses.[28]

For 2000 years or more, man has wrestled with problems of origin, reality and worth of the world he has found himself in. Daya Krishna says that gradually there has occurred a differentiation through which the problems regarding the constitution, origin, reality and worth concerning any particular group of objects have been separated from the problems concerned with reality as a whole. The former is known as science and the later, philosophy.[29] In the late twentieth century, cognitive science and artificial intelligence could be seen as being forged in part out of philosophy of mind. Philosophy is done primarily through reflection. It does not tend to rely on experiment. However, in some ways, philosophy is close to science in its character and method; some Analytic philosophers have suggested that the method of philosophical analysis allows philosophers to emulate the methods of natural science. This suggests that philosophy might be the study of meaning and reasoning generally; but some still would claim either that this is not a science, or that if it is, it ought not to be pursued by philosophers. All these views have something in common, whatever philosophy essentially is or is concerned with, it tends on the whole to proceed more abstractly than most natural sciences. It does not depend as much on experience and experiment and does not contribute as directly to technology. It clearly would be a mistake to identify philosophy with any one natural science; whether it can be identified with science very broadly construed is still an open question.

Philosophy and Mathematics
Mathematics uses very specific, rigorous methods of proof that philosophers sometimes try to emulate. Most philosophy is written in ordinary prose; and while it strives to be precise, it does not usually attain anything like mathematical clarity. As a result, mathematicians hardly ever disagree about results, while philosophers of course do disagree about their results as well as their methods. The philosophy of mathematics is a branch of philosophy of science; but in many ways mathematics has a special relationship to philosophy. Philosophy of mathematics is the study of philosophical questions raised by mathematics, such as the nature of numbers and what the nature and origins of our mathematical knowledge are.

This is because the study of logic is a central branch of philosophy, and mathematics is a paradigm example of logic. In the late nineteenth and twentieth centuries, logic made great advances and mathematics was proven to be reducible to logic. The use of formal, mathematical logic in philosophy now resembles the use of math in science, although it is not as frequent

Philosophy and Ethics

The term "ethics" (moral philosophy) comes from the Latin word, *ethica*; its Greek equivalent is *ethos*, which means "custom, habit." It is a major branch of philosophy. It is the study of values and customs of a person or group. It covers the analysis and employment of concepts such as right and wrong, good and evil and responsibility. It is divided into four primary areas: meta-ethics, normative ethics, descriptive ethics and applied ethics.

There are two main strands of thought—non-realism and realism—that attempt to explain what ethical values and claims are actually about. It suggests that moral values are creations, dependent on people's feelings and goals regarding themselves and others or on their belief systems. Another group of meta-ethical theories, called 'realism', by contrast, hold that moral value is somehow an intrinsic property of the world and those ethical principles are simply discovered or intuited. Under this view, ethical values held by people can at best reflect an independent truth by which their validity must be judged. These theories may be derived from religious philosophy, natural philosophy or theology. Normative ethics bridges the gap between meta-ethics and applied ethics. It is the attempt to arrive at general moral standards that tell us how to judge right from wrong, or good from bad, and how to live moral lives. This may involve articulating the character or good habits that we should acquire, the duties that we should follow, or the consequences of our behaviour on ourselves and others.

The next one is descriptive ethics. Some philosophers rely on descriptive ethics and choices made and unchallenged by a society or culture to derive categories, which typically vary by context. This can lead to situational ethics. These philosophers often view aesthetics, etiquette and arbitration as more fundamental principles to imply, rather than explicitly state, theories of value or of conduct. According to these views, ethics is not derived from a top-down a priori philosophy but is rather strictly derived from observations of actual choices made in practice. Some consider aesthetics itself as the basis of ethics and a personal moral core developed through art and storytelling as very influential in one's later ethical choices. The last one is applied ethics. Politics is applied ethics—

that it was how cases were really resolved and that political virtues were in fact necessary in all matters where human morality and interests were destined to clash. The issue of abortion is an applied ethical topic since it involves a specific type of controversial behavior. But it also depends on more general normative principles, such as the right of self-rule and the right of life, which are litmus tests for determining the morality of the procedure. Applied ethics is used in determining public policy. But not all questions studied in applied ethics concern public policy.

Philosophy and Logic
While many cultures have employed intricate systems of reasoning and math, logic as an explicit analysis of the methods of reasoning received sustained development originally only in three places: India, in 6th century BC; China, in 5th century BC; and Greece, between 4th century BC and 1st century BC. The formally sophisticated treatment of modern logic descends from the Greek tradition, the latter mainly being informed from the transmission of Aristotelian logic. During the medieval period, logic became the main focus of philosophers, who would engage in critical logical analyses of philosophical arguments. However, in India, innovations in the scholastic school, called Nyaya, continued into the early 18th century. It did not survive long into the colonial period. In the 20th century, Western philosophers like Stanislaw Schayer and Kalus Glashoff tried to explore certain aspects of the Indian tradition of logic. Logic and the philosophy of language are closely related. Philosophy of language has to do with the study of how our language engages and interacts with our thinking. Logic has an immediate impact on other areas of study. Studying logic and the relationship between logic and ordinary speech can help a person better structure their own arguments and critique the arguments of others. Philosophical logic is the study of the more specifically philosophical aspects of logic. Gottlob Frege is regarded by many as the founder of modern philosophical logic. Traditionally, logic is studied as a branch of philosophy. Philosophy primarily concerned with logical analysis of scientific statements. Logic is the method of philosophising.[30] Philosophical logic has a much greater concern with the connection between natural language and logic. As a result, philosophical logicians have contributed a great deal to the development of non-standard logics as well as various extensions of classical logic and non-standard semantics for such logics.

Symbolic language is actually a species of formal logic and is distinguished from Aristotelian syllogistic logic, which deals solely with categorical propositions. Informal logic is the study of natural language arguments. The study of fallacies is an especially important branch of informal logic. Formal logic is the study of inference with purely formal content, where that content is made explicit. Symbolic logic is the study of symbolic abstractions that capture the formal features of logical inference. Formal logic is very often used with the alternate meaning of symbolic logic, whereas informal logic is any logical investigation that does not involve symbolic abstraction. While formal logic is old, dating back more than two millennia, most of symbolic logic is comparatively new and arises with the application of insights from mathematics to problems in logic. The conception of logic as the study of argument is historically fundamental and was how the founders of distinct traditions of logic, namely Plato and Aristotle, conceived of logic. Modern logicians usually wish to ensure that logic studies just those arguments that arise from appropriately general forms of inference. Immanuel Kant introduced an alternative idea as to what logic is. He argued that logic should be conceived as the science of judgment. The valid inferences of logic follow from the structural features of judgments or thoughts.

The character of modern knowledge is truth-functional and extensional. Scientific philosophy aims at logical analysis of scientific statements. The foundational axioms of formal sciences like logic are logically true and the theorems that follow from those axioms are provable.[31] The 'Organon', which was Aristotle's work on logic, introduced the syllogistic. The parts of syllogistic were the analysis of the judgments into propositions consisting of two terms that are related by one of a fixed number of relations, and the expression of inferences by means of syllogisms that consisted of two propositions sharing a common term as premise, and a conclusion that was a proposition involving the two unrelated terms from the premises. Modal logic is not truth conditional and so it has often been proposed as a non-classical logic. Logic as it is studied today is very different from the logic that was studied before, and the principal difference is the innovation of predicate logic. Whereas Aristotelian syllogistic logic specified the forms that the relevant part of the involved judgments took, predicate logic allows sentences to be analysed into subject and argument in several different ways, thus allowing predicate logic to solve the problem of multiple generality that had perplexed medieval logicians. Mathematical discoveries in the early nineteenth century cleared the way for modern scientific philosophy.[32] Mathematical logic really refers to two distinct areas of research: the first is the application of the techniques of formal logic to mathematics and mathematical reasoning, and the second, in the other direction, the application of mathematical techniques to the representation and analysis of formal logic.

Conclusion

We have studied the various branches of philosophy and their relation with other disciplines. An important application can be found in epistemology, which aid in understanding the requisites for knowledge, sound evidence and justified belief. Aesthetics can help to interpret discussions of music, literature, the plastic arts and the whole artistic dimension of life. In general, the various philosophies strive to provide workers in their respective fields with a deeper understanding of the theoretical or conceptual underpinnings of their fields. Philosophy is often seen as an investigation into an area not sufficiently well understood to be its own branch of knowledge. What were once philosophical pursuits have evolved into modern-day fields such as psychology, sociology, linguistics and economics. But as such areas of intellectual endeavour proliferate and expand, so will the broader philosophical questions that they generate.

It is rather difficult to give an exhaustive list of the main divisions of philosophy, because various topics have been studied by philosophers at various times. Ethics, metaphysics, epistemology and logic are usually included. Other topics include politics, aesthetics and religion. In addition, most academic subjects have a philosophy; for example, the philosophy of science, the philosophy of mathematics and the philosophy of history.

Over time, academic specialisation and the rapid technical advance of special sciences led to the development of distinct disciplines for these sciences and their separation from philosophy. Mathematics became a specialised science in the ancient world, and natural philosophy developed into the disciplines of natural sciences over the course of the scientific revolution. Today, philosophical questions are usually explicitly distinguished from the questions of special sciences and characterised by the fact that they are the sort of questions that are foundational and abstract in nature and that are not amenable to being answered by experimental means. The definitions that are given above are closely related to philosophy or different schools of philosophy. Some of the philosophic schools originated even before the Christian era and some are of very recent origin. In the first part of this chapter, we looked at some important terms with a Christian perspective; in the last part of the chapter, we looked at them with a secular point of view.

Helpful Questions
1. Define philosophy, theology and Christian philosophy? How does Asian philosophy differ from Western philosophy?
2. Name the branches of philosophy.
3. How is philosophy related with other disciplines?

Chapter 2
Nature of Philosophy

This chapter gives you information about the historical perspective of philosophy. It will help you to understand the scope of philosophy in an easy manner. Students of philosophy will get an insight into the functions of philosophy as well.

The philosopher applies to the possibilities, the intellectual satisfaction inherent in his theories and convictions. Some encyclopedias have described philosophy in terms of intellectual inquiry and the use of critical analysis and reasoning, as well as dialogue or introspection, to solve intractable and fundamental problems. Different philosophers have had varied ideas about the nature of reason, and there is also disagreement about the subject matter of philosophy. Some think that philosophy examines the process of inquiry itself. Others think that there are essentially philosophical propositions, which is the task of philosophy to prove.

History of Philosophy

The history of philosophy is the study of philosophical ideas and concepts through time. History of philosophy is the study of what philosophers up until recent times have written, the interpretation of such philosophers, who influenced whom and so on. The history of philosophy can be approached either exegetically or critically. Issues specifically related to history of philosophy might include: How can changes in philosophy are accounted for historically? What drives the development of thought in its historical context? To what degree can philosophical texts from prior historical eras even be understood today? Western, religious or secular, have had their own unique schools of philosophy, arrived at through both inheritance and through independent discovery. Such theories have grown from different premises and approaches; examples of which include rationalism, such as the supernaturalistic philosophies and religions. History of philosophy seeks to catalogue and classify such development and therefore understand the development of philosophical ideas through time. There are many kinds of philosophy, dependent on the numerous human cultures. What are not controversial are the general types of problems included in philosophy.

Greek thought left its mark not only upon the content but also upon the form of Medieval Christian writing. Whereas Augustine was direct, personal and biblical, later medieval writing was often logical but formal, thorough but thoroughly dry. This is true in varying degrees of the two medieval thinkers who count for most in philosophical theology today, Anselm of Canterbury and Thomas Aquinas. Platonism percolated through to the medieval church by its influence upon individual theologians and through Neo-Platonists. Some of the Aristotle's ideas were absorbed as transmitted by the sixth-century philosopher-statesman Boethius. At the height of his power, Boethius was accused of treason and executed. While in prison he wrote his most famous work, *The Consolation of Philosophy*, which describes how the soul is able to rise above adversity and attain a vision of God through philosophic contemplation. In later centuries, it became a classic philosophical manual. But perhaps even more significant was his plan to translate into Latin the works of Plato and Aristotle, his philosophical commentaries and original works on logic. These helped to shape the philosophical vocabulary and questions on the later Middle Ages.

Medieval philosophy is the philosophy of Western Europe and the Middle East during what is now known as the medieval era or the Middle Ages, roughly extending from the fall of the Roman Empire to the Renaissance period. Medieval philosophy is defined partly by the process of rediscovering the ancient culture developed by the Greeks and the Romans in the classical period, and partly by the need to address theological problems and to integrate sacred doctrine (in Christianity and Judaism) and secular learning. Some problems discussed throughout this period are the relation of faith to reason, the existence and unity of God, the object of theology and metaphysics, the problems of knowledge, of universals, and of individuation. The Middle Ages are commonly dated from the 4th-century fall of the Western Roman Empire until the end of the 15th century. Philosophy did not begin with the Middle Ages, but the

Middle Ages bear witness to the development of the Christian philosophy and the Christian faith. For one thing, they began to take each other seriously as never before. In the early centuries of the church, individual thinkers had alternately flirted with and denounced philosophy. For good or ill, philosophical ideas entered the bloodstream of medieval theology, and this in turn affected the life and thought of Christianity in later ages. Medieval thought was a curious mixture of Christian faith and pagan philosophy. The church had a monopoly of learning and most medieval philosophers were clerics. They were amateurs in the sense that they were non-professionals; they did it because they loved it. The church has inherited from its past its Scriptures and writers like Augustine. From them it learned and thought doctrines of God, creation and salvation. But it also inherited a good deal of Greek philosophy. And many of its best minds were concerned to bring the church up to date and produce a synthesis of the two. In the Middle Ages, two basic types of theology began to crystallise. On the one hand, there was *natural theology* according to which a genuine knowledge of God and of his relationships with the world could be attained by rational reflection on the nature of things without having to appeal to Christian teaching. And on the other hand, there was *revealed theology*, which was concerned with what was disclosed to man by God through the revelation recorded in the scriptures. *Revealed theology* goes back to biblical revelation and *natural theology* goes back to the classical Greek Philosophy of Plato and Aristotle.

The Middle Ages witnessed the first sustained urbanisation of northern and western Europe. Modern European states owe their origin to the Middle Ages, and their political boundaries as we know them are essentially the result of the military and dynastic achievements in this tumultuous period. Science, technology, agricultural production and social identity changed drastically during this period. The knowledge of philosophy was very limited during that period of time. Theology during this period was largely confined to the monasteries and is therefore called monastic theology. The theologian found himself faced with the question of the relation between faith (theology) and reason (philosophy). The attempt to harmonise the faith and reason became the motive force of medieval Christian thought. The impact of philosophy led to a new approach to theology—Scholastic theology or Scholasticism. The impact of philosophy on theology began in the 11th century with the emergence of reason (philosophy) as a method to be used in theology. In the following centuries, the role of reason was further expanded. In the 13th century, theology entered a new and more dangerous phase. Philosophy now appeared not just as a tool for use in theology but as a rival system of thought. Thomas Aquinas attempted to make a synthesis between faith and reason. He tried to show that the philosophy of Aristotle could be consistently held alongside Christian theology.[33]

In the 14th and 15th centuries, there was an increasing skepticism about the possibility of harmonising theology and philosophy. The medieval period spans from some thousand years. The Medieval theologians wrestled with the problem of the relation between faith and reason. Medieval Philosophy can be signified as Christian philosophy because of two reasons: (1) the philosophy of the medieval period is influenced by Christianity and (2) medieval philosophy mainly dealt with issues between the church and the state. There were quarrels between the Pope and Kings of the European countries about the supremacy of the church and the state. In the light of this issue, there were many philosophers who came into the scene in support of or in opposition to the Pope. In the sixteenth century, Church Reformers made a considerable impact on the history of Western philosophy. Luther and Zwingli did not wish to break the link between the church and the state. Their aim was not to found a new church, but to reform the old one. But the radical Reformers went beyond this and they established another church. Zwingli laid the foundations for Swiss Protestantism and Reformed theology. While Reformers like Martin Luther may be seen as somewhat original thinkers who began a movement, Calvin was a great logician and systematiser of that movement, but not an innovator in doctrine. Calvin's publications spread his ideas of a properly reformed church to many parts of Europe and from there to the rest of the world.

Seventeenth- and eighteenth-century philosophy is known as 'Modern Philosophy.' Seventeenth-century philosophy was dominated by the need to organise philosophy on rational, skeptical, logical and axiomatic grounds, such as the work of Rene Descartes, Blaise Pascals and Thomas Hobbes. This type of philosophy attempts to integrate religious belief into philosophical frameworks, and, often to combat atheism or other unbeliefs, by adopting the idea of material reality, and the dualism between spirit and matter. The eighteenth-century philosophy deals with the period often called the early part of 'The Enlightenment' in the shorter form of the word, and centres on the rise of systematic empiricism, following after Sir Isaac Newton's natural philosophy. Thus Diderot, Voltaire, Rousseau, Montesquieu, Kant and the political philosophies embodied by and influencing the American Revolution are part of the Enlightenment. Other prominent philosophers of this time were David Hume, Adam Smith and Francis Hutcheson. Then next in the history of philosophy is the period of postmodern philosophy. Some philosophers subdivide the postmodern philosophy into two: (1) Early postmodern philosophy (1800-1900) and (2) Later postmodern philosophy (1900 -2000). Postmodern philosophy is usually considered to begin after the philosophy of Immanuel Kant at the beginning of the 19th century. German idealists, such as Hegel, expanded on the work of Kant by maintaining that the world is entirely rational and its nature is fundamentally knowable. Contemporary philosophy (2000-2100) began by the beginning of the twenty-first century. Much philosophy in this period concerns itself with explaining the relation between the theories of the natural sciences and the ideas of the humanities or common sense.

The term "scholasticism" refers to those medieval schools of thought that were concerned with defining and systematising the Christian understanding of reality, which was above all concerned with the relations of God with the world. Different schoolmen had different approaches. There was no one generally-accepted system. The Realists followed Plato in holding that universals were real. The things that we see and touch are really copies of an eternal archetype that in some way has brought them into being. The Nominalists took the opposite view. They rejected the idea of universals altogether. They believed that there was no such thing as goodness apart from particular good things, and that all such general, abstract words were merely a manner of speaking. The Conceptualists steered a middle course. They took the view of Aristotle that universals do, in fact, being to the realm of thought, but they also stand for something which is actually there that gives unity to the diversity of the world of our experience.

Idealism seemed to present a spiritual bulwark against the rising tides of materialism and secularism. It seemed to offer a rational basis for Christianity. Philosophers before Hegel had not given any importance to history in their understanding of Reality. With Hegel the history of the World, which is the autobiography of the Absolute Spirit, is an integral part of the philosophical reflection. Rejecting idealism, other philosophers, many working from outside the university, initiated lines of thought that would occupy academic philosophy in the early and mid-20th centuries: In the late 19th century and early 20th century, several forms of pragmatic philosophy arose. The ideas of pragmatism in its various forms developed mainly from discussions that took place with Charles Sanders Peirce and

William James. Husserl initiated the school of phenomenology. Kierkegaard and Nietzsche laid the groundwork for existentialism. Frege's work in logic provided the tools for early analytical philosophy. Mill's utilitarianism and Marx and Engel's Marxism dominated discussions in political philosophy until Rawls' 1971 work *A Theory of Justice*. There has been both a history of philosophy and a philosophy of history. History sees philosophy as merely an occurrence among other occurrences, while philosophy claims to judge the very validity, meaning and reality of history.[34] History has been understood as the developing self-actualisation of reality and in this sense has been regarded as identical with philosophy.

Scope of Philosophy
The scope of philosophy in the ancient understanding, and the writings of the ancient philosophers, was all intellectual endeavours. This included the problems of philosophy as they are understood today, but it also included many other disciplines, such as pure mathematics and natural sciences such as physics, astronomy and biology. Bimal Matilal writes:[35]

> A philosophical position is hardly considered as established or vindicated unless it has answered its critics and responded to the objections of its opponents.... . The opponents usually hold a different view, disagreeing with the philosopher, and record his disagreements giving some reasons or counter-arguments. But sometimes the opponents may simply disagree and refute the propositions of the philosopher without holding any particular doctrine of his own.

Karl Marx said that "philosophers try to interpret the world, but the task is to change it." Aristotle said that "all men by nature desire to know." Philosophy is a subject that influences many aspects of our lives and our understandings of our expressions. Philosophy has claimed to be knowledge rather than opinion. Modern philosophy started with a universal doubt in quest of a mathematical certainty that shall renew the very possibility of doubt and we are as far removed from any agreement as before. Philosophising the necessary life-touching field of thoughts is the need of the hour. Philosophers have to be in search of more possibilities of philosophising the high morale and philosophic conceptions in the practical-oriented system. The scope of philosophy is very high in this contemporary world of thought.

The goal of a philosophy based on self-evident axioms reached its height with Spinoza's Ethics, which expounded a pantheistic view of the universe where God and Nature were one. This idea then became central to the Enlightenment from Newton through to Jefferson. The ideas of

Pascal, Leibniz, Galileo and other philosophers of the previous period also contributed to and greatly influenced the Enlightenment. There was a wave of change across European thinking as exemplified by Newton's natural philosophy, which combined mathematics of axiomatic proof with mechanics of physical observation, a coherent system of verifiable predictions.

Search for wisdom is said to be the goal of philosophy. By wisdom, one can broadly mean ideas, insights in understanding the world, in its judgments about its truth and their religious and ethical implications, questioning and challenging the presuppositions of these judgments.[36] In olden days, higher learning or development of knowledge was called philosophy and highly learned scholar or lover of knowledge was called philosopher. Now the scope of philosophy has greatly increased. Generally, it has the following three major divisions:

i. Metaphysics: (a) Theology; (b) Metaphysics regarding soul; (c) Science of universe; (d) Science of creation; and (e) Cosmology.

ii. Epistemology: Theory of knowledge

iii. Axiology: (a) Logic; (b) Ethics; and (c) Aesthetics

There are good reasons for presenting the scope of philosophy, for the most part, and I trust this chapter will clarify. The principal reason is that philosophical analysis is really no more than a tool for exploring and clarifying a set of ideas. It does not in any way attempt to impose an alien system on Christian philosophy. It simply takes a given subject matter, in this case, the doctrines of the creed, and examines them for their meaning and plausibility. The skills and methods of philosophical analysis are to be applied to these doctrines chiefly in order to probe and explain their coherence.

Functions of Philosophy

The function of philosophy is to distinguish the different kinds of reasoning, to discuss the weight we should give to each and the contexts in which each is appropriate. Just as reasoning is of different kinds so the conclusions reached have not the same logical status.[37] The function of philosophy in relation to religion is to enquire what kind of statements are religious statements and what the criteria are as we judge them true or false. It will also enquire the logical status of different religious terms such as grace, spirit, resurrection etc. Philosophy enables us to see more clearly what our beliefs mean. Philosophy as a 'general' discipline that has something to do with 'life' and especially with 'reasoning'. Few genuine properties shared by all philosophers can be found as far as its function is concerned. But the ways in which different thinkers characterise philosophy can be important as a normative statement about how philosophy should be done. The task is made more difficult by the fact that the use and meaning of the word *philosophy* has changed throughout history. In antiquity, it encompassed almost any inquiry; for Descartes, it was supposed to be the Queen of the Science; in the time of David Hume, metaphysics and morals could be roughly translated as the human sciences, while analytic philosophy likes to define itself roughly as inquiry into concepts.

The function of the philosopher is neither to understand nor change it; his function is merely to clarify certain conceptual confusions in which he finds himself involved when thinking about certain problem. In a sense, every person changes the world, whatever we may mean by this term, in some way and understands it to some degree and is engaged in philosophic confusions and makes an attempt at their philosophical clarification, to some extent.[38] Philosophy is simultaneously a name for the conceptual that arises in thinking about any subject and the attempt at the clarification of those confusions. Here is a region, a realm, a set of problems. It only needs a name and we submit that the word 'philosophy' can adequately perform this function. Philosophical analysis and evaluation shall have to be brought upon certain important areas of human thought and experience whereby we have the emergence of the philosophy of art, of mathematics, of history, of science, of education and so on. All these are now considered as different disciplines. General artists, mathematicians and educational theorists have welcomed philosophical clarifications and the dialogue with philosophers. When philosophy asks: What is goodness? What is rightness? Then it is classified as moral philosophy or ethics because it is dealt with the moral judgment.[39] When it asks: What is argument? What is fallacy? Then it can be classified as logic because one set of beliefs is entailed by another set. When philosophy asks How is the mind related to the body or is human behaviour determined or free? How space is related to time? then it is classified as metaphysics. When philosophy asks How do you know? Does man posses certain notions and ideas innately? then it is the theory of knowledge or epistemology. Over time, academic specialisation and the rapid technical advance of the special sciences led to the development of distinct disciplines for these sciences, and their separation from philosophy. Mathematics became a specialised science in the ancient world, and 'natural philosophy' developed into the disciplines of the natural sciences over the course of the scientific revolution. Today, philosophical questions are usually explicitly distinguished from the questions of the special sciences and characterised by the fact that they are the sort of questions that are foundational and abstract in nature, and which are not amenable to being answered by experimental means.

The function of philosophy would thus mainly consist in an analysis and experience of confusions which stand in the way of such a scientific study. Any misconception about the function of philosophy can stand powerfully in the way of such deepening. It is the task of philosophy to be self-conscious of its function and avoid dictating the limits to either science or religion. For every kind of study and thinking, the help of philosophy is necessary and no subject can be studied systematically in its absence. Thus, in almost all the subjects, either they are separate philosophical ideas or they are accepted as a part of philosophy. According to William James, giving an exhaustive list of the main divisions of philosophy is difficult, because various topics have been studied by philosophers at various times. Ethics, metaphysics, epistemology and logic are usually included. Other topics include politics, aesthetics and religion. In addition, most academic subjects have a philosophy; for example, the philosophy of science, the philosophy of mathematics and the philosophy of history.

Function of Christian philosophy must also be thoroughly discussed. Examining the Christian faith philosophically helps us to express it in an articulate way. The intellectual understanding of the Christian faith is the ability to express it with more clarity. As Christians, we should be ready to give an answer and the reason, or the rational account to everyone, if we may be asked (Gk. *Logion*; 1 Peter 3:15). This means that we must give some place to rational argument. All evangelists and preachers reason when they preach the gospel.

Role of the Philosopher
All over the world, the stresses and strains of living are increasing. Technology is quickening the pace of life, but thought patterns are unable to keep abreast of the conditions created by technological development. They have become ominously outmoded, for while nuclear weapons are in man's hand, his thinking remains primitive and tribalistic. What is the role of the philosopher in this situation? Civilisations have crumbled due to internal decay and external onslaughts. Our contemporary human society faces an alarming debasement of values and the external threat of

environmental deterioration, which, however, is of our own making the need of the world, defines the philosopher's role for the day. The lover of wisdom, the philosopher, can discover and share understanding about the royal road to unshakable happiness and spiritual well-being. The philosopher's role may be to restore to him a sense of perspective, and set him on the path of self-knowledge. Unfortunately, philosophy has come to be regarded as a theoretical and academic preoccupation, not meant to be applied to the practical task of providing the background and insights to assuage the world's travail, or engage the attention of individuals who are in quest of fundamental principles to guide them in daily life. Philosophy is needed to convince the ill-educated mind to disavow the irrational and the near-sighted and rise to the heights beyond the rational, to the all-embracing awareness of truth that is the true religious consciousness. Anand Amaladass writes:

> Philosophy must aid people to live rightly; its light must ray out to teach men and women how to lead purer and nobler lives. In other words, the need of the day is for a philosophy that is religious, not in the conventional, sectarian, narrow sense, but as a power to purify the mind of prejudice and the heart of its selfishness. Conversely, we may say that the world needs a religion that is made noble and universal by the light of philosophy.[40]

It is one thing to define the role of the philosopher in terms of the formal object of his inquiry, differentiating his role from that of a sociologist or an anthropologist, since each discipline has a specific scope and thrust. And it is another thing to talk about the role of the philosopher as a person involved in society, committed to the truth he perceives as a thinker. His role is not to be seen as dissociated from his lifestyle.

Philosophy transcends on the one hand its culture in the sense that the 'wisdom' of one culture is potentially available to the people of another culture. On the other hand, this 'wisdom tradition' even as it transcends its culture, remains immersed within its cultural setting and presuppositions and in that sense it is not universally available for the assent of the rational mind. So the 'wisdom' is always culturally rooted. There has been also a search for wisdom across the cultures. Every culture is confronted with questions and challenges from outside. Philosophy is a permanent process of enlightenment; it is not an art of what one can make of man, but what he can make of himself. There was a time, in the Christian Middle Ages, when philosophy used to be treated as the servant maid of theology, and then came another time, from the middle of the 19th century almost to this day, when philosophy was assigned the place of a servant maid to the sciences. If philosophy should be treated as anyone's servant, it could and should only be the family of man as such: philosophy as serving man in creating genuine humane and humanitarian conditions among human beings.

Besides this impersonal stance of philosopher to reality from the earlier times, in the contemporary period they take philosophy as a profession, means of livelihood; a way of 'doing' rather than way of 'being.' For a philosopher who considers philosophy as an intellectual, impersonal enterprise, and reduces it to a part-time profession, the question regarding the role of philosopher poses little problem. The task of the philosopher is not to directly interfere with public life; he is normally not the one having the practical means and the political power to bring about social change. His task is that of a caretaker, a custodian who, based on his subtle reflection on the principle to what we can know and on an open discourse with others, shows the way of how, on what maxims we should act in order to safeguard the future of man – the basic assumption, of course, being that to secure the future of mankind is a desirable aim.[41]

Purpose of Philosophising

The philosopher as thinker is to be a 'dweller' on the earth, making it his 'home' and being at peace with others, with the nature and with himself: The challenge to be thinkers implies also that we be 'holy' thinkers. Such a role of philosophers as thinkers of the Divine brings Heideggerian thought-structure closer to Eastern thought, according to which there is no difference between thinking of reality or philosophising and thinking of the Divine or theologising. 'Philosophy is an adventure' and philosophers are to be adventurous. According to Gabriel Marcel, "Philosophy has no weight and no interest whatever unless it sounds an echo in our life." Kant writes:

> Philosophy is a mere idea of a possible system of knowledge which exists nowhere in concerto. We can only learn to philosophize, that is to exercise the talent of reason, according to its general principles... however with reservation of the right of the reason to investigate the sources of these principles themselves, and of either accepting or rejecting them[42]

Anand Amaladass suggested that only one can be said to philosophise who neither submits to any authoritative text nor to any exemplary individual thinker; since for the philosopher there is no sacred texts nor are there holy nor wise men in possession of truth as such.[43] The question about the role of the philosopher is connected with the role of philosophy. So, three points emerge from the views expressed by the two distinguished philosophers mentioned above. First, philosophy, which is for the sake of the people, has an important part to play in society. Second, there are problems or questions of everyday life covering the entire range of philosophy. Making a distinction between 'pure philosophy' and 'applied philosophy'; we can say that some of the problem, e.g. question about God, the knowledge of the external world, the knowledge of other minds, questions about good and bad, right and wrong, fall in the area of pure philosophy, and some others such as abortion, euthanasia, sexual immorality, world hunger, civil disobedience, capital punishment, professional ethics, etc., are dealt with in applied philosophy. Third, philosophy must help one to realise oneself. Self-realisation is the basic factor one can achieve through philosophy.

Conclusion

History of philosophy will help us understand better both ourselves and those with whom we might disagree. We need to read about the past in order to understand the present. By studying the thought of the past generations we can be challenged where our views are defective and helped to see our own pet ideas in a proper perspective. We can easily understand that our own grasp of truth might be less than perfect and that it is possible to learn from those with a different perspective. The adherents of Christian philosophy must understand its goal very clearly. People of other religious groups have been frequently challenging us with regard to the uniqueness and finality of the Christian faith. But we should reaffirm that Christian faith is unique and Christianity is not compatible with cults, the occult, non-Christian religions and secular movements. When we share the gospel or discuss the Christian faith with those who have no experience of Christian faith, it is necessary to find some common ground, which is appropriately reasoning and logical. At the same time, we should understand that Christian faith by its very nature cannot be understood without Christian experience.

Helpful Questions

1. Briefly describe the history of philosophy.

2. What do you know about the functions of philosophy?

3. What is the role of the philosopher?

CHAPTER 3

Origin of Western Philosophy

This chapter will help you to understand the origin of philosophy in Greece. It will also give you an idea of the contribution of Greek philosophers to philosophy.

Ancient Greece was the cradle of western civilisation. Earliest known-thinkers (500 BC) are called Pre-Socratic Philosophers. They were not satisfied with the mythological explanations that were offered by the prevalent Greek polytheistic religion. They were also known as Cosmologists. They wrestled with two puzzling questions of human life:[44] (1) They observed that the world is made of many different kinds of things. They disagreed on what they conceived as the unifying stuff of physical nature—was it water, air, fire? (2) Likewise they were puzzled by the obvious fact that nature undergoes transformation. They realised that everything is under constant change. Does the one change into many? Then how is it one? The 'problem of change' was the second enigma they set to solve out.

Greek philosophy is the first of the philosophies of the West. It focused on the role of reason and inquiry. There is considerable discussion about why Athenian culture encouraged philosophy, but a popular theory says that it occurred because Athens had a direct democracy. It is known from Plato's writings that many sophists maintained schools of debate, were respected members of society, and were well paid by their students. Another theory explains the birth of philosophical debate in Athens with the presence of a slave labour workforce which performed the necessary functions that would otherwise have consumed the time of the free male citizenry. Freed from working in the fields or other manual economic activities, they were able to participate in the assemblies of Athens and spend long periods in discussions on popular philosophical questions. Students of Sophists needed to acquire the skills of oration in order to influence the Athenian Assembly and thereby increase respect and wealth. In response, the subjects and methods of debate became highly developed by the Sophists.

Ancient philosophy may be divided into three periods: the Pre-Socratic period, the Socratic period, and the post-Aristotelian period. The pre-Socratic period was characterised by metaphysical speculation, often preserved in the form of grand, sweeping statements, such as 'all is fire, or all changes.' The Socratic period is named in honour of the most recognisable figure in Western philosophy, Socrates, who, along with his pupil, Plato, revolutionised philosophy through the use of the Socratic method, which developed the very general philosophical methods of definition, analysis and synthesis. While no writings of Socrates survive, his influence as a skeptic is transmitted through Plato's works. Plato's writings are often considered basic texts in philosophy as they define the fundamental issues of philosophy for future generations. These issues and others were taken up by Aristotle, who studied at Plato's school, the Academy, and who often disagreed with what Plato had written. Philosophy became a much wider subject in the post-Aristotelian period.

Pre-Socratic Period
Pre-Socratic period covers the period of philosophy until Socrates came into scene. They were known as Sophists. The word "philosopher" was accepted by Socrates later; however, philosophical teachings were prevalent even before Socrates.

The Ionian Dawn
The earliest philosopher-scientists are generally mentioned by the name of the place to which they belonged. They hailed from the Greek colony called Ionia; so they are called the early Ionians.

Thales of Miletus in Ionia
He belonged to 6th century BC. Some of the authorities want to be more precise and claim that he was born about 624 B.C. and died about 550 BC. We learn from Herodotus that the life of Thales belonged to the reigns of Layettes and Croesus, kings of Lydia, and that he was still living shortly before the fall of Sardis in 546 BC. We are also told that at an earlier date, he had predicted the eclipse of the Sun that put an end to a battle between Lydians and the Medes. That was in 585 BC.

The great renown of Thales was due to his assertion that the first or primitive ground of all things is water: from water everything originates and to water everything returns.[45] Along with this is associated the view that the world is like a flat disc floating on water. In ancient mythology there were indeed views about some water-god creating everything in the universe. What Thales did was to scrap the concept of god and retain water only as the first cause. It must have been a very courageous step to take, the whole point of which was to try to understand nature in terms of a purely natural phenomenon free all mythic imagination of the past.

Anaximander of Miletus

The ancients described him sometimes as a disciple of Thales, sometimes simply as his contemporary. He defined his primitive matter, in connection with which he is supposed to be the first to use the term principle, as the eternal, infinite, indefinite ground, from which in order of time, all arises, and into which all returns. It comprehends and rules all the spheres of the universe. It underlies every individual cause of the finite and mutable. But it is itself infinite and indefinite. Ancient Greek philosophy, proposes to interpret Anaximander's position as follows: Once upon a time the four elements of which the world is made lay in a more stratified form: earth, which is the heaviest, at the centre, water covering it, mist above the water, fire embracing all. Here are a few fragments of Anaximander that have reached us.

The Non-Limited is the original material of existing things; further, the source from which existing things derive their existence is also that to which they return at their destruction, according to necessity; for they give justice and make reparation to one another for their injustice, according to the arrangement of time. The essential nature, whatever it is, of the Non-Limited is everlasting and ageless. The Non-Limited is immortal and indestructible.

Anaximenes

The third great philosopher to carry forward the Ionian tradition was either a disciple or a contemporary of Anaximander. Instead of water, however, he conceived it as air. "Air is constantly in motion and has the power of motion inherent in it and this motion brought about the development of the universe from air." As the operating process of this development Anaximenes named two opposite processes: (1) rarefaction and (2) condensation. Rarefaction is the same thing as heat or growing hot, and condensation is identified with growing cold. The air by rarefaction becomes fire, and the fire borne aloft upon the air becomes the stars. By the opposite process of condensation, air first becomes clouds and, by further degrees of condensation, becomes successively water, earth and rocks. The world resolves again in the course of time into primal air.

Only one full sentence of Anaximenes' work has survived: "As our soul, being air, holds us together, so do breath and air surround the whole universe." The first philosophers, as Farrington shows, were men of an active type, drawing their thoughts from the experience gained through technique. So their interest was in the material world and the fundamental principles underlying it.

The Pythagorean School
With Pythagoras Greek Philosophy takes a new turn from naturalism or materialism of the early Ionians to a peculiar blend of science and mysticism. Pythagoras, the founder of the school, came from Samos, an island near Miletus, and his date is generally accepted as 582-500 BC. But he immigrated to south Italy, where he is said to have founded some kind of society or brotherhood maintaining morality and discipline, order and harmony of the whole community. In any case, there were two aspects in the thoughts and ideas introduced by the Pythagorean School. These were mathematical, on the one hand, and mystical, on the other. The former was of very decisive historical significance while the latter was indicative for marked regression in Greek thought. The mathematical zeal of the Pythagoreans culminated in the theory of number.

Pythagoras preached the doctrine of the immortality of the soul, the human body being a prison for it. Release and transmigration of soul is possible through contemplation and ritual practices. To woo the people they applied the method of double tradition—mathematics and mysticism. He somehow inter-mingled science and religious fervour. The peculiarity of Pythagorean philosophy is that it invented number theory as the key to the riddle of the universe. The emphasis on number is a landmark in the history of science, no doubt, but difficulty arose when the Pythagoreans formulated the theory that the number is the fundamental framework of the world. According to Pythagoras everything in the universe, corporeal or incorporeal, is numerable. In the very aspect of things in the universe, there is number.

Heraclitus: New Turn
Heraclitus of Ephesus flourished about the year 513 BC. He was surnamed by his successors as the Dark. He wrote a work entitled *On Nature*, which

survives for us only in fragments. Further, he conceived in his own way for the first time in European thought that this basic fact about the world, namely ceaseless motion or perpetual becoming, was due to the inner contradiction operating in the world. Heraclitus says: "Everything is in a state of flux; nothing subsist nor does it ever remain the same."[46] Reality is understood as a dynamic becoming. This universal principle is better characterised as *Becoming*, rather than *Being*, since everything is and is not, Heraclitus hereby expressed that everything is *Becoming*. Not merely does origination belong to it, but passing away as well; both are not independent, but identical. It is a great advance in thought to pass from *Being* to *Becoming*, even if, as the first unity of opposite determinations, it is still abstract. To him, the fundamental character of reality is change.

He represented a continuation of the tradition and made a natural principle, namely fire, the basic stuff of everything. At the same time, his stupendous advance from the Ionians must not be overlooked. The world, which is the same for all, has not been made any god or man; it has ever been, is now, and ever shall be, ever-living fire, kindled by measure, quenched by measure. The best symbol to express the constantly changing one-in-many is fire. Heraclitus concluded that everything is fire. Thus, the primary substance, according to Heraclitus, is fire. But his fire is not primary in the sense of being original. His world has no origin. It has existed always. Nothing is permanent. To him, difference is essential to unity. Unity exists in the tension of opposites. Opposites are composites. Reality is one and many.

Heraclitus' sayings— "The world, as entity out of everything, was created by none of the gods or men, but was, is and will be eternally living fire, regularly becoming ignited and regularly becoming extinguished...."—is a very good exposition of the principles of dialectical materialism. Heraclitus is said to have written one book, encyclopedic in scope, in oracular style. His remark on one and many as well as the change is so closer to the Buddhist analysis of reality, which asserts that *sarvam anityam*—everything is impermanent. David Hume's philosophy of skepticism also supports it. Heraclitus is the forerunner of the great idea of 'dialectic' according to Hegel and Marxist philosophers. For them, reality is understood as a dynamic becoming.

There are criticisms too. Parmenides is in front to oppose the philosophic concepts of Heraclitus with special reference to 'nothing is permanent.' It is against our self-experience, which is real. There are permanent laws in physical nature. It is the task of philosophers to understand the multiple change of reality.

The Eliatics

The name of the school was derived from Elea, a town in south Italy. The most prominent philosopher representing the school was Parmenides and Zeno, both of whom were citizens of Elea. But the reputed founder of the school was Xenophanes.

Xenophanes

Xenophanes was, primarily speaking, not a philosopher in the strict sense. His interest was mainly in religion, and as a religious leader, he was evidently much influenced by the mysticism of the Pythagoreans. Though born about the year 576 BC at Colophon in Ionia, he cast aside all that was positive in the scientific achievements of the early Ionians. Views are summed up as follows: "The idea of the unit of God, and the polemic against the anthropomorphism of the popular religion, this is his starting point. God, for him, is an eye: understanding, ear; unmoved, undivided, undisturbed ruling all through thought; and like to men neither in form nor understanding. In this manner, mainly intent on diverting from God all terms and predicates of finitude, and establishing his unity and immutableness, he enunciated at the same time this his true nature as his highest philosophical principle without however negatively carrying out, by polemically turning it against finite being."

Parmenides

He was born in the last quarter of the sixth century B.C., he could have undergone in his early life, some influence of Pythagoreanism and it is presumed that he could even have been a member of the Pythagorean order. His philosophical poem begins with some kind of mystical vision, which must have been inspired by the mystery religions of the ancient Greeks. This part of his poem, though showing his religious bent of mind, has little or no philosophical interest. The real philosophical interest of the poem is to be found in the remaining portion of his poem, which is divided into two main parts called the Way of Truth and the Way of seeming.

In the Way of Truth Parmenides gave his own theory of the nature of the universe. One of its most original features is the categorical denial of the evidence of the senses. The fundamental character of the reality is permanent, not change, 'being' and not 'becoming', one and not many. There is only one stable being; plurality and change are illusions. Being is called absolutism. There exists only one absolute reality and nothing else. He held the view of ontological monism. To him, the way of reason is the only way, reveals the truth, that reality is one and stable. In the Way of Seeming, which follows, the evidence of the senses is accepted. In his view, the Way of Truth refers to the intelligible world, the Way of Seeming to the sensible world. The way of Seeming may be regarded as a preparation for the Way of Truth. According to Parmenides, one immutable being, understood only by pure reason, is the exclusive reality. The world of multiplicity and change, known to us by our everyday experience of practical life, is only an illusion.[47]

> The fundamental character of reality is permanence, not change, being and not becoming, one and not many. There is only stable being. Plurality and change are illusions. If 'A' is being and 'B' is being, A is the same as B. A can not become B, for both are being. Parmenides held the view of 'Ontological Monism'; being (Ontos) is one (monos). It is also called 'Absolutism'; there exists only one absolute (independent and unrelated) reality and nothing else.

In explaining a changing multiple world of things, Parmenides reached a wrong conclusion. It is evident that we perceive multiplicity and change in the things of the world. His philosophic conflict with Heraclitus stimulated subsequent Greek philosophers to make a search for more balanced and moderate views. He also contributed in the field of epistemology or the theory of knowledge. To him, there are two ways of knowing—sense experience and reason. Moreover, his ontological monism or absolutism is similar to the Advaita philosophy of Shankaracharya (A.D. 600). Changing reality is illusory for both of them. But its paradoxical teaching of Heraclitus became famous—"being versus becoming, one versus many, permanent versus change, and experience versus rationalism."

Zeno

A disciple of Parmenides, Zeno wanted to prove the master's thesis—mainly which only the One Immutable Being is real—by a series of most tricky arguments designed to prove that multiplicity and movements must be unreal inasmuch as these are infested with internal contradictions. Zeno argued that since what we thus see cannot be logically tenable, the observed movement must be our illusion.

Zeno wrote a book entitled *Attack* in defense of Parmenides' theory of *Being* as One and Indivisible. He controverted the opposite proposition that Things are Many and showed how two contradictory conclusions are to be derived from the same. He held that the unchanging being to be real and relegated all becoming and change to the realm of the unreal.[48]

Empedocles: Science and Idealism

There was another philosopher who paved the path for atomism. He was Empedocles. Empedocles was a statesman and an orator, a physicist and a physician, sometimes supposed by the ancient Greeks even as a prophet. He was assumed to have flourished in the middle of the fifth century B.C. The four recognised forms of matter had not been 'Earth, Air, Fire, and water', but 'Earth, Mist, Fire, and Water.' Empedocles substituted Mist by Air and even went to an experimental demonstration of its physical reality. Apart from the four elements, Empedocles spoke no doubt of the forces of Love and Hate, which went to the making of the world of multiplicity. Empedocles wrote two poems—*On Nature and Purifications*.

The Atomists

If the experiment of Empedocles proves that nature works by unseen bodies, it bore a magnificent philosophical result in the speculations of the atomists, the atoms being too minute to be directly perceived. The founders of the atomic hypothesis were Leucippus and Democritus. Little is really known about their lives. But it is generally believed that Leucippus was born about 440 B.C. and he came from Mellitus. Democritus was born in the Ionian colony of Abdera about 460 B.C. Thus, both the philosophers were connected with the early materialistic tradition of Ionia. As a matter of fact Ionian materialism reached its culmination in the philosophy of the atomists. The word "atom" literally means the uncut table or the ultimate indivisible. Thus the idea seems to have been small and smaller parts; we are logically led to a point beyond which we cannot subdivide it into still smaller parts. The smallest unit of matter thus arrived at is the atom.

Ancient science had clearly established the fact that Nature works by unseen bodies. Modern science has devised progressively better methods of seeing the unseen. Yet Democritus says that each of the individual bodies is heavier in proportion to its excess. Democritus said there was only one kind of motion, that due to vibration. As the atoms move they collide and become entangled in such a way as to cling in close contact to one another, but not so as to form one substance of them in reality of any kind whatever, for it is very simple-minded to suppose that two or more could ever become one. Democritus says that the spherical is the most mobile of shapes; and such is mind and fire. Everything in the world ultimately consists of such minute particles. With the revival of the atomic theory in modern science, particularly by Dalton, there is a great deal of renewed interest in the atomism of the ancient Greeks.

Anaxagoras: The First Idealist

Anaxagoras was born about the year 500 BC. Soon after the Persian War, he took his abode in Athens. He lived there till, being accused of blasphemy, he was forced to flee to Lampuscus, where he died. It was he who transplanted philosophy to Athens, which then became the centre of Grecian culture. His *On Nature* was much in circulation. Hegel greatly admired the first introduction of the principle of 'The Mind' by Anaxagoras. This principle of Mind according to Anaxagoras introduced order into the mass of primitive constituents of things, conceived by him as Fire, Air, Earth and Water. Anaxagoras describes this intelligence as spontaneously operative, unmixed with anything, the ground of all motion, but itself unmoved, everywhere actively present, and of all things the finest and purest. It was only the necessity of a moving cause possessed at the same time of designing activity, which had brought him to the idea of an immaterial principle. His Mind is in strictness, therefore, only a mover of matter: in this function its entire virtue is almost quite exhausted. All Things were together, infinite in number and in smallness, for the small also was infinite. And since all were together, nothing was distinguishable because of its smallness.

At any rate, with Anaxagoras the first period of Greek philosophy is said to have come to its end. This was partly because of the triumph announced for the principle of subjectivity—of the Mind—and partly because of the transplantation of philosophical activity to Athens. Anaxagoras was the author of only one book, which sold at Athens for one *drachma*. The philosophical concepts of Anaxagoras versus Democritus became very important among the philosophers. Their problem was not epistemological, but metaphysical, or materialism versus spiritualism. For Democritus, the world was created by atoms (atomism); but for Anaxagoras, the world was created by a spiritual principle that transcends the cosmic reality. Anaxagoras rejects materialism.

The Sophists

Theoretically speaking, the Sophists expressed the boundless egoism of their time, both in public and in private. They were prominent in Greece until the period Socrates monopolised the field of philosophy by way of criticising the Sophists.

Protagoras

The first sophist of any eminence we are told of was Protagoras who flourished around 440 B.C. He professed to be teacher in Sicily and Athens and he was the first philosopher blatantly demanding payment for teaching. The main point of his teaching is that there exists no world other than that of individual sensation, just as in practical life there was no sense anywhere outside personal gratification. Nor did he show any reverence for the accepted gods. In the open market he is said to have declared, "As for the gods, I am unable to know whether they are or whether they are not; for there is much that prevents us from knowing these things, as well the obscurity of the subject as the shortness of the life of man."

Accordingly, his book on the gods was burnt in the open market. Protagoras was the author of two books – *Truth* (also called *Regulatory Arguments* or On Being) and *On the Gods*. Here are some of the surviving fragments: "Of all things the measure is Man, of the things that are, that they are, and of the things that are not, that they are not. Art without practice, and practice without art, are nothing. Education does not take root in the soul unless one goes deep."

Gorgias

The most celebrated sophist after Protagoras was Gorgias who flourished in 427 B.C., and was about the greatest orator of his time. The main point of his teaching was that nothing exists, or if something exists it cannot be known, or communicated. The first generation of Sophists (Protagoras, Gorgias) was of honourable men; the second generation, whom these men reared, was professing scoundrels. Gorgias is one of the earliest authors to compose a manual of Rhetoric. Some of his model orations have survived. As to his philosophical views we have to rely on later writers' comments.

Socratic Period

Three famous Greek philosophers—Socrates, Plato and Aristotle—are included in the category of the Socratic period. Their main philosophical teachings will be discussed briefly here. It is obvious that they are prominent figures among Greek philosophers. They reshaped the nature of philosophy and through them philosophy became an important subject of study and a special department in almost all universities of the world.

Socrates (470-399 B.C.)

Out of the philosophical chaos created by the Sophists came a philosopher giant, Socrates. He was born in 470 B.C. and is known to have a predilection for discussing the meaning and purpose of life with youths in particular, convincing them of their ignorance and rousing in them the slumbering seeds of knowledge. Socrates was a key figure in transforming Greek philosophy into a unified and continuous project. He was the most outstanding personality of Greek antiquity. He was an itinerant Guru in Athens.

He used the pedagogic method (Socratic Method), which was considered by many as his own. His method was not monologue, rather dialogue. He called this the midwifery method. He would ask questions and let them think and answer.[49] Socrates' awareness of his own ignorance allowed him to discover his errors as well as the errors of those who claimed knowledge based upon falsifiable or unclear precepts and beliefs. Philosophy for Socrates was more a matter of living a noble life than changing to a body of dogmas. His philosophy is wholly individual practice; life and doctrine cannot in his case be separated. He taught, "man, know yourself." To him, truth is in everyone's heart and truth is within. If one knows the good, one will do good. Obstacle is ignorance; virtuous behaviour flows from knowledge. He said, "man, know yourself and you will be virtuous."

He studied under several Sophists. He examined common but critical concepts that lacked clear or concrete definitions, such as beauty and truth, and the virtues of piety, wisdom, temperance, courage and justice. But he rejected the relativity of truth, justice and the Unitarian approach of the Sophists. He discovered the ethical truth that helps man to be virtuous and wiser. He said that every human is pregnant with the truth and the teacher is nothing more than a helpful 'midwife.' He emphasised the ethical truth that helps human beings to be wiser and more virtuous, than discovering the speculative truth of cosmology. Socrates said that "virtuous behaviour necessarily flows from knowledge and the ignorance is the obstacle to a good moral life. If a man knows himself, he will be virtuous."[50] Socrates wrote nothing, but inspired many disciples, including many sons of prominent Athenian citizens (mainly Plato), which led to his trial and execution in 399 B.C. on the charge that his philosophy and sophistry were undermining the youth, piety and moral fibre of the city. He was offered a chance to flee from his fate but chose to remain in Athens, abide by his principles and drink the poison hemlock.

Apparently, the corrupt life of Athenians proved for Socrates too derogatory to live. He, therefore, found in death a good riddance. In his dialogue *Phaedo*, Plato wants us to believe that Socrates had the sense to add a quaint humour to it. He was brought twice before the Athenian senators who accused him of corrupting the youth by turning them away from the gods of Athens. He was finally condemned by the senators to drink a deadly poison—hemlock. His last words were addressed to his friend Crito: I owe a cock to Esclapius: Will you remember to pay the debt?' Esclapius was the god of healing, and it was customary to sacrifice to him when one had recovered from an illness. The meaning of the image is then that Socrates, by death, was recovering from a long disease, which was life.

We know more about Socrates only through the writings of Plato, his disciple. Many of the writings of Plato survived. Aristotle, the disciple of Plato, criticised Socrates' teaching on the role of free will. The will can be in conflict with the intellect. A man who knows what is good can still remain not doing it. Knowledge is sufficient to make people virtuous. He reduced the role of will to being the faithful servant of human knowledge. But the Upanishads agree with him that ignorance or *avidya* is the root of all evils. Even Leibniz (1670 AD) supports the view through his concepts that the human will always follows the best reason presented to it by the intellect. Secondly, Socrates taught that every truth is within. But it is not right, not all truth is within. The self must not be erected as a universally valid principle. However, he was the most outstanding teacher of the moral conscience of humanity. He was concerned with individual ethics, not social ethics.

Plato (428-348 B.C.)
The death of Socrates was followed by certain rather minor tendencies that developed in Greek philosophy. There are the Cynic, Cyrenaic and Megaric schools associated specially with the names of Antisphene, Aristippus and Euclid respectively. None of these, however, made any great impact on Greek thought. Then Plato came to the scene, perhaps the greatest name in Greek philosophy. Born in a noble Attic family in 429 B.C., Plato came under the influence of Socrates at a time when his political ambition was arrested for good by the return of democracy, which he hated as intensely as the naturalistic tradition of the early Ionians. This led him to philosophical Idealism and as a matter of fact he became its greatest exponent in European thought. The crux of his philosophical view is his Ideal theory. Plato was Socrates' most important student. He made three trips to Cicily to be the teacher of the young king.

Plato founded the Academy in Athens, the first European university and wrote 24 dialogues, which applied the Socratic method of inquiry to examine philosophical problems. *The Republic* is the best of all works of

Plato. His metaphysical dualism is to be specially mentioned. To him, there are two kinds of reality—material or physical and spiritual. First is the spacio-temporal reality, which can be perceived by the senses only. This reality is always in constant flux. The latter is the universally true, unchanging and eternal reality. His anthropological dualism was more prominent than the rest of his teachings. Man is composed of a material body and a spiritual soul. Man's soul is the true reality although he belongs to both the worlds. Jean Mercier writes:[51]

> The immortality of the human soul is thus the cardinal doctrine of Platonist anthropology. His famous dialogue, the 'Phaedo', contains an account of the 'proofs' he gave in favour of the immortality of the human soul. One argument was that the soul being spiritual is imperishable. Further he argued that what pre-exists from all eternity must also eternally post-exist.

Some central ideas of Plato's dialogues, such as the Theory of Forms, are that the mind is imbued with an innate capacity to understand and contemplate concepts from a higher order pre-eminent world. Concepts are more real, permanent and universal than representative of the things of this world, which are only changing and temporal. The idea of the immortal soul is superior to the body and the idea of evil is simple ignorance of truth. The true knowledge leads to true virtue and the art is subordinate to moral purpose. The society of the city-state should be governed by a merit class of propertyless philosopher king, with no permanent wives or paternity rights over their children, and be protected by an athletically gifted, honourable, duty bound military class. In the later dialogues, Socrates figures less prominently, but Plato had previously woven his own thoughts into some of Socrates' words.

In the dialogue called *Sophists,* Plato described the struggle between materialism and idealism as the battle of gods and Giants—the Giants are materialists of course while the gods are idealists: George Thomson shows that the controversy for him was not purely theoretical. This is evident form Plato's mature work called *The Laws.* "They say that earth, air, fire and water all exist by nature or chance, not by art, and that by means of these wholly inanimate substances there have come into being the secondary bodies – the earth, sun, moon and stars. Set in motion by their individual properties and mutual affinities, such as hot and cold, wet and dry, hard and soft, and all the other combinations formed by necessity from the chance admixture of opposites—in this way heaven has been created and everything that is in it, together with all the animals and plants, and the seasons too are of the same origin—not by means of mind of God or art but, as I said, by nature and chance."

In his *Republic* and *Laws*, Plato is wholly occupied with the problem of managing men, not at all with the problem of the control of the material environment. Accordingly the works, if full of political ingenuity, are devoid of natural science. By an ingenious piece of sophistry Plato prove, in the same passage of the *Republic*, that it is not the man who *makes* a thing, but the man who *uses*, it, who has true scientific knowledge about it. "The user, who alone has true science, must impart his science to the maker, who then has correct opinion." Plato held the view that only reason gives us the knowledge of ideas, conceptions or essences which alone real in nature. Reason is then the faculty or that power of the soil which contemplates the universal in all things.[52] This doctrine effectively exalts the position of the consumer in society and reduces the status of the producer. In explaining the philosophy of Plato, few things are to be mentioned with much emphasis:

i. Plato represented the greatest tragedy in Greek philosophy—the tragedy of a great thinker pleading for myths and falsehood, though considering this falsehood as beneficial for the society considered ideal by him, or to put it more concretely, slavery.

ii. Plato criticised democracy, condemns tyranny and proposes a three-tiered, merit-based structure of society, with workers, guardians and philosophers, in an equal relationship, where no innocents would ever be put to death again, citing the philosophers' relentless love of truth and knowledge of the forms or ideals, concern for general welfare and lack of propertied interest as causes for their being suited to govern.

iii. Plato was the champion of a spiritual world that transcends the empirical reality. He was not a theist. For him, the spiritual world is made of a multiplicity of ideas. St. Augustine proposed a theistic metaphysics where the Platonist philosophy supports the content of the divine mind.

iv. His metaphysical dualism is to be specially mentioned. To him, there are two kinds of reality-material or physical and the spiritual realities, the spacio-temporal reality and the eternal reality. It is comparable to the dualism professed by the Indian philosophical system of Samkhya.

v. His anthropological dualism describes man as composed of a material body and a spiritual soul. Man's soul is the true reality although he belongs to both the worlds. It leads to arguable consequences, which Aristotle first assailed. His anthropology is more ideological than philosophy.

Plato posited a basic cosmological argument in *The Laws*. He argued that motion in the world and in the cosmos was 'imparted motion' that would have required some kind of 'self-originated motion' to set it in motion and to maintain the motion. Plato also posited a 'demiurge' of supreme wisdom and intelligence as the creator of the cosmos in his work *Timaeus*. For Plato, the demiurge lacked the supernatural ability to create *ex nihilo* or out of nothing. The demiurge was only able to organise the 'anake.' The 'anake' was the only other co-existent element or presence in Plato's cosmology. Plato is not a theist; he is an outspoken champion of a spiritual world that transcends the empirical reality. Plato discusses the problem of knowledge in *Theaetetus* and makes Socrates say that knowledge does not consist in impression of sense; rather in reasoning about them; in that only and not mere impressions, truth and being can be attained.[53]

Aristotle (384-322 B.C.)

Plato's most outstanding student was Aristotle, perhaps the first truly systematic philosopher. Aristotle was born in 384 B.C.—the son of a physician who was also a friend of the king of Macedon. The profession of his father perhaps drew him to scientific pursuits. His interest in philosophy was largely inspired by his association with Plato, under whom he studied for about twenty years. But they fell out and Aristotle is said to have uttered a memorable sentence then: "Dear is Plato; but dearer, truth." After the death of Plato, he left Athens and went to the court of Hermeias, prince of Atarneous, in Mysia. In 343 B.C. Philip, king of Macedon, appointed him tutor to his son Alexander, who was then only thirteen years old. When Alexander went off to Persia with a view to conquering the East, Aristotle came back to Athens and founded the 'Lyceum.' Aristotle had to leave Athens as interested circles accused him of blasphemy. So, after thirteen years of teaching, he left Athens. Referring to the fate of Socrates, he said that the Athenians might not sin a second time against philosophy. He died in exile in 322 B.C. at Chalcis on account of the anti-Macedonian reaction in Athens.

Aristotle wrote mostly in dry prose and it is sometimes claimed that his writings were free from Hellenic specialty. He was acknowledged as the founder of logic, natural history, psychology and the theory of morals.

He wrote on all possible subjects including physics, ethics, metaphysics, etc. The foundation of his metaphysics was the theory of Causation, which was taken in a far wider sense than is done in our time. Aristotle finds that there are four kinds of causes: the material, the efficient, the formal and the final. Moreover, the same four causes are to be found both in human and cosmic production.

Aristotelian analysis of all propositions into those of the subject-predicate type has undoubtedly had a tremendous influence on the substance-attributes view of reality.[54] Aristotle also put forth the idea of a first cause, often referred to as the 'Prime Mover' or 'Unmoved Mover' (*primus motor*) in his work *Metaphysics*. For Aristotle too, as for Plato, the underlying 'stuff' of the universe always was in existence and always would be. Aristotle posited an underlying *ousia* (an essence or substance) of which the universe is composed, and it is the *ousia* that the Prime Mover organised and set into motion. The Prime Mover did not organise matter physically, but is instead a Being who constantly thinks about thinking itself, and who organised the cosmos by making matter the object of aspiration or desire.' The Prime Mover was, to Aristotle, a 'thinking on thinking,' an eternal process of pure thought. Thomas Aquinas called him 'the philosopher', while Dante referred to him as the 'Master of those who know.' He is the champion of philosophy of all ages.

Aristotelian logic was the first type of logic to attempt to categorise every valid syllogism. A syllogism is a form of argument that is guaranteed to be accepted, because it is known to be valid. A crucial assumption in Aristotelian logic is that it has to be about real objects. The application of Aristotelian logic is preceded by having the student memorise a rather large set of syllogisms. For Aristotle "God is the first Cause or Unmoved mover. His God is pure actuality, not subject to change. He is pure thought and pure self-consciousness, with no concern for the interior world of substances. His is a philosophical God. Therefore He is not a God to worship. God is a first Mover, the Lord of the Universe and its Ruler." Aristotle provided the first formulation of what is called the cosmological argument for the existence of God, later used by Thomas Aquinas and several other philosophers. God's existence is established as the necessary first cause of a changing universe. Aristotle's anthropology is radically opposed to the dualistic view of Plato. Man is a rational animal composed of matter and form. Soul is not being, but a principle. The human soul is not separable and therefore the idea of human soul's immortality is meaningless. Man is also rational, transcending animality by his intellectual power and free will. The distinction between *being* and *becoming* is fundamental to both Plato and Aristotle. Nothing is unchanging in this world. Everything is subject to change and decay, which is becoming. In contrast to this world of change, there is a realm of *being* that is unchanging and eternal. Reality is the realm of eternal unchanging *being* and this changing world of becoming is but a pale of reflection of reality.[55] Aristotle's philosophy was entirely different from his teacher Plato. Goethe the great German philosopher compared the philosophy of Aristotle with a pyramid in connection with its broad basis, while the philosophy of Plato was compared with an obelisk or a tongue of fire shooting up to the heavens above. Jean Mercier compared their philosophy in the following words:[56]

> While Plato was 'an idealist' who regarded the transcendent spiritual world of eternal ideas and values as the true reality and contemptuously looked down on the shadowy world of ordinary experience, Aristotle was 'an empiricist' who favoured the concrete, particular changing things of nature and human life and gathered knowledge about them to discover their immanent (not 'transcendent') unifying principles. He rejected the mystical approach of Plato and adopted a scientific approach prolonged by philosophical reflection. Philosophy, he said, begins with wonder and observation of the empirical reality on the basis of which reason is led to bring out theories to explain the facts.

Aristotle's philosophy can be summed up in the following sentences:[57] Metaphysics is the study of substances. Concrete individual things are real. He called them substance. A substance is a unity of form (idea, essence) and matter. Matter and form are inseparable respects of every individual substance. They make up the 'hylomorphic composition' (*hylo-*matter); *morphe* (form). Aristotle overcame Plato's dualism through his hylomorphic theory. For substances undergo two types of change: developmental or accidental change and radical or substantial change. Hylomorphic theory accounts for all cases of substantial change, when one substance becomes another substance. To explain accidental change, Aristotle introduced another internal composition. The world of substances and events is regulated by four causes: (1) The material cause: the material he used to make statue (marble); (2) The formal cause: the form, the idea is still in the mind of an artist; (3) The efficient cause: the work of the artist as well as the tools; and (4) The final cause: the purpose, to beautify it to earn his livelihood.

Post-Aristotelian Period
Epicureanism, Stoicism and Neo-Platonism will be discussed importantly. The Bible speaks of Epicureanism and Stoicism. Apostle Paul and his

companions met them in the midst of their missionary journey. Some of their encounters and teachings were dealt with in the Scripture. We should get a grasp of these two. Neo-Platonism is placed prominently in the field of Christian philosophy because of its influence on the writers of the New Testament and the Hellenistic Christian philosophers.

Epicureanism (342-271 B.C.)

Epicurus (341-270 B.C.) was a champion of Epicureanism. He was a fierce adversary of Stoicism. The Epicureans derived their name from Epicurus, a philosopher of Attic descent, who's 'Garden' at Athens rivaled in popularity with the 'Porch and the Academy.' The doctrines of Epicurus found wide acceptance in Asia Minor and Alexandria (95-50 B.C.). Epicurus believed that man's primary problem was the double fear of the gods and of punishment after death. His solution was simple—deny the interest of the Greek gods in the affairs of men and adopt an atomistic metaphysics that denies any possibility of human immortality. The atoms naturally dissipate at death, leaving no possibility of consciousness, and thus the fear of punishment after death is absolutely irrational. Obviously, resurrection would not be a possibility.

The object of Epicurus was to find in philosophy a practical guide to happiness. His philosophy was based on Democritus' materialistic understanding of reality. Epicurus aimed at freeing people from the fear of the gods and the fear of death. Man should enjoy life here and now and seek its lasting pleasures because there is no life after death. True pleasure and not absolute truth was the end at which he aimed; experience and not reason was the test on which he relied. It is obvious that a system thus formed would degenerate by a natural descent into mere materialism; and in this form, Epicureanism was the popular philosophy at the beginning of the Christian era. In place of the noble ethical doctrine of Stoicism, Epicurus substitutes a pragmatic hedonistic, utilitarian, self-centred view of life. The antithetical approaches of Zeno and Epicurus have their parallel in the contrasting Indian Philosophical teachings of *Yoga* and *Tantra*. Yoga advocates self-control and restraint, but Tantra teaches the opposite view of letting-go and unimpeded indulgence. When St. Paul addressed Epicureans and Stoics, Acts 17:18, at Athens, the philosophy of life was practically reduced to the teaching of these two antagonistic schools. Epicureanism was not atheistic, but it was ardently naturalistic.[58]

Stoicism (280 B.C.)

A new political situation arose in Greece with the conquest of the Roman Empire. Individual ethical preoccupations overtook the metaphysical syntheses. Philosophical thought reached into a new zone. Practical philosophies had been prioritised with moral and religious emphases. The Stoics and Epicureans, who are mentioned together in Acts 17:18 represent the two opposite schools of practical philosophy, which survived the fall of higher speculation in Greece.

Stoicism is one of these types of philosophies. Zeno of Citium, (B.C. 280) was the founder of this school. He derived its name from the painted *portico* (*stoa*) at Athens, in which he taught. Zeno was followed by Cleanthes (B.C. 260); Cleanthes was followed by Chrysippus, (B.C. 240), who was regarded as the founder of the Stoic system. Among their most prominent representatives were Zeno and Antipater of Tarsus, Seneca and Marcus Aurelius. They regarded God and the world as *power*, and its manifestation on matter as being a passive ground, in which dwells the divine energy. Their ethics were a protest against moral indifference, and to live in harmony with nature, conformably with reason and the demands of universal good, and in the utmost indifference to pleasure, pain and all external good or evil, was their fundamental maxim. This philosophy advises people to have an impassive attitude of indifference to pleasure and pain. Everything in our human life is divinely appointed and therefore we should worry about nothing. Submission to destiny is the great stoic virtue. Several famous Romans were attracted by the Stoic philosophy, such as Seneca, minister of the emperor Nero, and the emperor philosopher Marcus Aurelius (170 AD). Jean Mercier summed up this philosophy in the following words:[59]

- Stoicism has its foundation on metaphysics of cosmic pantheism. Stoicism is the first clear pantheistic system of the West. For a pantheist, the world is as real as the divine reality of which it is a partial manifestation.

- The universe is like a big fire with two constitutive principles: The active fire and the passive fire. The active fire is the soul of the universe which is signified as the Divine Immanent Reason or the impersonal law of the cosmos. The latter is the material world ruled by the divine soul.

- Man's soul is a spark of the divine fire. The Stoic man is the ascetic who controls his lower instincts and he shall be non-violent, altruistic and compassionate. His destiny is to submit to the divine cosmic rule. To be free means to surrender to the divine law, to rebel against it is foolishness.

- Some early Christians were impressed by the Stoic ethics such as self-control, asceticism, etc. They were also attracted by the Stoic inclination for the universal indifference, its lack of enthusiasm, the absence of joy and faith and a life of commitment to a personal divinity.

Stoicism, which lies in a supreme egotism, teaches doctrines of the fatherhood of God, the common bonds of mankind, the sovereignty of the soul. The ethical system of the Stoics has been commonly supposed to have a close connection with Christian morality (Acts 17:18), but the morality of stoicism is essentially based on pride, that of Christianity is based on humility; the Stoics upholds individual independence, the other upholds absolute faith in another (God); the one looks for consolation in the issue of fate, but the other in Providence; the Stoics are limited by periods of cosmic ruin, the other looks for consolation is consummated in a personal resurrection. Stoics are ultimately pantheistic, and thus man was. Stoicism is deterministic, even fatalistic and the very concept of resurrection seemed to deny the finality of death

Neo-Platonism (250 A.D.)

Neo-Platonism is a collective designation for the philosophical and religious doctrines of a heterogeneous school of speculative thinkers who sought to develop and synthesise the metaphysical ideas of Plato. The doctrine kept its essentially Greek character, however. By extension, the term is applied to similar metaphysical theories expounded in medieval, Renaissance and modern times. Doctrinally, Neo-Platonism is characterised by a categorical opposition between the spiritual and carnal, elaborated from Plato's dualism of Idea and Matter; by the metaphysical hypothesis of mediating agencies, the *nous* and the world soul, which transmit the divine power from the One to the many; by an aversion to the world of sense; and by the necessity of liberation from a life of sense through a rigorous ascetic discipline.

Plotinus was the founder of Neo-Platonism. He was born in Egypt. He joined a Persian expedition to the East. After coming to Rome, he became the spiritual leader of a religious school. He is considered as the most 'oriental' of all the Greek philosophers. His way of life as a 'guru' (teacher) of a sect and the mystico-religious inclinations of his thought makes him the most eastern of the Greek philosophers and Plotinus' philosophy can be summed up in four important points.[60] (a) His metaphysics is monistic, though not pantheistic. It is a synthesis of Parmenides (Reality is one) and Plato (the primacy of the Spirit). He called the absolute 'the One'; because the one is totally transcendent, it is everything known, beyond thought. From the 'One' proceeds or emanates the first Being, the Nous or *Logos*. (b) Logos is an intermediate between the One and the universe. Then from this *logos* emanates the soul of the world, then the individual souls, etc. The world comes from the One; but not identical to the One. Everything is ultimately destined to return to the one. (c) For Plotinus, man as a spiritual soul trapped in a physical body, participates in the cosmic process of reinstatement into the One through mystical union. Plotinus' metaphysics should be mentioned with two important accounts—the unity of the absolute reality and its relationship with the world. Plotinus' solution satisfies our understanding on acknowledging the unity of the absolute reality, where Plato failed. (d) Moreover, he taught that the finite world derives, proceeds necessarily from the One. The idea of causing 'to be' is attested for the first time. Aristotle failed to explain that the absolute is the cause of the world's existence.

The word soul, however, because it is intermediate between the *nous* and the material world, has the option either of preserving its integrity and imaged perfection or of becoming altogether sensual and corrupt. The same choice is open to each of the lesser souls. When, through ignorance of its true nature and identity, the human soul experiences a false sense of separateness and independence, it becomes arrogantly self-assertive and falls into sensual and depraved habits. Salvation for such a soul is still possible, the Neo-Platonist maintains, by virtue of the very freedom of will that enabled it to choose its sinful course. The soul must reverse that course, tracing in the opposite direction the successive steps of its degeneration, until it is again united with the fountainhead of its being. The actual reunion is accomplished through a mystical experience in which the soul knows an all-pervading ecstasy.

The elements of asceticism and unworldliness in Neo-Platonism appealed strongly to the Fathers and Doctors of the Christian Church. The early Christian prelate St. Augustine, in his *Confessions*, acknowledged the contribution of Neo-Platonism to Christianity and indicated the profound influence exerted by its doctrines on his own religious thinking. Although a number of medieval theologians and philosophers, notably the German mystic Meister Eckhart, were deeply influenced by Neo-Platonism, Roman Catholic dogmatists condemned its unorthodox tenets. In the 15th century, however, Neo-Platonism became more generally accepted. The German Roman Catholic speculative philosopher Nicholas of Cusa and other mystics sought to overcome the doubt arising from the limitations of human knowledge by espousing the theory of direct human intuition of God, a theory closely akin to the Neo-Platonic doctrine that the soul in a state of ecstasy has the power to transcend all finite limitations.

Conclusion

Ancient Greece was the cradle of Western philosophy. We have already discussed that Philosophy is generally said to begin in the Greek cities of western Asia Minor (Ionia) with Thales of Miletus, who was active around 585 B.C. and left as the *opaque dictum*, "All is water." His most noted students were Anaximamenes Miletus ("All is air") and Anaximander. Other thinkers and schools appeared throughout Greece over the next couple of centuries. Among the most important were Heraclitus ("All is fire, all is chaotic and transitory"), Anaxagorus ("reality is so ordered that it must be governed by Mind"), the Pluralists and Atomists ("the world is composite of innumerable interacting parts"), the Eliatics, Parmenides and Zeno ("All is One and change is impossible") and the Sophists ("truth was no more than opinion and for teaching people to argue fallaciously to prove whatever conclusions they wished"). This whole movement gradually became more concentrated in Athens, which had become the dominant city-state in Greece.

We have already encountered the three fundamental metaphysical options: atheism (Epicurus), theism (Aristotle) and pantheism (Zeno). On the whole, pantheism has never found much favour among Western philosophers. In the East, on the contrary, the pantheistic system has flourished. The fact is that Christianity, Judaism and Islam abhor pantheistic metaphysics while Hinduism, Taoism and Mahayana Buddhism are well-disposed towards it. Agnosticism teaches that the beings of the world cannot lead to the 'Being' of the one for the One is beyond being. The One is unknowable and without attributes.[61] In many ways, Greek philosophy paved the way for both modern science and modern philosophy. Clear unbroken lines of influence lead from early Greek philosophers to the Renaissance, the Enlightenment and the secular sciences of the modern day.

Helpful Questions

1. Write short notes on the Pythagorean School, the Eliatics and the Sophists.
2. How does Platonism differ from Aristotelianism?
3. Describe briefly Epicureanism and Stoicism.

Part 2
History of Christian Philosophy

Three major schools of philosophy prevailed before the Christian era. These schools of philosophy influenced early Christian writers—(a) Platonism, founded by Plato; (b) Aristotelianism, founded by Aristotle; and (c) Stoicism, founded by Zeno. Although they remained distinct schools of thought, they greatly influenced one another in the early Christian era. By the Christian era, much of Greek philosophy had built on Plato and Aristotle in such a way as to teach clearly that there is one supreme transcendent God. Historical perspective of philosophy has been dealt with in the first part of the book. Philosophical developments in various periods will be discussed in Part 2. We will also look at how great philosophers from different parts of the world have contributed to this very important field of thought. Philosophy with its general outlook is briefly sketched here.

The progress of Christian Philosophy in history naturally divides itself into six main periods:

1. *Early (ancient)*, from the first century AD to the third century AD, foundation was laid for Christian Philosophy; Christian truths were established with some practical adaptations of Greek thought by Roman writers

2. *Medieval*, from the fourth to the fifteenth century, Greek thoughts were utilised for the systematisation of Christian dogma; speculation was mainly referred to the ecclesiastical orthodoxy

3. *Reformational*, Protestant Christian Philosophy was formed against Roman Catholicism in the sixteenth century

4. *Modern*, in the seventeenth and the eighteenth centuries, in which thought became free to speculate upon all the problems presented by reason and experience, though it only realised its liberty fully in the hands of Locke, Hume and Kant

5. *Postmodern* philosophy encompasses the philosophical developments through experiments, existence and language in the nineteen and twenty centuries. Soren Kierkegaard, Paul Tillich, G. Marcel, Charles Peirce, William James and Ludwig Wittgenstein were the important Christian philosophers in the period of Postmodern philosophy.

6. *Contemporary*, it bears witness to the philosophical developments in the twenty-first century. Contemporary philosophy is very new in origin; it is a growing field of philosophical thought.

Philosophical teachings of Jesus and Apostle Paul are dealt with in the first part. Then the philosophy of Hellenistic Church Father and its impact on Christian philosophy get a special mention. The following chapters of the second part of the book deal with the medieval, modern, postmodern and contemporary philosophies and the relation between theology and philosophy. Historically, the term "Western Philosophy" refers to the philosophical thinking of Western civilisation, beginning in ancient Greece. We have already learned about these in the fourth chapter, "Origin of Western Philosophy." Medieval Philosophy is Christian Philosophy. Western Philosophy is also known as 'European Philosophy.' Apart from Greek philosophy, all of the Western philosophy is 'Christian Philosophy' itself or closely related to it in one way or other. The word "philosophy" itself originated in the West. Christian philosophy has had a tremendous influence on and has been greatly influenced by Western religion, science and politics. In the West, 'philosophy' is an expansive and ambiguous concept.

Chapter 4

Early Christian Philosophy

This chapter focuses on Christian Philosophy, especially its foundation. It will also give you a brief description of early Christian philosophers and an understanding of the philosophy of Hellenistic Christian Philosophers.

The philosophic concepts of Jesus Christ and Apostle Paul will be discussed in the first part of the chapter. Jesus Christ really laid the foundation for Christian Philosophy. Apostle Paul elaborated the Christian philosophy that was established by Jesus Christ. We can find so many philosophic concepts in Paul's epistles. Paul was the one who learned about Platonic philosophy whereby he was able to logically establish his theological viewpoints. Some of his theological concepts are quite similar to Platonic philosophy, which greatly influenced St. Augustine.

Hellenistic Christian philosophers made use of this philosophical monotheism as an obvious point of contact. A typical second-century Platonist would hold in to it, but with the Platonic element being dominant. Neo-Platonism, founded by Plotinus, was a revised form of Platonism. It stressed the ultimate transcendence of God. It deeply influenced many Christian thinkers from the fourth century onwards.[62] Hellenistic Christian philosophers were Gentile Greeks and Romans. As they came to grips with their Christian faith and presented it to their contemporaries, they were forced to relate it to the thought patterns of their society—Greek philosophy. They had to grapple with the inherent contradiction between the Greek and biblical concepts of God.

Foundation of Christian Philosophy

Judaism and Greek Philosophy

Many different forms of sacrifice are mentioned in the Old Testament, which tell us about the Israelite understanding of God and his relationship with his people. Salvation depends on God and it can be achieved through his covenants, not through sacrifices. The ritual of sacrifices may be a way for the covenant people to approach God. God drew the people of Israel into fellowship with himself. The sacrifices enabled the people to express their relationship with God in three ways: (1) *To thank God for His goodness* (Lev.7:12; 1:10-13), (2) *to share fellowship with God* (Lev.3:5) and (3) to make atonement for their sins (Lev. 4, 5, 16 ch.). This Judaistic method of sacrifices as God commanded to the Israelites gives implications to the once-for-all sacrifice of the Lord Jesus Christ on the Cross of Calvary. Judaism in a sense has been a preparation for the Coming of the Lord in this universe for the atoning sacrifice. Although the whole Jewish community did not realise it, many Jews believed in Jesus and so a new community emerged—Jewish Christians.

Israel was given a conditional Mosaic covenant as the demonstration of God's holiness, which was his standard. Those who would enter into fellowship with a Holy God would also have to have His holy standard. That would be accomplished through forgiveness—promised in the new covenant (Jer.31: 31-34). The prophetic books give further details of how that will be achieved. Isaiah and Zechariah picture not only a reigning Messiah, but also a suffering Messiah through whom God provides forgiveness. Many of the prophetic books detail the climatic age when at Messiah's return, the nation Israel is repentant, forgiven and restored to the land that was promised to her (Deut.30: 1-10) The nations of the world will also enter into blessing. In God's programme of dealing with Israel and the gentiles to bring them to the place of blessing, a repeated theme of the Old Testament is the continuing sin of the human race and the grace of God to restore an errant humanity. It is God's promise to David, however, that indicates that David's greater son will be the one through whom this future kingdom will be inaugurated (2 Sam.7: 12-16). In this magnificent statement, God promises David that his dynasty in issuing the Messiah will never be terminated and the Messianic kingdom rule will be forever. What is the purpose of it all? The Book of Zechariah concludes with no appropriate emphasis; the holiness of God. God's purpose in wooing sinful people back to fellowship with Himself is to bring glory to His name. God is Holy and all that will enter into fellowship with Him must be Holy. The day when a regenerated people in a restored world worship God in His holiness, the millennial kingdom shall be established.

Philosophical perspective of the history of the intertestamental period has to be carefully observed because of its influence on the New Testament teachings. The teaching of the Pharisees especially reveals the tendency to dualism or deism in later Judaism; they interposed between God and the world various agents of mediation, the law, the word, the name, the glory of God and a host of angels, good and bad. They also fostered a new hope of the future, under the double form of the Messianic kingdom, and of resurrection and immortality. Jesus Christ came into the world as the 'Messiah' of the Jewish expectation. When the time had fully come, Jesus came into this world (Gal. 4:4). Jesus Christ came to fulfill the Law and to establish a new covenant with His people. Judaism of Jesus' time could not grasp the reality that Jesus is the Messiah, and as a result, they crucified Him. The Jewish drift became the cause of the entrance of the gentiles into the kingdom of God, which means reconciliation.

When the term "philosophy" is used in an academic context, it typically refers to the philosophical tradition begun with the ancient Greeks. Philosophy is an enquiry into reality as a whole. We have already encountered the three fundamental metaphysical options: atheism (Democritus and Epicurus), theism (Aristotle) and pantheism (Zeno). Greek philosophy in the early Christian era drew close to biblical Christianity. The task of early Christian philosophers was to express the faith in relation to their Greek heritage. This meant expressing it in Greek terms without distorting it. They have succeeded in a larger extent in doing this. By this careful and culturally relevant approach, Greek thought influenced Christian thought. At the same time, most of the elements in Greek thought that were contrary to biblical Christianity have to be rooted out. Christianity also came to be seen in a Greek way. Christian philosophical concepts were made common to the Greek world. Comparing and contrasting Christian philosophy with Greek philosophy helped the people in a few centuries to evaluate their faith. In many ways, Greek philosophy paved the way for both modern science and modern philosophy. Clear unbroken lines of influence lead from early Greek philosophers to the Renaissance, the Enlightenment and today's secular sciences.

Plato influenced the first Christian thinkers, especially St. Augustine, who was attracted by the highly 'spiritual' idealism of his philosophy. St.

Thomas Aquinas (1250 AD) became the defender of Aristotelianism during the Christian middle ages. Aristotelianism is the philosophy of those who use Aristotle's methods and doctrines in their own thought. Aristotle developed and systematised the extensive Greek learning and as a result his writings became a source of inspiration in many centuries and in many nations.[63] The history of Aristotelianism has also been determined by the availability of Aristotle's writings. When Aristotelian science was superseded, Aristotelianism as a comprehensive explanatory system was doomed. With historical studies and new translations of Aristotle continuing to appear, Aristotelianism appears to be guaranteed a continuing life.

We read of the concept of *logos*, the philosophical expectation of the Greek word *logo*, which means "word" or "science" in John 1:1. The term was current in the philosophical literature from Heraclitus down through the Stoics to Philo, a Jewish philosopher in the first half of the first century. It was a very useful term with definite apologetic significance and value for commending the gospel to the gentile world. It was also of value for an entrance into the Jewish community, where the concept of the 'word of the Lord' gave the term immediate meaning. The background for John's use of the term was the Old Testament context. The moral principles of Socrates were being developed with a more directly ethical interest by the Cyrenaics and Epicureans into a system of Hedonism and by the Cynics and Stoics into a doctrine of intuitive right and duty, resting inconsistently upon a pantheistic and materialistic view of the universe. But the spiritual and ethical elements in Stoicism became only second to Platonism in the preparation of the Greek world for Christianity. Jesus Christ is the culmination of the Greek expectation of *logos*. We can say that in a sense that Greek philosophy is the *preparatio eveangelica* for the Christ to be manifested in the Greek world.

Hellenism is the traditional designation for the Greek culture of the Roman Empire in the days of Jesus and Paul and for centuries after. Classical philosophies of the Greeks had already expired and diluted beyond recognition except for small bands of continuators of the traditions of the Pythagoreans, of Plato and of Aristotle. The new philosophies of the Hellenistic world were those of the Cynics, Skeptics and increasingly the Stoics; these thinkers bring us into the world of Hellenistic philosophy. Slowly, a more integral and rounded tendency emerged within Hellenism; in certain respects, in opposition at times to it in regard to one philosophical problem or another.

Jesus Christ—Philosopher of Philosophers

The disciples of Jesus Christ and other followers wrote what Jesus had taught his followers. The teachings of Jesus can be summed up as Moral Philosophy and Religious Philosophy. Jesus Christ summed up the whole Bible in the following manner: "Love your God and love your neighbour." It is, of course, true that Jesus might not have used the word 'philosophy.' There is no direct mention of it anywhere. But the teachings of Jesus Christ are highly philosophical. However, as we normally say that Jesus is the *Leader of leaders* or *the Teacher of teachers*, it is appropriate to say that Jesus Christ is the *Philosopher of philosophers*; he is the greatest philosopher the world has ever seen.

Life and Teachings

The life and teachings of Jesus as recorded in the Gospels form the basis of Christian Philosophy. Like Socrates, Jesus Christ taught very deep principles of human life, the universe and God, but he did not write anything. There is no record of any writing by Jesus on systematic philosophy or theology in the formal sense. Several accounts of his life and many of his teachings are recorded in the New Testament and form the basis for some Christian philosophies. If He had written his view of reality in His own words as a separate volume, it would have been possible to review history from his perspective and gain a greater understanding of his intellectual dimension of understanding. In some senses, it is almost inconceivable that no such document was created because with his standard of forethought to the realisation path of those in his wake it should surely have been of benefit. Jesus put himself through the extremes of challenges. He spent so much time thinking from the point of others that those emotions passed through him in advance.

Jesus began his education while still young. Luke wrote that Jesus was sitting in the temple among the teachers "listening to them and asking them questions." And we read that all who heard him were amazed at his understanding and his answers (Luke 2:46, 47). He entered into public ministry at the age of thirty only. So he had enough time to develop his knowledge of the Old Testament and of the traditional writings and teachings of the rabbis. He demonstrated again and again his knowledge of the Old Testament. His own words often related to the traditional teachings of the rabbis.

Over the years, Jesus had evidently listened and learned to good effect. He understood how people felt and what they believed. His teaching was built on this good foundation. He would realise first what they were to realise only later and rarely did they exist in the same moment. Having proven a standard of divine love what was to remain but the challenge to come back again and raise that standard again for real. He had always gone through the extremes of worst first as if it were the end of the continuum of infinity. He could then come back from that and be headed in the direction of the ultimate of heavenly expression and so that was what he chose as a challenge to himself.

Being God, it is a matter of shame and degradation to be housed in the carnal body and subject to its animal impulses. In the body, he is nailed to the cross of matter and the worst of his painful sacrifice and of his humbling himself to be born of a virgin is his subjection to the carnal appetites of the animal. He must finally dissolve the physical elements of the veil of the temple and the *ekstasis* (ecstasy) described as the consummation of the drama of initiation in the Mysteries. The word "ecstasy" literally means "standing out", and it referred to the actual freeing of the soul from the physical body. It is the resurrection, when the tomb of flesh is broken asunder, the gates of death are opened, and the dead are raised incorruptible.

Ethical Philosophy

The ethical philosophy of Jesus Christ has to be specially noted at this crucial period of time. What He taught the people over twenty centuries ago is relevant even today. Jesus Christ gave importance to teaching the people of the time the values of human life. He severely criticised the Pharisees and the Sadducees who perverted the Old Testament scripture and imposed upon the people the unnecessary human-made laws that caused the deterioration of the moral standard of life. He encouraged the followers to lead the simple life that is helpful for self and society. His concept of morality is signified with the inward purity and outward service. He gave a new definition of the life in the world. To Jesus Christ, we are created for serving the community or doing to others. The ethical philosophy of Jesus Christ is the best of this type the world has ever seen. Famous leaders like Mahatma Gandhi had been deeply influenced by the ethical teachings of Jesus Christ.

The New Testament Ethics is founded upon the Gospel of Jesus Christ. Wherever the Gospel is introduced, it makes ethical demands. The New

Testament ethics cannot be understood without reference to the Gospel and the Gospel has no meaning without reference to Christ. We can see the Christian ethical standards and tradition beginning to grow in the New Testament. The ethics portrayed by Christ seem to be an excellent model for future ethicists and ethical people alike, but some so-called religious philosophers ignore it. Jesus' contribution to Moral Philosophy is especially noteworthy. Matthew records six examples of Jesus' revising of the prevalent moral code of the Law. The moral code was prescribed and explained by the Rabbis, which was then revised by Lord Jesus Christ in the New Testament. First, Jesus meant that anger is the passion that impels murder and so it is as offensive as murder itself. Even to say 'fool' is an offense leading to hell. So, the importance of reconciliation in good time is demanded (Matt. 5:21-26). A lustful gaze is equal to committing adultery (Matt.5:27-30). Jesus rejected divorce unless one will be guilty of adultery (Matt.5:31, 32). Since swearing cannot make one hair white or black, it should be replaced by a plain 'yes' or 'no' (Matt. 5:33-37). Jesus, replacing the old system, taught that if anyone strikes you on the right cheek, turn to him the other also (Matt.5:40). f) Instead of hating one's enemies one should love them and thereby become the children of the heavenly Father (Matt. 5:43-45).[64]

Religious Philosophy
The religious philosophy of Jesus Christ carries a special meaning in the New Testament. He addressed the Lord as 'Father.' He encouraged His followers by way of introducing God as immanent. Moreover, He revealed Himself as the Son of God and that He and the Father are one. The followers were satisfied with His teachings about prayer, fasting and worshipping God Almighty. Jesus Christ taught people to trust the Lord for every need of life. He taught and preached about the kingdom of God to those who worried about the restoration of the Kingdom. Also, He told them that His Kingdom is not of this world; rather, it is a spiritual kingdom. Christ knows that the world can only know of His reality if His disciples are truly one in deed and word. As the Father and Christ are one in external appearance and inward essence so Christ prays that the world might see true personal oneness of the outer and inner man in His disciples and thus be introduced to the one who made such possible. Ronald B. Mayers writes:[65]

> Man is personal! God is personal! Christ manifests the congruent personality of both in one person! A glimpse of this personal emphasis can be seen in Paul's argument from the personal nature of the Athenians to the absurdity of believing the ultimate is impersonal.

Jesus was never against Judaism, but He spoke against the unrighteous acts of the Pharisees, priests and Rabbis of Judaism. He loved the Jews as His own people and did many miracles and good works for them. Jesus was always overcrowded wherever He travelled. The Jews accepted Him as Messiah. Jesus was neither against the Old Testament nor the Jewish community. He rather taught that the Old Testament was a necessary but preliminary step to the completion of salvation. Jesus repeatedly connected His ministry and mission with the Old Testament. This is a direct factor in our Lord's message that has an apologetic significance. Though addressed to a predominantly Jewish community, an apologetic based on the typology and fulfillment of the Old Testament had an immediate and continued appeal. According to Jesus' teaching, the Jews do not need to give up their Old Testament faith in order to accept Christianity. They only need to realise that anticipation has become actualisation, that shadow had been replaced by reality. Christianity does not replace or obliterate Judaism, but completes it. Christianity is Judaism fulfilled.

Apologetics of Jesus
The words and deeds of Jesus are recorded on numerous occasions as defending Himself and it stands as the sign of apologetic in the thoughts and actions of Jesus Christ. Also, it is very clear that Jesus or His disciples were giving explicit reasons for 'who Jesus is and what is His teaching.' The Holy Bible gives ample evidence for His defense through His discourse with John's disciples.[66] First, He defended the non-fasting practices of His disciples contrary to the practices of the Pharisees and John's disciples (Matt. 9:14-17). Second, the empirical evidences of His messianic fulfillment is pointed out that they could hear and see the lame walking, the blind seeing, the deaf hearing, the leper cleansed and the dead raised to life again (Matt. 11:26). Jesus used the word defense (apologia) in Luke 12:11-12. The English word "apologetics" is derived from *apologia*.

Jesus drives the tempter away by the Scripture (Deut. 8:3; 6, 13, 10, 20; cf. Matt.4ch. and Luke 4ch.). At the hour of His death, He recited Psalm 22. So, Scripture was a part of His life. Because Jesus knew the Scripture well, so He contradicted again and over again of Judaic traditions, which was derived from it (Matt. 5; Mark 7) and repeatedly spoke certain words of the law (Matt.5: 38 ff.: 19:1ff). Christ used the traditional texts (Word of God) freely and in doing so He showed Himself Superior to all bondage to the latter (Luke 5:18 ff; Isa.41: 2ff.). He never preached this in any way of critical manner and he followed the ancient prophets. Jesus was concerned too that His followers should understand and benefit from

God's revelation of Himself as recorded in the Scripture (Matt.5:17; Matt.9:16, 17). Jesus made use of all three parts (The law, Poetical Books and Prophetical Books) of the Hebrew Scriptures in His teachings (Matt.12:29-31; Luke 4:18, 19; Isa. 61:1, 2; John.13:18). If we separate the New Testament from the Old Testament and study the revelation of God in Christ Jesus apart from the whole record of how God has made Himself known to men, we hinder our understanding of God and the world, and of world and his destiny. In the New Testament, there are many quotations from the Old Testament, such as "Have you read…" and "It is written… ." (Matt.12:3, 5; Luke 20:17, 24:46). In several cases, an event is described as fulfilling what is written in the Old Testament (Matt.13:14; John19:28). The words and deeds of Jesus Christ were based on the word of God. Many a time, He defended his teaching of the spiritual truth of God through the Scripture.

Biblical Philosophy
Jesus Christ came to fulfill the law and the prophets, and out of His filial consciousness of God, He propounded answers to the practical demands of His time. His doctrine of God the Father was based on the biblical philosophy, which transcended all dualism. In the kingdom of heaven, the good would ultimately prevail over the evil. The law of love expressed the ideal of conduct for man as individual, and in his relation to society and to God, the supreme and ultimate reality.

Jesus' way of approaching the Scripture is worthy of special mention. It was Jesus' custom to go to the synagogue on the Sabbath day (Luke 4:16). He read the Scripture portion that says about His ministry, which is known as the "Nazareth Manifesto." Jesus rejected the literalist approach used by Satan at the time of His temptation in the wilderness. At the same time, he rejected the method of interpreting the Law by way of emphasising the trivial things through minutely detailed explanation and ignoring the weightier matters (Matt. 23, 23, 24). Jesus pointed out on another occasion the central axis of God's dealing with humanity, that is, death and resurrection. Although the cross and resurrection of Jesus were the one-time experience of an individual, they reflect the suffering and glory of God.

Conclusion
The centrality of the person of Jesus Christ is, in one way or another, a feature of all the historical varieties of Christian belief and practice. Christians have agreed in their understanding and definition of what

makes Christ distinctive or unique. Certainly, they would all affirm that his life and example should be followed and that his teachings about love and fellowship should be the basis of human relations. In Christian teaching, Jesus cannot be less than the supreme preacher and exemplar of the moral life, but for most Christians, his life and work mean more than that. They focus on the death and resurrection of the Lord Jesus Christ who came into this world with the purpose of dying for the redemption of humanity.

Hellenistic Christian Philosophy

Hellenism is the traditional designation for the Greek culture of the Roman Empire in the days of Jesus and Paul, and for centuries after. Classical philosophies of the Greeks had already expired and diluted beyond recognition except for small bands of continuators of the traditions of the Pythagoreans, of Plato and Aristotle. The new philosophies of the Hellenistic world were those of the Cynics, Skeptics, and increasingly, the Stoics; these thinkers bring us into the world of Hellenistic philosophy. Slowly, a more integral and rounded tendency emerged within Hellenism, but also in certain respects in opposition at times to it in regard to one philosophical problem or another.

Here are some of those thinkers most closely associated with Hellenistic Christian philosophers, listed more or less in a chronological order. The period of Hellenistic Christian philosophers can be specially noted as from second century to fifth century (AD 100 to 500). They were the earliest Christian writers outside the New Testament, belonging to what is called "sub-apostolic age." The Hellenistic Christian philosophers are specially known as the Apologists and Polemicists. They help us to understand the transition from the apostolic church of the first century to the Catholic Church, which began in the second century.

The early church was divided into the Greek-speaking East and the Latin-speaking West. The earliest gentile Christianity was Greek and the New Testament was written in Greek. Even in the West, the earliest churches were Greek-speaking.[67] The first traces of Latin Christianity are found in North Africa, and the African Tertullian was the first important Latin Christian writer. The Greek- and Latin-speaking churches co-existed happily in the early centuries and after the collapse of the Roman Empire, the two churches drifted apart, becoming the Eastern Orthodox and Roman Catholic churches.

Justin Martyr

In the early church, there was a kind of love-hate relationship with secular philosophy. Justin was born of Greek parents early in the second century. The Greek-speaking church father Justin Martyr (died c165) had long been a student of philosophy before he became a Christian.

Conversion and Writings

Before becoming Christian, he was attached to a Stoic philosopher and then to an Aristotelian philosopher. Later, he went to a well-known Platonist. Then he met an old man by the sea and through whom he became Christian. Even then he still wore the pallium, the philosopher's cloak, proclaiming that the Christian faith was the "only reliable and profitable philosophy." Justin was known as the "Defender of Faith." Justin never gave up being a philosopher. It was Justin who developed the logos doctrine for Christian apologetics as a means of relating philosophy and Christianity.[68] The constant contrast of philosophy and Christianity makes Justin Martyr a very important apologist.

Justin was not just a Christian, seeking to relate Christianity to Greek philosophy; rather he was a Greek who had come to see Christianity as the fulfillment of all that was best in philosophy, especially in Platonism. Only three works of Justin survive: (1) Dialogue with Trypho, (2) 1 Apology and (3) 11 Apology. He was resolutely opposed to paganism and found no time for syncretism. Justin portrayed Jesus Christ as the fulfillment of the best in Greek philosophy. He also held that Plato and other Greek philosophers had borrowed some of their ideas from the Old Testament.[69] Justin anchored his Christian faith in his Greek heritage. He did not renounce Greek philosophy even after he became a Christian. Since then he became a better philosopher and really a true philosopher.

His Philosophy

He looked for the truth in Greek philosophy. He argued that the divine *Logos* (Word or Reason) had enlightened thinkers like Socrates to see the errors of paganism. The logical conclusion of such enlightenment was Christianity. Justin Martyr welcomed the Greek philosophy with open-mindedness and accepted as a precious gift of God. For Justin, Greek philosophy is the precious God's gift that had led him to Christian faith.[70] He underestimated the role of the other philosophers, while comparing with Christ by way of accepting the supremacy of Christ and His teaching as complete and perfect. For him, the imperfect must be corrected and tested by the Perfect who is Christ. He said that Christ is vastly superior to Socrates. Justin signified the magnanimity of Christ in his 11 Apology:[71]

> For next to God we worship and love the word, who is from the unbegotten and ineffable God, since he also became man for our sake, that by sharing in our sufferings he might also bring us healing. For all those writers were able to see reality darkly, through the seed of the implanted Word within them.

Justin spent his last years at Rome, teaching until he was arrested and put on trial. He was martyred for the sake of Christian faith. Justin's approach of seeing continuity between his Greek past and his Christian faith was continued by Clement and Origen at Alexandria. But Tertullian at Carthage was opposed to the philosophical viewpoint of Justin Martyr.

Irenaeus of Lyons

Irenaeus was bishop of Lugdunum in Gaul, which is now Lyon, France. He was a disciple of Polycarp, the Bishop of Smyrna, who was said to be a disciple of Apostle John. He treated his opponents with disdain. His primary means of rebuttal was scripture and tradition, the latter being the public proclamation of the truth in the churches established by the apostles.

His life and Writings

Irenaeus was a Greek, but born in Asia Minor into a Christian family. He might be born in the first half of the second century and died at the beginning of the third century. He is best known for his writings, arguing for the unity of God and against Gnosticism. He was a "man against heretics."

During the persecution of Marcus Aurelius, Irenaeus was a priest of the Church of Lyon. The clergy of that city, many of whom were suffering imprisonment for the faith, sent him (in 177 or 178) to Rome with a letter to Pope Eleuterus concerning Montanism. Returning to Gaul, Irenaeus succeeded the martyr Saint Pothinus and became the second Bishop of Lyon. He was influenced by Justin. He became a bridge between early Greek theology and Western Latin theology.

His writings were formative in the early development of Christian Theology and he is recognised as a saint by both the Eastern Orthodox Church and the Catholic Church; both consider him a Father of the Church. He was a notable early Christian apologist. Irenaeus wrote a number of books, but the most important that survives is *Adversus Haereses* (Against

Heresies).[72] The purpose of *Against Heresies* was to refute the teachings of various Gnostics groups; apparently, several Greek merchants had begun an oratorial campaign praising the pursuit of Gnostics in Irenaeus' bishopric. *Against Heresies* was one of the best surviving descriptions of Gnosticism. Irenaeus also wrote *The Demonstration of the Apostolic Teaching*, an Armenian copy of which was discovered in 1907. This work seems to have been an instruction for recent Christian converts. Various fragments of other works by Irenaeus have been found, and many lost works by him are attested by other ancient writers. These include *On the Subject of Knowledge, On the Monarchy, or How God is not the Cause of Evil* and others.

Irenaeus was an important figure defending the four main Gospels in the New Testament in 170, stating in his "Against Heresies." He was the first Christian writer to list all four of the now canonical Gospels as divinely-inspired. Irenaeus was also the first to assert that the Gospel of John was written by John the Apostle, and that the Gospel of Luke was written by Luke the companion of Paul. Irenaeus' works were first published in English in 1885 in the Ante-Nicene Fathers' collection. *Against Heresies* constitutes a minute analysis and refutation of the Gnostic doctrines. He appeals to the prophecies to demonstrate the truthfulness of Christianity.

Concept of God
The central point of Irenaeus' philosophy is the unity of God in opposition to the Gnostics' philosophy. According to Gnosticism, God has been divided into a number of divine 'Aeons', and their distinction between the utterly transcendent 'High God' and the inferior 'Demiurge' who created the world. Irenaeus developed the logos theology. His emphasis on the unity of God is reflected in his corresponding emphasis on the unity of salvation history. Irenaeus repeatedly insists that God created the world and has been overseeing it ever since this creative act; everything that has happened is part of his plan for humanity. The essence of this plan is a process of maturation. Irenaeus believes that humanity was created immature, and God intended his creatures to take a long time to grow into or assume divine likeness.

According to Irenaeus, the high point in salvation history is the advent of Jesus. Irenaeus believed that Christ would always have been sent, even if humanity had never sinned; but the fact that they *did* sin determines his role as a saviour. He sees Christ as the new Adam, who systematically *undoes* what Adam did: thus, where Adam was disobedient concerning

God's edict concerning the fruit of the Tree of Knowledge, Christ was obedient even to death on the wood of a tree. In addition to reversing the wrongs done by Adam, Irenaeus thinks of Christ as recapitulating or summing up human life. This means that Christ goes through every stage of human life, from infancy to old age, and simply by living it, sanctifies it with his divinity. Irenaeus argues that Christ did not die until he was older than conventionally portrayed.

Against Gnosticism
For him, Gnosticism is not Christian, nor was it a higher knowledge, but inventive imagination. He was best known as a Polemicist.[73] In his criticism of Gnosticism, Irenaeus made reference to a Gnostic gospel that portrayed Judas in a positive light, as having acted in accordance with Jesus' instructions. Scholars typically regard the Gospel of Judas as one of many Gnostic texts, showing one of many varieties of Gnostic beliefs of the period.

According to the Gnostic view of Salvation, creation was perfect to begin with; it did not need time to grow and mature. Gnosticism was a radically different religion from orthodox Christianity. Irenaeus employed a number of arguments against Gnosticism. It can be summed up in three points[74]: (1) Irenaeus described the different Gnostic systems in detail; he sought to expose the ludicrous nature of many of their beliefs; (2) he challenged the Gnostic claims to secret apostolic traditions; and (3) in opposition to the radically different Gnostic beliefs, Irenaeus' appeal to tradition was correct in that it serves to prove his case against Gnosticism.

Original Sin
He argued that original sin is latent in humanity, and that it was by Jesus' incarnation as a man that he "undid" the original sin of Adam, thus sanctifying life is guaranteed for all mankind. Irenaeus maintained the view that Christ is the Teacher of the human race through whom wisdom would be made accessible to all. Irenaeus conceives of our salvation as essentially coming about through the incarnation of God as a man. He characterises the penalty for sin as death and corruption. God, however, is immortal and incorruptible, and simply by becoming united to human nature in Christ he conveys those qualities to us. Irenaeus, therefore, understands the atonement of Christ as happening through his incarnation rather than his crucifixion, although the latter event is an integral part of the former.

Antichrist

Irenaeus identified the Antichrist, another name of the apostate Man of Sin, with Daniel's Little Horn and John's Beast of Revelation 13. He sought to apply other expressions to Antichrist, such as 'the abomination of desolation,' mentioned by Christ (Matt. 24:15) and the 'king of a most fierce countenance,' in Gabriel's explanation of the Little Horn of Daniel, chapter 8. But he is not very clear how 'the sacrifice and the libation shall be taken away' during the 'half-week' or three and one-half years of the Antichrist's reign. He interpreted the three and one-half 'times' of the Little Horn of Daniel 7 as three and one-half literal years. Antichrist's three and a half years of sitting in the temple are placed immediately before the second coming of Christ. They are identified as the second half of the 'one week' of Daniel 9. Irenaeus is the first of the church fathers to stress the mystic number 666. The solution of this numerical riddle has intrigued ecclesiastical writers from that time forward. He considered the Beast-Antichrist to be the recapitulation of all apostasy, in whose number 666 he found curious symbolism of Noah's age and the size of Nebuchadnezzar's golden image.

Millennium

Irenaeus declares that the Antichrist will be terminated by the second advent with the resurrection of the just, the destruction for the wicked and the millennial reign of the righteous. The general resurrection and the judgment follow the descent of the New Jerusalem at the end of the millennial kingdom. Irenaeus calls those heretics who maintain that the saved are immediately glorified in the kingdom to come after death, before their resurrection. He said that the millennial kingdom and the resurrection are actualities, not allegories, the first resurrection introducing this promised kingdom in which the risen saints are described as ruling over the renewed earth during the millennium, between the two resurrections.

Irenaeus held to the old Jewish tradition that the first six days of creation week were typical of the first six thousand years of human history. And he expected the millennial kingdom to begin with the second coming of Christ to destroy the wicked and inaugurate, for the righteous, the reign of the kingdom of God during the seventh thousand years, the millennial Sabbath, as signified by the Sabbath of creation week. He stresses five factors with greater clarity and emphasis than Justin: (1) the literal resurrection of the righteous at the second advent, (2) the millennium bounded by the two resurrections, (3) the Antichrist to come upon the heels of Rome's breakup, (4) the symbolic prophecies of Daniel and the

Apocalypse in their relation to the last times and (5) the kingdom of God to be established by the second advent.

Clement of Alexandria

Clement of Alexandria (AD 150-215) was the first member of the Church of Alexandria and one of its most distinguished teachers. He united Greek philosophical traditions with Christian doctrine and valued *gnosis* that with communion for all people could be held by common Christians. Clement of Alexandria welcomed the Greek philosophy with open-mindedness and accepted as a precious gift of God. Clement wrote that how the Law and prophets were to the Jews, in the same way Plato, Aristotle and other Greek philosophers were to the Greeks, as the preparation for Christ.

Life and Works

Athens is named as Clement's birthplace. He was born in a pagan Greek family in the middle of the second century. The thoroughness of his education is shown by his constant quotation of the Greek poets and philosophers. He traveled in Greece, Italy, Palestine and finally Egypt. He succeeded his teacher Pantaenus as the head of a Christian philosophical School at Alexandria sometime after 180.[75] One of his most popular pupils was Origen. During the persecution of Septimius Severus (AD 202), he left Alexandria and never returned.

He sought refuge with Alexander, the then bishop in Cappadocia from whom he brought a letter to Antioch in 211. He died in Asia Minor in 216. Clement's work was continued by his far greater successor Origen. Though he lays down at starting a purely spiritual conception of the Church, later the exigencies of his controversy with the Gnostics make him lay more stress on the visible church. As to his use of Scripture, the extraordinary breadth of his reading and manifold variety of his quotations from the most diverse authors make it very difficult to determine exactly what was received as canonical by the Alexandrian Church of that period.

His works were known as the boldest literary undertaking in the history of the Church. Clement attempted to set forth Christianity for the faithful in the traditional forms of secular literature. The second century was the hotbed of Gnosticism. Pantaenus and Clement after him sought to present an orthodoxy that was intellectually viable. They have shown that one can investigate philosophical and intellectual questions without being a heretic. Three major works of Clement survive, which are corresponding to the three stages of Christian instruction. The first book is an *Exhortation to the Greeks*, which is an apology. Second, *Tutor* is the manual of instruction for the new convert. It is a guide to outward conduct and is seen as a preparation for the reception of the spiritual doctrine. Third, *Carpet Bags* is a complex and strange work. His spiritual teaching is presented.[76] The first book deals with the religious basis of Christian morality, the second and third with the individual cases of conduct. Much of Clement's work has been published in recent years in the collection 'Sources Chretiennes', in particular by Alain Le Boulluec. Moreover, various authors preserved some fragments written by him. His thinking stands in the line of the Greek apologists. As he was from Alexandria, it is necessary to note Clement's use of allegory and his description of the perfect Christian as a 'true Gnostic.'

Clement on Philosophy

He saw truth in Greek philosophy, like Justin. For him, philosophy prepared the Greeks for Jesus Christ just like the Old Testament was to the Jews. Clement argued that Paul's warning against philosophy was meant "bad philosophy." He embraced much of the Greek worldview, but was careful to keep away from Gnostic heresy. The significance of Clement in the history of the development of doctrine is that he knew how to turn the simple church tradition into a world of philosophy. This attitude determines especially his treatment of non-Christian philosophy. He shows exhaustively that the philosophers owe a large part of their knowledge to the writings of the Old Testament, yet he seems to express his own personal conviction when he describes philosophy as a direct operation of the divine Logos, working through it as well as through the law and his direct revelation in the Gospel to communicate the truth to men.

Before the incarnation, knowledge of God was given to the Jews through the Law and the Greeks through philosophy, which was inspired by the *logos* (Christ). The *logos* became incarnate to impart knowledge and to serve as our model. It is true that the knowledge of the philosophers was elementary, fragmentary and incapable of imparting true righteousness; and it was far surpassed by the revelation given through the law and the prophets. Thus he emphasises the permanent importance of philosophy for the fullness of Christian knowledge, explains with special predilection the relation between knowledge and faith and sharply criticises those who are unwilling to make any use of philosophy. He pronounces definitely against the sophists and against the hedonism of the school of Epicurus. From philosophy he takes his conception of the Logos, the principle of Christian gnosis, through whom alone God's relation to the world and his revelation are maintained. Although he generally expresses himself unfavourably in regard to the Stoic philosophy, he really pays marked deference to that mixture of Stoicism and Platonism which characterised the religious and ethical thought of the educated classes in his day. Through his positive evaluation of Greek philosophy, his speculative bent and his deliberate lack of system, he was a contrast to the present Western writers of philosophy.

Against Gnosticism and Docetism

He vigorously opposed Gnosticism. In opposition to Gnostic denials of the goodness of marriage, Clement affirmed that it is a gift of God. Against the Gnostics, Clement emphasises the freedom of all to do good. What he offers is the communication of saving *gnosis*, leading men from paganism to faith and from faith to the higher state of knowledge. This true philosophy includes within itself the freedom from sin and the attainment of virtue. All sin has its root in ignorance, but the knowledge of God is followed by well-doing.

Faith is the foundation of all *gnosis*, and both are given by Christ. As faith involves a comprehensive knowledge of the essentials, knowledge allows the believer to penetrate deeply into the understanding of what he believes; and this is the making perfect, the completion, of faith. In order to attain this kind of faith, the "faith of knowledge", which is so much higher than the mere "faith of conjecture", or simple reception of a truth on authority, philosophy is permanently necessary. For him, Christianity is the true philosophy. There was with Clement the tendency for faith to mean orthodox Christianity and knowledge to mean Greek thought.[77] Clement was against Docetism as well. Docetism is the idea that Jesus Christ only appeared to be human. Clement affirmed that Jesus had a real body and that he ate and drank.

Ethical Teaching

Clement, in his ethical expressions, is influenced strongly by Plato and the Stoics, from whom he borrows much of his terminology. He laid great stress on the fulfillment of moral obligations. Clement strongly affirms the freedom of the will and the need for man to co-operate with God by accepting salvation. He apparently conceives of the possibility of repentance after death. He praises Plato for setting forth the greatest possible likeness to God as the aim of life; and his portrait of the perfect

Gnostic closely resembles that of the wise man as drawn by the Stoics. So he counsels his readers to shake off the chains of the flesh as far as possible to live already as if out of the body, and thus to rise above earthly things. His highest ideal of conduct remains the mortification of all affections, which may in any way disturb the soul in its career.

Salvation is obtained in relation to the church and through baptism one is made a member of the church. The knowledge of God leads to perfect love and to a mystic relationship with God, fully consummated only after death. Clement emphasised the antiquity and unity of the Catholic Church, the tradition handed down orally in the church from the apostles and the importance of interpreting the scriptures in accordance with the rule of the church.

Origen

Origen, another Christian philosopher (AD 185–255), was an early Christian scholar, theologian and one of the most distinguished of the early fathers of the Christian Church. He is thought to have been born at Alexandria and died at Caesarea Maritima. He is deeply indebted to the Platonic philosophy. He attempted to harmonise the philosophy of Christianity with some sort of unorthodox "Platonized Christianity." The outcome was the formulation of new philosophical thoughts like the pre-existence of soul, theory of reincarnation and the necessity of divine creation. We can see these thoughts in the philosophies of Plato and Plotinus.[78]

His Life and Training

Origen was educated by his father, Leonides, in elementary and scriptural studies. Origen's father was killed in the outbreak of the persecution during the reign of Septimius Severus in 202. Origen wished to follow in martyrdom, but was prevented only by his mother. Origen was taken under the protection of a woman of wealth and standing for a short time. Since his father's teaching enabled him also to give elementary instruction, he came to Catechetical School of Alexandria, whose last teacher was Clement of Alexandria, in 203. About 230, Origen entered on the fateful journey to Greece on some ecclesiastical mission, he paid a visit to Caesarea, where he was heartily welcomed and was ordained a priest. But Demetrius strongly disapproved his preaching before ordination while at Caesarea. Demetrius had been the first to introduce episcopal ordination in Egypt. The metropolitan accordingly convened a synod of bishops and presbyters, which banished Origen from Alexandria, while a second synod declared his ordination invalid. Origen accordingly fled from Alexandria in 231 and made his permanent home in Caesarea.

In 235, with the accession of Maximinus, a persecution raged; and for two years Origen is said, though on somewhat doubtful authority, to have remained concealed in the house of a certain Juliana in Caesarea of Cappadocia. Little is known of the last twenty years of Origen's life. He preached regularly on Wednesdays and Fridays and later daily. In 250 persecution of the Church broke out anew, and this time Origen did not escape. He was tortured, pilloried, and bound hand and foot to the block for days without yielding. Though he did not die while being tortured, he died after two years of injuries sustained. Had he died during persecution, he would have been declared a martyr, something that he would have greatly desired. A later legend, recounted by Jerome and numerous itineraries place his death and burial at Tyre.

His Works

Origen was teaching throughout the day and the greater part of the night was devoted to the study of the Bible and lived a life of rigid asceticism. From 212, Origen had acquaintance with Ambrose of Alexandria, whom he was instrumental in converting from Valentianism to orthodoxy. Ambrose was a man of wealth and he made a formal agreement with Origen to promulgate his writings, and all the subsequent works of Origen were dedicated to Ambrose. In 213 or 214, Origen visited Arabia; and Origen accordingly spent a brief time in Petra, after which he returned to Alexandria. Origen, though not ordained, preached and interpreted the Scriptures at the request of the bishops, Alexander of Jerusalem and Theoctistus of Caesarea. Of Origen's activity during the next decade little is known, but it was obviously devoted to teaching and writing.

Ambrose provided him with more than seven stenographers to take dictation in relays, as many scribes to prepare long-hand copies, and a number of girls to multiply the copies. At the request of Ambrose, he began writing many books. Origen was a prolific writer. But much of his work has been lost. Much of it survives only in translation. His major writings can be divided into four groups:[79] (1) Biblical: This list contains a massive edition of the Old Testament, the Hebrew Text, Commentaries (scholarly expositions), Homilies (practical and edificatory), Scholia (notes on particular passage); (2) First Principles: It was the first attempt to produce a systematic theology. It has dealt with God, world, freedom and the Scripture; (3) Against Celsus: It is his reply to Celsus' *true word*, a vehemently anti-Christian work; and (4) Practical Works: He wrote prayer and exhortation to martyrdom.

His Philosophy

Origen was thoroughly familiar with Greek philosophy. He studied under leading pagan philosophers. Origen was influential in integrating elements of Platonism into Christianity. He incorporated Platonic idealism into his conceptions of the Logos, and the two churches, one ideal and one real. He also held a strongly Platonic view of God, describing him as the perfect, incorporeal ideal. He espoused a Platonic view of eternal souls achieving perfection while escaping the temporary, imperfect material world. His important views are hierarchical structure in the Trinity, the temporality of matter, 'the fabulous pre-existence of souls' and 'the monstrous restoration.' Origen taught the doctrine of eternal generation, which came to be seen as orthodox. He argued this philosophically. The tension between orthodoxy and heresy in Origen is seen clearly in his doctrine of the Trinity. He taught the threeness of God and it was a graded Trinity. For him, Father is greater than the Son, who is greater than the Holy Spirit. His Trinity is known as a three-tier Trinity.

Origen, deeply loved by his pupils, preached and taught dialectics, physics, ethics and metaphysics; thus laying his foundation for the crowning theme of theology. He accordingly sought to set forth all the science of the time from the Christian point of view and to elevate Christianity to a theory of the universe compatible with Hellenism. He was severely criticised of philosophical doctrine in his time and later. Tony Lane writes:[80]

> It is paradoxical as one moves from Justin to Clement to Origen one encounters increasing hostility towards philosophy together with a steadily increasing absorption of philosophical ideas. The philosophical element was especially acute in Origen and his orthodoxy has been debated from his day to ours. In the fourth century there was a powerful anti-Origenist movement. In the sixth century he was formally condemned as a heretic. And yet he remains the single most influential father of Greek theology.

Origen was convinced that the doctrine of Christianity helped people to live the old ways behind and follow in the footsteps of Jesus. The whole treatise was studded with references to the change of life that Christianity had brought about in a many people. And he presented 'the best life' as a deciding factor. For Origen, change of life was important and not thought. Despite presenting arguments as proof, Origen always came up with the proof of deeds, either as lending support to his other arguments or as an argument which could not be refuted. We see it, for example, in his presentation of Jesus' humanity and divinity.[81] Two points shall not be neglected. First, Origen had fervent desire to be orthodox and his devotion to Jesus Christ. His dedication to the Christian service is to be appreciated. Second, his actual theology was totally permeated by Platonism.

Conclusion
Greek philosophy in the early Christian era drew close to biblical Christianity, at the same time remained different at various points. The task of the early Christian philosophers was to express the faith in relation to their Greek heritage. This meant expressing it in Greek terms, at the same time without distorting it. The Hellenistic Christian philosophers succeeded in a larger extent in doing this. By this careful and culturally relevant approach, Greek thought influenced Christian thought. At the same time, most of the elements in Greek thought which were contrary to biblical Christianity were rooted out. Christianity also came to be seen in a Greek way. Christian philosophical concepts were made common to the Greek world. Comparing and contrasting the Christian philosophy with Greek philosophy helped the people in few centuries to evaluate their faith and thus the outcome is 'Hellenistic Christian Philosophy.'

Helpful Questions
1. How do Jesus' teachings differ from the teachings of other Christian philosophers?
2. Prepare a paper on Alexandrian Christian philosophers.

CHAPTER 5

Medieval Christian Philosophy

This chapter gives a glimpse of the growth of philosophy in the West. It will help the reader to understand how Christian theologians were influenced by the medieval philosophy. It will also provide the reader with a bird's eye view of Christian Philosophy.

The Middle Ages are commonly referred to as the 'medieval period' or simply 'medieval.' This term comes from two Latin words: "medium" and "age." The term "Middle Age" was first coined by Flavio Biondo, an Italian humanist, in the early fifteenth century. The early Renaissance historians, in their glorification of all things classical, declared two periods in history, that of Ancient times and that of the period referred to as the Dark Age. Medieval philosophy was greatly concerned with the nature of God and application of Aristotle's logic and thought to every area of life. If God exists at all, surely He is the most important feature of the universe, and therefore worthy of study. One continuing interest in this time was to prove the existence of God through logic alone, if possible.

Medieval philosophy is "Christian philosophy." The philosophy of the medieval period is influenced by Christianity and sometimes 'used' to serve it. Philosophy is an autonomous discipline but at times, especially in the past, it has been strongly influenced by a religious context.[82] The Middle Ages are commonly dated from the fourth-century fall of the Western Roman Empire until the end of the fifteenth century. We cannot simply jump from Plotinus to Descartes and ignores 1200 years of 'Christian thought', which in their view, has nothing to do with genuine philosophy. But this is too facile and unjust a way of dealing with centuries of contextualised philosophy of Christian thinkers.

St. Augustine of Hippo

St Augustine (AD 354-430) developed classical Christian philosophy, largely by synthesising Hebrew and Greek thought. He drew particularly from the Greek pagan thinker Plato, Neo-Platonism and stoicism, which he altered and refined in light of divine revelation of Christian teaching and the Bible. It has often been said that both Catholicism and Protestantism stem from Augustine. The former takes from him its high view of the church and sacraments. The latter follows Augustine in his vision of the sovereignty of God, man's 'lostness' in sin and the grace of God that alone can bring salvation to man.[83] He is rightly called the Platonizer of Christianity, while St Thomas Aquinas, 800 years later, and was influenced by Aristotelian thought in producing his philosophical synthesis. Augustine's writings were surpassed in influence mainly until thirteen century.

Life and Works

St. Augustine was born of a pagan father and a Catholic Christian mother Monica as the eldest son in Thagaste, Tunisia (Algeria), a provincial Roman city in North Africa.[84] He was educated in Africa and baptised in Milan. Saint Augustine was of Berber descent and at the age of 11, Augustine was sent to school at Madaurus, a small Numidian city about 19 miles south of Thagaste. At age seventeen, he went to Carthage to continue his education in rhetoric. His early career was in philosophy and rhetoric, the art of persuasion and public speaking. At the age of thirty, Augustine had won the most visible academic chair in the Latin world, at a time when such posts gave ready access to political careers. Augustine renounced Manicheism which influenced him a lot in his student-life. He then became an enthusiastic student of Neo-Platonism.

In the summer of 386, Augustine underwent a profound personal crisis and decided to convert to Christianity. Key to this conversion was the voice of an unseen child he heard while in his garden in Milan telling him in a sing-song voice to 'tolle lege' ('take up and read') the Bible, at which point he opened the Bible at random and fell upon the Romans 13:13. Ambrose baptised Augustine on Easter Vigil in 387 in Milan, and soon thereafter in 388, he returned to Africa. On his way back to Africa, his mother died, leaving him alone in the world without family. Upon his return to North Africa, he created a monastic foundation at Thagaste for himself and a group of friends. In 391, he was ordained a priest in Hippo Regius, (now Annaba, in Algeria). In 396, he was made bishop of Hippo and remained as bishop in Hippo until his death in 430. Augustine died on August 28, 430, at the age of 75, during the siege of Hippo by the Vandals. Augustine was canonised by popular acclaim, and later recognised as a Doctor of the Church in 1303 by Pope Boniface VIII.

Augustine was one of the most prolific Latin authors, and the list of his works consists of more than a hundred separate titles. They include apologetic works against the heresies of the Arians, Donatists, Manichaeans and Pelagians, texts on Christian doctrine, notably De doctrina Christiana, exegetical works such as commentaries on Genesis, the Psalms and Paul's Letter to the Romans, many sermons and letters and the *Retractions*, a review of his earlier works, which he wrote near the end of his life. Apart from those, Augustine wrote *The City of God*, consisting of 22 books in 410 AD. Augustine has written a moving account of his conversion to Christianity in his "Confessions."[85] *The Confessions*, often called the first Western autobiography, is still read around the world. *Confessions* became a classic of both Christian theology and world literature.

His Philosophy

St. Augustine was interested to framing an overall Christian understanding of reality. He wrote his *Confessions*, which shows us clearly how he was drawn to Manichaeism and later came to the Christian faith. Manichaeism is a dualistic metaphysics of Good and evil. Augustine believed that the Platonic philosophy embodied important truths about aspects of reality. He was successful in his aim of getting Platonic ideas absorbed into the church's view of the nature of reality. St. Augustine seems to be the first to use natural theology in fifth-century Rome. Some of his philosophical concepts are given below.

Anthropological Dualism

Augustine endorsed Plato's dualistic philosophy of man. It is that man is a spiritual soul using a physical body. He believed in the immortality of the human soul, but he rejected the pre-existence of human soul, which was taught by Plato. To Augustine, the fulfillment of the fundamental aspiration of the human soul is possible only with a life after death. The anthropological concept of Augustine is very much similar to that of Plato. Jean Mercier writes:[86]

> Though Augustine endorsed Platonic dualistic anthropology and its speculative arguments for the soul's immorality, he remained open to the more relevant lessons of experience. Indeed he discerned that man's

natural desire for total happiness is another pointer to the possibility of life after death. This is an existential argument that does not need the support of anthropological dualism.

Augustine's concept of *man is a spiritual soul using a physical body* being endorsed Platonist dualism became a strong pointer to the Christian theologians. He acquiesced to Plato's arguments in favour of the immortality of the human soul, which also became a challenging concept in the biblical anthropology, a division of the systematic theology. At the same time, he was biblical in the sense that he did not accept the argument for the pre-existence of the soul advocated by Plato.

Divine Illumination

For Augustine, finite thoughts cannot be a sufficient explanation of the presence of infinite ideas and perfect values. Man's thoughts are caused by a divine illumination. Human mind receives its light from an external source, which must be infinite and perfect—which is God. God acts in the human mind in the way He illumines the mind. Augustine used this principle as an argument to prove God's existence. Divine illumination is the Augustinian philosophy to prove the existence of God. The philosophical theism finds its basis in this Augustinian philosophy. Augustine endorsed Plotinus' approach, equating the *Nous* with God's mind, which contains all ideas and values. Man's thoughts are caused by a divine illumination. God acts in the human mind as a sun that illumines it with its rays. Thus the light of the mind is a participated light. This approach to understand the origin of ideas was used by Augustine as an argument to prove God's existence. Finite minds alone cannot be a sufficient explanation of the presence of infinite ideas and perfect values. One must conclude that the human mind receives its light from an external source, which must be infinite and perfect: God himself.

Freedom and Evil

Human freedom is the cause of evil. God is not the cause of evil. He permits the evil because he has the power to transform evil in to good. Evil is explained as the wrong choice of free creatures. Augustine is credited with initiating the debate about God and evil. Jean Mercier wrote on Augustine's concept of freedom as:[87]

> His view on freedom is rather pessimistic. He remembered his experience before his conversion, when he was free to do what he liked and sinned, free also to adopt all kinds of false views and therefore erred. Once converted and under God's grace, he felt happy at not having to choose

anymore. Freedom for him was a double-edged sword, a dangerous power at man's disposal. Happiness flows from God's grace, not from human freedom.

Creation

In *The Literal Interpretation of Genesis*, Augustine took the view that everything in the universe was created simultaneously by God and not in seven calendar days like a plain account of Genesis would require. He argues that the six-day structure of creation presented in the book of Genesis represents a logical framework, rather than the passage of time in a physical way—it would bear a spiritual, rather than a physical, meaning, which is no less literal. Augustine also does not envisage the original sin as originating structural changes in the universe, and even suggests that the bodies of Adam and Eve were already created mortal before the fall. Apart from his specific views, Augustine recognises that the interpretation of the creation story is difficult, and remarks that we should be willing to change our mind about it as new information comes up.

With the Manicheans, Augustine debated the problem of evil. Against the view that there was an eternal evil principle opposed to God, Augustine argued that God was the sole creator and sustainer of all things. Evil was a deprivation of good. Augustine had debate with the Pelagians who argued that man should put himself right with God by doing good. Augustine debated the freedom of the will. Against the pagans who blamed the fall of Rome to invading hordes from the north on the corrupting, enervating influence of Christianity, Augustine wrote *The City of God*. It was the first attempt at a Christian philosophy of history. He saw the kingdom of God as the goal of all history. In *The City of God*, Augustine also defended what would be called today as young Earth creationism. In the specific passage, Augustine rejected both the immortality of the human race proposed by pagans and contemporary ideas of ages, such as of certain Greeks and Egyptians that differed from the Church's sacred writings. *City of God* provides a wide-ranging crystallisation of his thinking on history and society.

Doctrine of Predestination

His idea of predestination rests on the assertion that God has foreseen, from time immemorial, all the choices every person who would ever live on Earth would make, and whether they would co-operate with Grace or not. The number of the people God knows would be saved are the elect, the number whom God knows will not be saved are the reprobate. God has chosen the elect certainly and gratuitously, without any previous merit on their part. According to Augustine, God, in his creative decree, has expressly excluded every order of things in which grace would deprive man of his liberty, every situation in which man would not have the power to resist sin and thus Augustine brushes aside the predestinationism that has been attributed to him.

Against the Pelagians, Augustine also strongly stressed the importance of infant baptism. He believed that no one would be saved unless they have received baptism in order to be cleansed from the Original Sin. The Church of England disavowed the state of original sin in the 16th century. Non-conformist religions such as the Unitarians and the Quakers never held to the concept.

Augustine on Lust
Augustine struggled with lust throughout his life. He associated sexual desire with the sin of Adam and believed that it was still sinful, even though the Fall had made it part of human nature. In the *Confessions*, Augustine describes his personal struggle in vivid terms. For Augustine, the evil was not in the sexual act itself, but rather in the emotions that typically accompanied it. His view on freedom is rather pessimistic.[88] Freedom for him was a double-edged sword, a dangerous power at man's disposal. Happiness flows from God's grace, not from human freedom. What is evil? While it is real enough, it is not a 'reality', not a 'thing', but a privation, a lack of order, a disharmony in created realities. God is not the cause of evil; he permits evil because he has the power to transform evil into good. Evil is explained as the wrong choice of free creatures. To the pious virgins raped during the sack of Rome, he writes, another's lust cannot pollute thee. Chastity is a virtue of the mind, and is not lost by rape, but is lost by the intention of sin, even if unperformed. In short, Augustine's life experience led him to consider lust to be one of the most grievous sins and a serious obstacle to the virtuous life.

Influence as a Theologian and Thinker
Augustine was the outstanding figure in philosophy between the time of Plato and Thomas Aquinas, a period of 1,600 years. He introduced the fusion of Platonism and Christianity, made possible through his readings of Apuleius, Plotinus and Porphyry. Augustine remains a central figure, both within Christianity and in the history of Western thought, and is considered by modern historian Thomas Cahill to be the first medieval

man and the last classical man. In both his philosophical and theological reasoning, he was greatly influenced by Stoicism, Platonism and Neo-Platonism.[89] His early and influential writing on the human will, a central topic in ethics, would become a focus for later philosophers, such as Schopenhauer and Nietzsche. In addition, Augustine was influenced by the work of both Virgil and Cicero. St. Thomas Aquinas took much from Augustine's theology while creating his own unique synthesis of Greek and Christian thought after the widespread rediscovery of the work of Aristotle. While Augustine's doctrine of divine predestination would never be wholly forgotten within the Roman Catholic Church, finding eloquent expression in the works of Bernard of Clairvaux, Reformation theologians such as Martin Luther and John Calvin would look back to him as the inspiration for their avowed capturing of the biblical gospel.

Critical Remarks

Jean L. Mercier criticised the philosophic concepts of Augustine in the following sentences:[90]

(i) The Augustine's approach of the rapport between faith and reason, theology and philosophy was opposed by Aquinas and the modern supporters of philosophical autonomy. The failure to recognises the existing diversity of approaches led to the prejudicial one-sidedness of positivism (science only), rationalism (philosophical reason only) and fideism (religious faith only).

(ii) The Augustinian argument for God's existence—an anthropological argument that leads from man's mind to the affirmation of God—overshadows the classical cosmological argument of Aristotle, Aquinas and others.

(iii) Though Augustine endorsed Platonist dualistic anthropology and its speculative arguments for the soul's immortality, he remained open to the more relevant lessons of experience. This is an existential argument that does not need the support of anthropological dualism.

(iv) Aquinas corrected the over-pessimistic view of Augustine on freedom by showing the positive function it has to play in man's fulfillment.

(v) Augustine's view on evil raises more questions than it solves. On the one hand, how can the origin of evil be ascribed to the freedom of creatures. On the other hand, one does not see how the evil is always transformed in the good—that is the reason why God 'permits' evil.

(vi) Eastern Orthodox theologians, while they believe all humans were damaged by the original sin of Adam and Eve, have key disputes with Augustine about this doctrine and as such this is viewed as a key source of division between the East and the West.

(vii) His writings helped formulate the theory of the just war. He also advocated the use of force against the Donatists.

St. Anselm of Canterbury

Saint Anselm of Canterbury (1033-1109 AD) was an Italian medieval philosopher, theologian and church official who held the office of Archbishop of Canterbury from 1093 to 1109. Called the founder of scholasticism, he is famous as the originator of the ontological argument for the existence of God and as the archbishop who openly opposed the Crusades. He was a Benedictine monk. He realised that reason is useful for theological understanding. He was the first truly great theologian of the medieval western church.

Early Life

Anselm was born in the city of Aosta in Italy. His family was accounted noble and owned considerable property. His ministerial life falls into three periods of about fifteen years each: (1) Prior of Bec (1063-78), (2) an Abbot of Bec (1078-93) and (3) Archbishop of Canterbury (1093-1109).[91] In 1059, he left home, crossed the Alps and wandered through Burgundy and France. The following year, after spending some time at Avranches, he entered the abbey as a novice at the age of twenty-seven. Three years later, in 1063, Anselm was elected prior of Bec. He held this office for fifteen years, and then, in 1078 Anselm was elected abbot. Under his jurisdiction, Bec became the first seat of learning in Europe.

Anselm was consecrated in 1093 by the order of King William II. Anselm demanded of the king for acknowledging Urban II as pope in opposition to Antipope Clement III. In October 1097, he set out for Rome and spent some time at the little village of Schiavi, where he finished his treatise on the atonement, *Cur Deus homo*, and then retired to Lyons. Anselm returned to England and the remaining two years of his life were spent on the duties of his archbishopric. He died on April 21, 1109. He was canonised in 1494 by Alexander VI. Anselm was proclaimed as a Doctor of the Church in 1720 by Pope Clement XI. Eight hundred years after his death, on 21 April 1909, Pope Pius X issued an encyclical *Communion Rerum* praising Anselm and his ecclesiastical career and his writings. In the Middle Ages, Anselm's writings did not receive the respect and attention they deserved.

His Works

Anselm may be considered the first scholarly philosopher of Christian theology. In the history of thought Anselm is largely remembered for two things. Firstly, his important work on the atonement, *Why God Became Man*, in which he tried to set out the logic of the atonement. The other thing for which Anselm is remembered is his ontological argument. Here he tried to work out a logical demonstration of the existence of God. He describes God as *That than which no greater can be thought*.[92] Anselm wrote his first philosophical works, *Monologion* and *Proslogion*. These were followed by *The Dialogues on Truth, Free Will* and the *Fall of the Devil*. Anselm wrote many letters to monks, male relatives and others that contained passionate expressions of attachment and affection. These letters were typically addressed *dilecto dilectori*, sometimes translated as "beloved lover."

In his *Liber pro Insipiente*, Gaunilo, the monk, opposed Anselm on the ground that we cannot pass from idea to reality. Anselm replied to the objections of his contemporary, Gaunilo, in his *Responsio*. Anselm also authored a number of other arguments for the existence of God based on cosmological and teleological grounds. This demonstration is the substance of his works *Monologion* and *Proslogion*.

His Philosophy

The groundwork of Anselm's theory of knowledge is contained in the tract, *De Veritate*, in which from the consideration of truth as in knowledge, in willing and in things, he rises to the affirmation of an absolute truth, in which all other truth participates. This absolute truth is God himself, who is therefore the ultimate ground or principle both of things and of thought.

Foundation

According to the usual interpretations, Anselm was indulging in a piece of natural theology. He was trying to prove the existence of God without appealing to Christian faith and teaching. It adopts a kind of a two-step process in apologetics. Step one is to use philosophy to lay the foundations; step two is to introduce the Christian faith on the strength of the philosophical arguments. Anselm wrote: "Nor do I seek to understand that I may believe, but I believe that I may understand. For this too I believe, that unless I first believe, I shall not understand." The notion of God comes thus into the foreground of the system; before all things it is necessary that it should be made clear to reason, that it should be demonstrated to have real existence. For him, the content of the Christian faith is given by revelation, not by philosophy. But the believing theologian can then seek, by the use of reason, to understand more fully that which he believes. Reason can thus show the rationality and inner coherence of the Christian faith.

Creation and Trinity

Anselm, basing the rational grounds of the Christian doctrines of creation and of the Trinity, says that we cannot know God from himself, but only after the analogy of his creatures. The special analogy used is the self-consciousness of man. The peculiar double nature of consciousness, memory and intelligence represent the relation of the Father to the Son. The mutual love of these two, proceeding from the relation they hold to one another, symbolises the Holy Spirit.

Anselm started with presuppositions and assumed the existence of God as Trinity, together with God's character, the nature of man and his sin against God.[93] He undertook to make plain in his *Why did God become Man?* the rational necessity of the Christian mystery of the atonement. The theory rests on three positions: that satisfaction is necessary on account of God's honour and justice; that such satisfaction can be given only by the peculiar personality of the God-man Jesus; and that such satisfaction is really given by the voluntary death of this infinitely valuable person. Such a penalty can only be paid by God himself, and, as a penalty for man, must be paid under the form of man. Satisfaction is only possible through the God-man. Now this God-man, as sinless, is exempt from the punishment of sin; His passion is therefore voluntary, not given as due. The merit of it is therefore infinite; God's justice is thus appeased and His mercy may extend to man. This theory has exercised immense influence on church doctrine, providing the basis for the Roman Catholic concept.

Ontological Argument

St. Anselm advanced important argument for proof of the existence of God-Ontological Argument. Anselm is best known for the Ontological Argument for God's existence. God is that than which nothing greater can be conceived. But to exist is greater than not to exist. If God does not exist, then he would not be 'that than which nothing greater can be conceived.' Therefore, God exists. Basically, it says that God has all possible good features. Existence is good, and therefore God has it, and so exists.

This is an argument to prove God's existence. Anselm's general approach is summed up in a celebrated phrase that immediately precedes his ontological argument: *Credo ut intelligam* (I believe so that I may understand). It is not a case of proving first and then believing. We cannot believe theological truths for non-theological reasons. Rather, it is only when we encounter the living God in faith that we are in a position to grasp the truth of Christian faith. The task of philosophical theology is to examine the implications of this.[94] We have the idea of God and therefore God exists. For him, God is the idea of the highest perfection. And this idea of the highest perfection must exist. What is necessary must exist. The idea of God is the idea of a necessary being. His fame in the history of philosophy comes from the Ontological Argument, which he is the first to have proposed. The argument to prove God exists is as follows: "We have the Idea of God, therefore God Exists." Anslem had no hesitation in passing from idea of God to reality, from mental content (the logical) to reality (the 'ontic'): hence the 'onto-logical' approach. To him (a) God is the idea of the highest perfection—even the atheist is ready to agree with it—and (b) the idea of the highest perfection must exist, says Anselm, because if it does not, it is no longer the idea of the highest perfection.

Critical Remarks

(i) Anselm's reasoning has been the subject of controversy since he first published it in the 1070s. It was opposed at the time by the monk Gaunilo, in his *Liber pro Insipiente*, on the ground that we cannot pass from idea to reality.

(ii) Descartes, Leibniz, Spinoza and some other contemporary philosophers welcomed the ontological argument of St. Anselm.[95]

(iii) It was rejected outright by most philosophers, beginning with Aquinas and Kant for whom one can never pass from essence to existence, from idea to reality, from possibility to necessity.

(iv) Existence is not perfection as claimed by the ontological argument. Perfections are positive features of the essence; they may exist or not. One may acknowledge an existence being by experience or by inference, but not by 'logic.'

(v) For him, God's justice is appeased, and His mercy may extend to man. It can be said that Anselm puts the whole issue on a merely legal footing, giving it no ethical bearing, and neglects altogether the consciousness of the individual to be redeemed.

(vi) Anselm's basic position was very different. It was not a case of faith taking over where reason left off. In apprehending religious truth, faith and reason must go hand in hand. Faith is the act of self-commitment that puts a man into the right relationship with God.

Thomas Aquinas

Saint Thomas Aquinas (1225-1274 AD) was an Italian Catholic priest in the Order of Preachers, a philosopher and theologian in the scholastic tradition, known as *Doctor Angelicus, Doctor Universalis*. He is the foremost classical proponent of natural theology and the father of the Thomistic school of philosophy and theology. St. Thomas is held in the Roman Catholic Church to be the model teacher for those studying for the priesthood. Thomas Aquinas, probably the best-known religious philosopher of the Middle Ages, adapted the argument he found in his reading of Aristotle to form the cosmological argument. His conception of the *first cause* is the idea that the universe must have been caused by something that was itself uncaused, which he asserted was God.

Life and Works

Thomas Aquinas was born in or around 1225 as the younger son of his parents at *Count of Aquina* the kingdom of Naples.[96] After his early education at the monastery, when he was 16, he left the University of Naples, where he had studied for six years. Aquinas had come under the influence of the Dominicans (1244). Aquinas graduated as a bachelor of theology from the University of Paris. In 1248, he returned to Cologne, where he was appointed second lecturer. In 1252, Aquinas went to Paris for his master's degree. In 1256, Aquinas was named *doctor of theology* and began to lecture on theology in Paris and Rome and other Italian towns. Thomas Aquinas was the student of Albert the Great. He moved to Rome in 1261 and after two years, he attended the London meeting of the Dominican order. In 1268, he lectured in Rome and Bologna. From 1269 to 1271, Aquinas was again active in Paris. He lectured to the students, managed the affairs of the church and advised the king, Louis VIII, his kinsman, on affairs of state. Later, King Charles II brought him back to the professor's chair at Naples. In January 1274, Pope Gregory X directed Aquinas to attend the Second Council of Lyons. Aquinas died on March 7, 1274. On July 18, 1323, Pope John XXII pronounced Aquinas' sainthood at Avignon. In 1567, Pope Pius V ranked Thomas Aquinas with those of the four great Latin fathers: Ambrose, Augustine, Jerome and Gregory. In 1880, Aquinas was declared *patron* of all Roman Catholic educational establishments.

In 1272, Aquinas wrote homilies, disputations and lectures. He also worked diligently on his great literary work, *Summa Theologica*. Aquinas' *Summa Theologica* was deemed so important that at the Council of Trent, it was placed upon the altar beside the Bible and the Decretals. *The Suma Theologiae*, the latest critical edition of which runs into sixty volumes, has been described as the highest achievement of medieval theological systematisation and the accepted basis of modern Roman Catholic theology. In his *Encyclical* of August 4, 1879, Pope Leo XIII stated that Aquinas's theology was a definitive exposition of Catholic doctrine. Also, Leo XIII decreed that "all Catholic seminaries and universities must teach Aquinas's doctrines."

Background of Thomistic Philosophy

When Thomas Aquinas was born, the Roman Catholic Church was following the Augustinian tradition, which was platonic in nature. What was revealed in the Holy Scriptures was by the church taken to be the true source of knowledge. Religion and the word of God (Revelation) commanded the highest respect. At this stage, philosophy or reason had no place in the Christian church. Aquinas reintroduced Aristotelian philosophy to Christianity. Jean Mercier writes:[97]

> The thirteen century AD is the golden age of Christian philosophy and theology. It is marked by the foundation of the first European universities specially the one in Paris, by the dominant role played by two new religious orders, Franciscans and Dominicans, and by the intellectual ferment caused by the rediscovery of Aristotelian philosophy. The dominant figure of the times was the Dominican Thomas Aquinas, who occupied the chair of Theology at Paris and Rome and was a prolific writer of Philosophical and theological treatises, of which the most well-known is the 'Summa Theologica.'

Thomas Aquinas worked out a system of thought that would square with the dogmas of the church and harmonise science and faith. Thomas Aquinas attempted to harmonise the Christian faith and Aristotelian philosophy. He chose the empirical approach of Aristotle to build up his philosophical synthesis, making maximum use of Aristotle provided it did not conflict his understanding of the Christian faith. Thomas' system is like a two-storey house—Aristotelian philosophy provides the foundation and the first storey; Catholic Theology perfects and completes it by adding the second storey and the roof.[98] He asserts that thought has its proper activity by which it can draw from sense-experience the materials of knowledge that extends beyond the bounds of the world of sense. The fundamental aim of the system of St. Thomas Aquinas is to demonstrate the rationality of the universe as a revelation of God.

Thomistic Philosophy

The problem before St. Thomas Aquinas was that of the discovery of philosophical support for the tenants of revelation. To understand their concept of the individual soul, it is essential to grasp the fundamental of the philosophy on which they have built their concept of the soul, God and the world. During the scholastic period, western philosophy was occupied in developing and formulating the articles of the Christian faith and organising them into a rational system. Thomistic philosophy held an important place in this period.

Cosmological Argument

The cosmological argument is a metaphysical argument for the existence of God, or a *first mover* of the cosmos. It is traditionally known as an 'argument from universal causation', an 'argument from first cause' and an 'uncaused cause' argument. The cosmological argument does not attempt to prove anything about the first cause or about God, except to argue that such a cause must exist. Aquinas was a staunch advocate of the cosmological argument. There could not be an infinite chain of causes back into the past; there must have been an uncaused first cause. This is God. Aquinas also adapted this argument to prove the goodness of God. Everything has some goodness, and the cause of each thing is better than the thing caused. Therefore, the first cause is the best possible thing. Similar arguments are used to prove God's power and uniqueness. The knowledge of God is possible because He is the Being that causes finite beings to exist. He can be known by analogy. Thomas Aquinas wrote that essence and existence are inseparable. A pure existence is meaningless, as it is always something that exists.

Cosmological argument is most widely accepted by astronomers and astrophysicists. Though contemporary versions of the cosmological argument most typically assume that there was a beginning to the cosmic chain of physical or natural causes, the early formulations of the argument did not have the benefit of this degree of theoretical insight into the apparent origins of the cosmos. Plato's *demiurge* and Aristotle's *Prime Mover* referred to a being who, they speculated, set in motion an already existing 'stuff' of the cosmos. A millennium and a half later, Aquinas went on to argue that there is an *Uncaused Cause*, which is just another name for God. And to Aquinas, it remained logically possible that the universe has already existed for an infinite amount of time and will continue to exist for an infinite amount of time. In his classic *Summa Theologiae*, he posited that even if the universe has always existed, there is still the question of cause, or even of 'first cause.'

Revelation

In Aquinas' view, special revelation is equivalent to the revelation of God in Jesus Christ. The major theological components of Christianity, such as Trinity and Incarnation, are revealed in the teachings of the Church and the Scriptures and may not otherwise be deduced. Special revelation (faith) and natural revelation (reason) are complementary rather than contradictory in nature, for they pertain to the same unity: truth. For Thomas, the purpose of divine revelation is to perfect human philosophy (though it will oppose false, incorrect philosophy), but rather supplements it and brings it to completion and perfection.[99] However, he believed that human beings have the natural capacity to know many things without special divine revelation, even though such revelation occurs from time to time, 'especially in regard to faith.'

Similarly, in the Asian perspective, significance of the concept of man, his nature and destiny and words like 'soul', 'self', 'spirit', 'Atman', 'Jiva', 'purusha', 'Ruh' and 'Shruti' are held to be the essence or form of man's individuality. Human personality has become the current coin of thought, though it has been shaped up through the ages. Relation of experience and revelation and their significance to the thought of the "Middle Ages" thinkers—relation between the soul and the 'over soul'—was regarded as a matter of life and death.

Analogy

An important element in Aquinas' philosophy is his theory of analogy. Aquinas noted three forms of descriptive language: univocal, analogical and equivocal. Univocality is the use of a descriptor in the same sense when applied to two objects. Analogy, Aquinas maintained, occurs when a descriptor changes some but not all of its meaning. Analogy is necessary when talking about God, for some of the aspects of the divine nature are hidden and others revealed to finite human minds.

The knowledge of God is possible because he is the *Being* that causes finite beings to exist. Aquinas rejected Plotinus' view that *being* characterises only the effect but is inapplicable to the cause (the one). Plotinus concluded that the One is unknowable. Aquinas, on the contrary, contended that God can be known by analogy. In Aquinas' mind, we can know about God through his creation (general revelation), but only in an analogous manner. We can speak of God's goodness only by understanding that goodness as applied to humans is similar to, but not identical with, the goodness of God. Equivocation is the complete change in meaning of the descriptor and is an informal fallacy. Aquinas concludes that being an analogical, not univocal. All our concepts are univocal, but *being* is not a concept, not univocal because there are many different modes of being. Aquinas's teaching on analogy is especially relevant in the light of the fierce debates on the meaning and nature of language—especially religion, metaphysics and moral language—which have raged in British philosophy over the past century.

Theology and Philosophy
Aquinas viewed theology as a science, the raw material data of which consists of written scripture and the tradition of the church. These sources of data were produced by the self-revelation of God to individuals and groups of people throughout history. Faith and reason, while distinct but related, are the two primary tools for processing the data of theology. Aquinas was the founder of a new philosophical synthesis called *Thomism* in which he endeavoured to harmonise the Christian faith and the Aristotelian philosophical approach. Unlike Augustine, he recognised that theological knowledge and rationale knowledge need separate treatment. He chose the empirical approach of Aristotle to build up his philosophical synthesis. Tony Lane writes:[100]

> Thomas' aim was to construct a synthesis between reason and faith, philosophy and theology, Aristotle and Catholic doctrine. He followed Aristotle's philosophy, but not blindly. Occasionally he felt the need to correct him, as with his opinion concerning the age of the universe. But generally he followed him because he believed him to be right. He maintained that Aristotelian philosophy and Catholic theology could be held together, with no conflict between the two.'

Aquinas blended Greek philosophy and Christian doctrine by suggesting that rational thinking and the study of nature, like revelation, were valid ways to understand God. The ultimate goals of theology, in Aquinas' mind, are to use reason to grasp the truth about God and to experience salvation through that truth.

Nature of God

Aquinas felt that the existence of God is neither self-evident nor beyond proof. In *Summa Theologica*, he considered in great detail five rational proofs for the existence of God. These are widely known as the 'Five Ways.' He proposed five positive statements about divine qualities: (1) *God is simple*, without composition of parts, such as body and soul, or matter and form. (2) *God is perfect*, lacking nothing. That is, God is distinguished from other beings on account of God's complete actuality. (3) *God is infinite*, that is, God is not finite in the ways that created beings are physically, intellectually and emotionally limited. This infinity is to be distinguished from infinity of size and infinity of number. (4) *God is immutable*, incapable of change on the levels of God's essence and character. (5) *God is one*, without diversification within God's self. The unity of God is such that God's essence is the same as God's existence.[101] Through this concept of God, Aquinas distanced himself from Plotinus for whom the Absolute is not being but the undifferentiated One and Aristotle for whom the Absolute mover is not the cause of finite reality.

Essence and existence are inseparable; essence alone is a mere idea of concept. A pure existence is meaningless as it is always something that exists. Thus in a substance, a universal essence is actualised in a concrete, particular existence. The perfection of the divine being does not allow for any limitation; He is pure self-existent, the being whose essence is to exist. He is pure Act without potency; the infinite existence that causes finite limited beings to exist by participation.

Aquinas argued that God, while perfectly united, is also perfectly described by three interrelated persons. These three persons (the Father, the Son and the Holy Spirit) are constituted by their relations within the essence of God. The Father generates the Son (or the Word) by the relation of self-awareness. This takes place through the Incarnation of the Word in the person of Jesus Christ and through the indwelling of the Holy Spirit within those who have experienced salvation by God. Thomas goes on to present the doctrine that cannot be reached without Christian revelation—the Trinity, the incarnation of Jesus Christ, the sacraments, the resurrection of the body, etc. These doctrines are beyond the grasp of unaided reason, but they are not contrary to reason.

Nature of Jesus Christ

In *Summa Theologica*, Aquinas begins his discussion of Jesus Christ by recounting the biblical story of Adam and Eve and by describing the negative effects of the original sin. The purpose of Christ's Incarnation was to restore human nature by removing 'the contamination of sin,' which humans cannot do by themselves. 'Aquinas argued against several specific contemporary and historical theologians who held differing views about Christ.

In response to Plotinus, Aquinas stated that Jesus was truly divine and not simply a human being. Against Nestorius, who suggested that God merely inhabited the body of Christ, Aquinas argued that the fullness of God was an integral part of Christ's existence. However, countering Apollinaris' views, Aquinas held that Christ had a truly human (rational) soul as well. This produced a duality of natures in Christ, contrary to the teachings of Arius. Aquinas argued against Eutyches that this duality persisted after the Incarnation. Aquinas stated that these two natures existed simultaneously yet distinguishably in one real human body, unlike the teachings of Manichaeus and Valentinus. In short, 'Christ had a *real body* of the same nature of ours, a *true rational soul*, and together with these, *perfect deity*.'

Goal of Human Life

In Aquinas's thought, the goal of human existence is union and eternal fellowship with God. Specifically, this goal is achieved through the beatific vision, an event in which a person experiences perfect, unending happiness by comprehending the very essence of God. This vision is a gift from God given to those who have experienced salvation and redemption through Christ while living on earth. This ultimate goal carries implications for one's present life on earth. Aquinas concurred with Aristotle in recognising the unity of man: one substance composed of body and soul. But he disagreed with him when he stated, like Plato, that the human soul, being spiritual, can subsist without its material support. The human soul is separable, therefore immortal.

Aquinas stated that an *individual's will* must be ordered towards right things, such as charity, peace and holiness. He sees this as the way to happiness. Aquinas orders his treatment of the moral life around the idea of happiness. The relationship between will and goal is antecedent in nature 'because rectitude of the will consists in being duly ordered to the last end.' Those who truly seek to understand and see God will necessarily love what God loves. Such love requires morality and bears fruit in everyday human choices.

Sacraments

Thomas is also famous for his teaching on the Eucharist. He expounded the doctrine of transubstantiation, which had been barely stated at the 'Fourth Lateran Council in 1215.[102] There are seven sacraments: Baptism, Confirmation, Holy Eucharist, Penance, Extreme Unction, Holy Orders and matrimony. The Holy Eucharist is the greatest of the sacraments. This is because it is the real presence of the Body and Blood of Christ. It perfects the other sacraments. For Aquinas, the visible sacrifice is the sacred sign of the invisible sacrifice. A thing may be called a sacrament either by having a certain hidden sanctity, and in this sense, a sacrament is a sacred secret, or by having some relationship to this sanctity. Sacraments are made necessary because humans have sinned. The main effect of the sacraments is grace; Grace perfects the soul and allows participation in the Divine Nature.

Furthermore, sacraments build the character of the spirit or soul. Therefore, the effects of the sacraments are justification. This is an interior effect. There are three reasons why sacraments are necessary to the salvation of humans: First, it is in the nature of humans to be led by things corporeal and sensible to things that are spiritual and intelligible. Second, by sinning, humans have subjected themselves to corporeal things; therefore, it is proper that the remedy have a corporeal side, leading to the spiritual. Third, humans are prone to direct their activity towards material things. The sacraments are the signs by which humans gain knowledge of spiritual and intelligible goods. It is necessary for salvation that humans united together in the name of true religion. Therefore, sacraments are necessary for man's salvation. The power of the sacraments is from God alone. It does not matter that the minister of the sacraments may be a sinner or evil.

Critical Remarks

(i) Thomism is typical 'Christian philosophy' in the best sense of the word. Unlike the Augustinian approach, it clearly affirms autonomy of the philosophical activity. Welcoming the Christian faith in a common, harmonious search for truth is able to satisfy both the philosopher and the believer.[103]

(ii) The foundation of Aquinas' cosmological argument as well as the Augustinian anthropological approach is better to be signified as the principle of casualty. Aquinas takes the evidence of the principle for granted wherein it is stated that 'whatever reality cannot be explained by itself must be explained by another reality.'

(iii) How far can human language be used to describe transcendent realities? Plotinus had already implicitly taken the lead. Aquinas' thesis that God can be known by analogy was intended to refute this skepticism.

(iv) Thomistic anthropology is a curious blend of Aristotle, Plato and Christian doctrine. While for Plato, the spiritual soul is a complete essence, for Aquinas it is an 'incomplete' essence, a concession he makes to Aristotle.

(v) Aquinas pointed out that valid statements about God were analogical. It has to be shown that there is a genuine correspondence between language and its object. Having said what we have said about the inadequacies of the old proofs of the existence of God, we cannot fall back on them to establish an analogical relationship between God and the world.

The foundations of religion according to St. Thomas Aquinas are rational. Augustine lays emphasis on basic faith in accepting God's revelation. Thomas makes a clear distinction between reason and faith. For him revealed truths are not contrary to reason. It is a matter of revelation. Faith is a matter of will. He makes a distinction between rational and trans-rational approaches. He signified philosophy as rational and tried to reconcile both to understand the mysteries of God. It was St. Thomas Aquinas who saved the church from this dogmatism by introducing Aristotelian philosophy into it and developing it in a very thorough manner.

John Duns Scotus

John Duns Scotus (1265-1308 AD) is known as the 'subtle doctor' whose hair-splitting distinctions were important contributions in scholastic thought and the modern development of logic. Scotus was also Professor, University of Paris, but not at the same time as Aquinas. Duns Scotus is considered one of the most important Franciscan theologians and was the founder of Scotism, a special form of Scholasticism.

His Background

Duns Scotus was born in Scotland, not far north of the English border. Ordained a priest, in 1291, in Northampton, England, he studied and taught at Paris (1293-1297) and Oxford and probably at Cambridge as well.[104] He was expelled from the University of Paris for siding with Pope Boniface VIII against Philip the Fair of France. Finally, he came to Cologne, Germany, in 1307. He died in Cologne and is buried in the Church of the

Minorities in Cologne. His sarcophagus bears the Latin inscription: 'Scotia brought me forth. England sustained me. France taught me. Cologne holds me.'

He wrote commentaries on Peter Lombard's *Sentences*, which is a synthesis of his various sets of lectures on *Sentences*. It is an important work, outlining his thought as a whole. Duns' second important work is "Various Questions." It was of course his last work. Duns never wrote *Summa Theologica*. He died young. His writings were not easy to read, due partly to his style and partly to the fact that he died before he could present his thought in a definitive form.

His Philosophy

Along with Aquinas, he is one of the two giants of Scholastic Philosophy. He came out of the Old Franciscan School. His thought is not easy to follow. In the sixteenth century, the Humanists and Protestant Reformers were not so polite about his absolute style. Later, philosophers were not so complimentary about his work; for instance, the modern word "dunce", which developed from the name "Duns", given to his followers in the 1500s.

Existence of God

Duns said that the existence of God can be proven only *a posteriori* through its effects. The Causal Argument he gives for the existence of God is that an infinity of things that are essentially ordered is impossible, as the totality of caused things that are essentially caused is itself caused, and so it is caused by some cause which is not a part of the totality, for then it would be the cause of itself; for the whole totality of dependent things is dependent and not on anything belonging to that totality. The argument is relevant for Scotus' conception of metaphysical inquiry into being by searching the ways into which beings relate to each other. Duns believed that reason and philosophy could prove the existence of God and some of His attributes, such as His infinity.[105] But much that Thomas believed to be demonstrated by reason and Duns held to be known only by revelation. Christian doctrines like God's goodness, justice, mercy and predestination are accepted by faith alone, not proved by reason.

Metaphysics

Metaphysics includes the study of transcendentalism; so-called because they transcend the division of being into finite and infinite and the further division of finite being into the ten Aristotelian categories. The study of the Aristotelian categories belongs to metaphysics. There are exactly ten categories, Scotus argues. The first and most important is the category of substance. The other nine categories, called accidents, exist in substances. The nine categories of accidents are quantity, quality, relation, action, passion, place, time, position and state.

Duns elaborates a distinct view on hylemorphism, with three important strong theses that differentiate him. He held that (a) there exists matter that has no form whatsoever, or prime matter, as the stuff underlying all change, against Aquinas; (b) that not all created substances are composites of form and matter; and (c) that one and the same substance can have more than one substantial form; for instance, humans have at least two substantial forms, the soul and the form of the body. Although Duns Scotus was a scholastic realist in that he treated universals as real, he did not accept the Thomistic distinction between existence and essence. Duns followed Aristotle in asserting that the subject matter of metaphysics is *being qua being*. Being in general was the first object of the intellect.

Logic
Duns was perhaps one of the most influential medieval logicians, in the ranks of Peter Abelard and William of Ockham. He was the one of the first medieval logicians to break from Aristotle's statistical model of possibility and necessity and to consider instead the concept of logical possibility. Duns stressed the primacy of the will. Reason shows the will what is possible, but the will is free to choose whichever option it wants to. The freedom of the will means that it does not simply follow whatever reason dictates. His theory moves from considering modal notions with respect to different ways the actual world is arranged at certain times to one where modal notions are considered with respect to conceptual consistency. This interpretation of possibility and necessity thus foreshadows Leibniz's possible world's conception of modality.

Theology
Duns was an Augustinian theologian. He is usually associated with voluntarism, the tendency to emphasise God's will and human freedom in all philosophical issues. Duns' stress on the freedom of God means that the role of reason and philosophy is necessarily limited. Duns suggested that the Son would not have become incarnate if man has not sinned; thus the incarnation would have been a free choice on God's part, not a necessity imposed upon Him by man's sin. Duns believed that reason and philosophy could prove God's existence and some of His attributes.[106]

Duns struggled throughout his works in demonstrating his univocity theory against Aquinas' analogy doctrine. Indeed Duns' theology has been called 'a counterblast to Thomism'. Much of his writing was in conscious opposition to Thomas Aquinas. Thomas believed in the primacy of reason and knowledge over the will. But Duns in contrast stressed the will. Reason shows the will what is possible, but the will itself is free to choose whatever of these it will. The *freedom of the will* means it does not simply follow whatever reason dictates.

Perhaps the most influential point of Duns Scotus' theology was his defense of the Immaculate Conception of Mary. Duns Scotus devised the following argument: Mary was in need of redemption like all other human beings, but through the merits of Jesus' crucifixion, given in advance, she was conceived without the stain of the original sin. This argument appears in Pope Pius IX's declaration of the dogma of the Immaculate Conception. This theory was defined as dogma in 1854 by Pope Pius 1X. Pope John XXIII recommended the reading of Duns Scotus' theology to modern theology students. John Duns Scotus was a theologian, philosopher and logician. Some argue that during his tenure at Oxford, the systematic examination of what differentiates theology from philosophy and science began in earnest. He was one of the most influential theologians and philosophers of the High Middle Ages, nicknamed *Doctor Subtilis* for his penetrating manner of thought.

William of Ockham

William of Ockham (AD 1288-1348), an English Franciscan friar and scholastic philosopher, was born at Ockham near Woking in Surrey. He is considered, along with Thomas Aquinas and Duns Scotus, one of the major figures of medieval thought and found himself at the centre of the major intellectual and political controversies of the fourteenth century.

His Life and Works

William of Ockham joined the Franciscan order at a young age. He is believed to have studied theology at University of Oxford from 1309 to 1321, but never completed his master's programme. Ockham was summoned before the Papal court of Avignon in 1324 under charges of heresy. After studying the works of John XXII and previous papal statements, Ockham concurred with the Minister General. He believed that John XXII was himself guilty of heresy for refusing to accept the Franciscan claim. Fearing imprisonment and possible execution, Ockham and other Franciscan sympathisers fled Avignon. In 1328, they took refuge in the court of the Holy Roman Emperor Louis IV of Bavaria, who was also engaged in dispute with the papacy. Ockham was excommunicated for leaving Avignon, but his philosophy was never officially condemned. He spent much of the remainder of his life writing about political issues, including the relative authority and rights of the spiritual and temporal powers. After Michael of Cesena's death in 1342, he became the leader of the small band of Franciscan dissidents living in exile with Louis IV. Ockham died probably in 1348 in the Franciscan convent in Munich, Bavaria.

William of Ockham also produced significant works on logic, physics and theology. William of Ockham wrote *Summa Logica in* 1341. Eventually, Ockham came to think that this intentional realm of 'fictive' entities was not needed, while he was writing his *Summa of Logic*. In logic, Ockham worked towards what would later be called De Morgan's Laws and considered ternary logic, that is, a logical system with three truth values, a concept that would be taken up again in the mathematical logic of the 19th and 20th centuries. While at Munich, William wrote extensively on church-state relations, mainly against the Pope. He held that the highest authority in the church is not the Pope but a General Council including lay representation. The views on monarchial accountability espoused in his *Dialogus* (1348) greatly influenced the Conciliar movement and assisted in the emergence of liberal democratic ideologies.

His Philosophy

Scholasticism and Nominalism

In Scholasticism, Ockham advocated a reform both in method and content, the aim of which was simplification. Ockham incorporated much of the work of some previous theologians, especially John Duns Scotus. From Scotus, Ockham derived his view of divine omnipotence, his view of grace and justification, much of his epistemology and ethical convictions. He reacted to and against Scotus in the areas of predestination, penance, his understanding of universals and his view of parsimony.

According to the *Quodlibets*, a so-called intellectio-theory, a universal concept is just the act of thinking about several objects at once; metaphysically it is quite singular and universal only in the sense of being predicable of many. As a pioneer of Nominalism, some consider him the *father of modern epistemology*, because of his strongly argued position that only individuals exist, rather than supra-individual universals, essences or forms and that universals are the products of abstraction from individuals by the human mind and have no extra-mental existence. He denied the real existence of metaphysical universals and advocated for the reduction of ontology.

Ockham is sometimes considered an advocate of conceptualism rather than nominalism. He believed that universals have no 'real' existence at all in Aristotelian categories, but are purely 'intentional objects' more or less in the sense of modern phenomenology; they have only a kind of 'thought'-reality. Such 'fictive' objects were metaphysically universal; they just were not real.

Ontological Parsimony

One important contribution that he made to modern science and modern intellectual culture was through the principle of parsimony in explanation and theory building that came to be known as Ockham's Razor. 'Ockham's razor' or Law of Economy', the methodological procedure that bears his name, is best known. This is the principle of simplicity—'the simplest explanation is the best', or 'it is futile to multiply hypotheses when a few will suffice.'[107] William applied this principle to medieval theories about universals. He opened the debate over universals, which was already resolved earlier by Peter Abelard. He turned this into a concern for ontological parsimony; the principle says that one should not multiply entities beyond necessity.

His skepticism to which his ontological parsimony request appears in his doctrine that human reason can prove neither the immortality of the soul nor the existence, unity and infinity of God. These truths, he teaches, are known to us by Revelation alone. For Ockham, the only truly necessary entity is God; everything else is contingent. He thus accepts the Principle of Sufficient Reason, rejects the distinction between essence and existence and advocates against the Thomistic doctrine of active and passive intellect.

Natural Philosophy

Ockham holds that Mathematics must be applied to other categories, such as the categories of substance or qualities, thus anticipating modern scientific renaissance while violating Aristotelian prohibition of *metabasis*. Ockham was arguably important in physics for his view, apparently an application of his razor that motion is essentially self-conserving in itself without need of any causal force. Arguably, Ockham's view only came to be accepted in Einstein's anti-Newtonian Cartesian relativistic geometrico-kinematical science of motion that eliminates all forces and reduces dynamics to Minkowskian geometrico-kinematics. It is partly derived from Parisian scholastic impetus theory that the continuation of uniform straight motion in the absence of any resistance would be caused by an internal inherent force of inertia. This was contrary to the contemporary impetus theory of Buridan of Paris and to the much later view of Newton.

Theory of Knowledge

In the theory of knowledge, Ockham rejected the scholastic theory of species, as unnecessary and not supported by experience, in favour of a theory of abstraction. This was an important development in late medieval epistemology. He also distinguished between intuitive and abstract cognition; intuitive cognition depends on the existence or non-existence of the object, whereas abstractive cognition 'abstracts' the object from the existence predicate. It is not yet decided among interpreters as to the role of these two types of cognitive activities.

He held that all true knowledge is acquired empirically—through the senses. The only reality to be known as individuals, and they are known by sense experience. Theologians must rely simply on God's revelation, and reason can offer no more than supporting probable arguments. This is the end of the synthesis between faith and reason[108]. Ockham's stress on empirical knowledge is inherited from Duns, having been based on freedom, helped to pave the way for the rise of modern science in the seventeenth century.

Political Theory

Ockham was one of the first medieval authors to advocate a form of church-state separation and was important for the early development of the notion of property rights. William taught that the Pope has no secular power and that the emperor can depose the Pope. He is also increasingly being recognised as an important contributor to the development of Western constitutional ideas, especially those of limited responsible government. His political ideas are regarded as 'natural' or 'secular', holding for a secular absolutism.

Critical Remarks
   i.   His natural philosophy is partially derived from Parisian scholastic impetus theory.
   ii. From Scotus, Ockham derived his view of divine omnipotence, his view of grace and justification, much of his epistemology and

ethical convictions, although he reacted to and against Scotus in the areas of predestination and penance.

iii. The views on monarchial accountability espoused in his *Dialogus* greatly influenced the conciliar movement and assisted in the emergence of liberal democratic ideologies.

iv. Ockham's position is known as the 'modern way' in contrast to the 'old way' of Thomas Aquinas and Duns Scotus. It dominated the thinking of the late Middle Ages.

v. Martin Luther and some other Protestant theologians were greatly influenced by Ockham's philosophical concepts.

Conclusion

The Middle Ages witnessed the first sustained urbanisation of northern and western Europe. Modern European states owe their origins to the Middle Ages, and their political boundaries as we know them are essentially the result of the military and dynastic achievements in this tumultuous period. Science, technology, agricultural production and social identity changed drastically during this period; but as far as the history of Christianity is concerned, this period was known as 'the Dark Age.' The knowledge of philosophy was very limited in that period of time. Theology during this period was largely confined to the monasteries and is therefore called monastic theology. The impact of philosophy on theology began in the eleventh century with the emergence of reason (philosophy) as a method to be used in theology. In the following centuries, the role of reason was further expanded. In the thirteenth century, theology entered a new and more dangerous phase. Philosophy now appeared not just as a tool for use in theology but as a rival system of thought. Thomas Aquinas attempted to make a synthesis between faith and reason. In the fourteenth and fifteenth centuries, there was increasing skepticism about the possibility of harmonising theology and philosophy. The medieval period spans a thousand years. Medieval Christian Philosophers wrestled with the problem of the relation between faith and reason.

In this chapter, we learned that Middle Ages became the chief instrument of the great systematic theologians of the church. St. Augustine tried to bring Plato's ideas and to represent them as the creative and formative principles within the world, which he conceived as a system of development, rising by spiritual gradations from lower to higher forms and culminating in God, who is the uncaused cause of all things. But underneath all the forms there still remained matter as an antithetical element, and Aristotle concealed the dualism of Plato. The Middle Ages form the middle period in a traditional schematic division of European history into three ages: the classical civilisation of antiquity, the Middle Ages and Modern Times. They were a period of great cultural, political and economic change in Europe. The Middle Ages witnessed the first sustained urbanisation of northern and western Europe. Modern European states owe their origins to the Middle Ages, and their political boundaries as we know them are essentially the result of the military and dynastic achievements in this tumultuous period. The Middle Ages are commonly dated from the 5th-century fall of the western Roman empire until the end of the 15th century.

Helpful Questions

1. Describe briefly the Augustinian influence on Christian philosophy.

2. What do you know about Thomistic philosophy?

3. Evaluate critically the philosophy of Anselm.

CHAPTER 6

Reformational Christian Philosophy

This chapter deals with the philosophical thoughts of Church Reformers. It will also enhance the reader's understanding of Reformational philosophy.

Martin Luther, Erasmus, John Calvin and Zwingli were the Reformation Christian Philosophers. It covered the history of Christian philosophy from 1500-1600 AD. There was a revival of interest in the classical past, which was known as 'Humanism', in all over Europe; especially in the north, there was a distinctively Christian Humanism led by Erasmus. The pioneer of the Reformation was Martin Luther. His teaching had spread widely throughout Germany and then further in all Eastern Europe and Scandinavia. In Zurich, Zwingli began to preach reform. He was an independent thinker, although he was influenced by Luther. Protestantism was split into two streams: Lutheran and Reformed (Swiss) Protestantism. John Calvin, a Frenchman, was a Reformed theologian. He took the leading after Zwingli and so the Reformed faith is often known as Calvinism.

Reformational philosophy is a movement pioneered by Herman Dooyeweerd and D. H. Th. Vollenhoven that seeks to develop philosophical thought in a radically Christian direction. We will elaborately study their philosophical perspectives later. Reformational philosophy began with the 'Renaissance' (1500 AD), a landmark in European history pointing to the end of Christian medievalism and beginning of a process that led to contemporary secularism. The influence of the Renaissance aided the breaking of the power of the papacy, in the establishment of Protestantism, and the right of free enquiry. The reformation insists on the right of the individual reason to determine the sense of the inspired scripture. The foundations of papal power were to be shaken by the earthquake of the Protestant Reformation and it is said that the Pope would retain control over no more than Italy and Spain.

Desiderius Erasmus

Desiderius Erasmus Roterodamus (1466-1536) was born with the name Gerrit Garretson on October 27, 1466, in Rotterdam as an illegitimate son of a priest. He was a Dutch Humanist and theologian. Erasmus was a classical scholar who wrote in a 'pure' Latin style. Although he remained a Roman Catholic throughout his lifetime, he was critical of what he considered the excesses of the Roman Catholic Church.

Life and Works

He was educated by the Brethren of the Common Life. He studied in a series of monastic or semi-monastic schools. In 1495, with the bishop's consent and stipend, he went on to study at the University of Paris and from 1495 he became a freelance scholar, travelling widely throughout Europe. For a time he was in Cambridge.[109] He stayed at Queens' College, Cambridge. From 1521, he settled in Basel and died there itself in the year 1536. From 1506 to 1509, he was in Italy and spent part of the time at the publishing house of Aldus Manutius in Venice. In 1488, he was ordained to the Catholic priesthood and reluctantly took vows as an Augustinian canon at Steyn at about the age of twenty-five. Soon after his priestly ordination, he got his chance to leave the monastery when offered the post of secretary to the Bishop of Chambray. Pope Leo X later made the dispensation permanent. Erasmus died in 1536 in Basel and was buried in the Munster cathedral, in the same city. According to tradition, his last words were 'Dutch for *Dear God.*'

Erasmus wrote prolifically and edited many works. Erasmus supervised the publication of many editions of the early church fathers. Erasmus wrote both on ecclesiastic subjects and those of general human interest. His more serious writings began early with the "Handbook of the Christian Soldier" (1503), translated into English later by William Tyndale. *The Praise of Folly* was written in 1509 at the home of his friend Thomas More. *The Praise of Folly* is a handbook of a Christian Knight on civility in children and many other works. In 1516 Erasmus published an edition of the New Testament printed in Greek with his own Latin translation. Erasmus' Greek New Testament became known as *Textus Receptus*. Immediately after the publication of his *Paraphrases of the New Testament*, he began a popular presentation of the contents of several books. These were published in Latin but were quickly translated into other languages. *Education of a Christian Prince* (1516) was written as advice to the young king Charles of Spain, later Charles V, Holy Roman Emperor. In 1524, he wrote 'the Freedom of the Will', an attack on Luther's doctrine that the fallen human will is in bondage and unable to do any good.[110] The most important work of this last period is the *Ecclesiastes* or 'Gospel Preacher' (1536), in which he comments on the function of preaching.

Erasmus was sympathetic with the main points in the Lutheran criticism of the Church. He had great respect for Martin Luther, and Luther always spoke with admiration of Erasmus' superior learning. Luther hoped for his co-operation in a work that seemed only the natural outcome of his own. In their early correspondence, Luther expressed boundless admiration for all Erasmus had done in the cause of a sound and reasonable Christianity and urged him to join the Lutheran party. When Erasmus hesitated to support him, the straightforward Luther felt that Erasmus was avoiding the responsibility due either to cowardice or a lack of purpose. Erasmus believed that there was room within existing formulas for the kind of reform he valued most. In 1524, Erasmus, having been forced by Pope and others, wrote an attack on Luther's doctrine of the bondage of the Human.

His Philosophy

Freedom of the Will
Twice in the course of the great discussion, he allowed himself to enter the field of doctrinal controversy, a field foreign to both his nature and his previous practice. One of the topics he dealt with was the freedom of the will, a crucial point. In his "Freedom of the Will" (1524), he lampoons the Lutheran view on free will. He lays down both sides of the argument impartially. The 'Diatribe' did not encourage any definite action; this was its merit to the Erasmians and its fault in the eyes of the Lutherans. In response, Luther wrote his "On the Bondage of the Will", 1525, which viciously attacks the 'Diatribe' and Erasmus himself, going so far as to claim that Erasmus was not a Christian. When the city of Basel was definitely and officially 'reformed' in 1529, Erasmus gave up his residence there and settled in the imperial town of Freiburg in Breisgau.

The Sacraments

A test of the Reformation was the doctrine of the sacraments and the crux of this question was the observance of the Eucharist. In 1530, Erasmus published a new edition of the orthodox treatise of Algerus against the heretic Berengar of Tours in the eleventh century. He added a dedication, affirming his belief in the reality of the Body of Christ after consecration in the Eucharist.

Erasmus' Sileni Alcibiadis

Erasmus' *Sileni Alcibiadis* (1515) is one of his most direct assessments of the need for Church reform. The term *Sileni* can be understood as something on the inside is more different than what one sees on the outside. Erasmus lists several Sileni and then questions whether Christ is the most noticeable *Silenus* of them all. The Apostles were Sileni since they were ridiculed by others. He believes that the things that are the least ostentatious can be the most significant. For instance, one cannot see the most special aspects of humans. The Scriptures also have Sileni. Erasmus believes that the Church constitutes all of the Christian people. People call them priests, bishops and Popes; but they only serve the Church. He criticises those that spend the Church's riches at the people's expense.

Legacy

Extraordinary popularity of his books has been shown in the number of editions and translations that have appeared since the sixteenth century, and in the undiminished interest excited by his elusive but fascinating personality. Ten columns of the catalogue of the British Library are taken up with the bare enumeration of the works and their subsequent reprints. Today, in his home town of Rotterdam, the University has been named in his honour. However, Rotterdam has ignored the life of one of its famous citizens for a long time. Research in 2003 showed that most Rotterdammers believe Erasmus was the designer of the 'Erasmusbridge' in Rotterdam. This shocking information led to the founding of the Erasmushuis, a house dedicated to celebrate the legacy of Erasmus.

Conclusion

Moderate Catholics felt that he had been a leading figure in attempts to reform the Church, while Protestants recognised his initial support for Luther's ideas and the groundwork he laid for future Reformation. His preference was for a liberal Catholic reform. Although he remained a Roman Catholic throughout his lifetime, he was critical of what he considered the excesses of the Roman Catholic Church. His disciples were found among Roman, Lutheran and Reformed theologians. Although Erasmus enjoyed the support of successive Popes, his teaching was condemned in Paris in 1527. As the counter-reformation progressed, his ideas were seen as dangerous and all his works were placed on the index of forbidden books in 1559. On the one hand, it was good that he wanted to reform the Roman Catholic Church by way of living as a Roman Catholic and, on the other hand, this attitude cannot be justified because a true seeker after truth must stand for the truth and speak against the falsehood.

Martin Luther

Martin Luther (1483-1546) was a German Christian philosopher and church reformer. Luther's theology challenged the authority of the papacy by emphasising the Bible as the sole source of religious authority and the church as a priesthood of all believers. According to Luther, salvation is attainable only by faith in Jesus as the messiah, a faith unmediated by the Church. These ideas helped to inspire the Protestant Reformation and changed the course of Western civilisation.

His Life

Martin Luther was born to Hans Luther and Margarethe on November 10, 1483, in Eisleben, Germany, then part of the Holy Roman Empire. He was baptised the next morning on the feast day of St. Martin of Tours. His family moved to Mansfield in 1484, where his father was a leaseholder of copper mines and smelters and served as one of four citizen representatives on the local council. Luther's mother was a hard-working woman. Hans Luther sent Martin to Latin schools in Mansfield, then Magdeburg, in 1497, where he attended a school operated by a lay group called the Brethren of the Common Life and Eisenach in 1498. At the age of seventeen in 1501, he entered the University of Erfurt and received his master's degree in 1505. He enrolled in law school at the same university that year but dropped out almost immediately.

Luther, later, was drawn to theology and philosophy and entered a closed Augustinian monastery in Erfurt on July 17, 1505, and studied theology.[111] He was taught the 'modern way' by the disciples of Gabriel Biel. In 1507, he was ordained to the priesthood, and in 1508 began teaching theology at University of Wittenberg. He received a Bachelor's degree in biblical studies on March 9, 1508, and another Bachelor's degree in the *Sentences* by Peter Lombard in 1509. On October 19, 1512, he was awarded his Doctor of Theology and, on October 21, 1512, was received into the senate of the theological faculty of University of Wittenberg, having been called to the position of *Doctor* in the Bible. He spent the rest of his career in this position at the University of Wittenberg. From 1510 to 1520, Luther lectured on the Psalms, the books of Hebrews, Romans and Galatians. He became convinced that the doctrine of justification by faith alone is the central truth of Christianity. He began to teach that salvation or redemption is a gift of God's grace, attainable only through faith in Jesus as the messiah. On October 31, 1517, Luther wrote to Albert, Archbishop of Mainz and Magdeburg, protesting the sale of indulgences. He enclosed in his letter a copy of his *Disputation of Martin Luther on the Power and Efficacy of Indulgences*, which came to be known as *The 95 Theses*.[112] It was his disputation as a scholarly objection to church practices, and the tone of the writing is accordingly 'searching, rather than doctrinaire.' Luther married Katharina Von Bora on June13, 1525, one of a group of 12 nuns he had helped escape from the Nimbschen Cistercian convent in April 1523. Luther's marriage set the seal of approval on clerical marriage. Bearing six children, Katharina helped earn the couple a living by farming the land. Luther confided to Stiefel on August 11, 1526. His marriage to Katharina von Bora set a model for the practice of clerical marriage within Protestantism.

Luther, in 1517, nailed a copy of the *95 Theses* to the door of the Castle Church in Wittenberg that same day—church doors acting as bulletin boards of his time—an event now seen as sparking the Protestant Reformation and celebrated every October 31 as Reformation Day. The *95 Theses* were quickly translated from Latin into German, printed and widely copied, making the controversy one of the first in history to be fanned by the printing press. Within two weeks, the theses had spread throughout Germany; within two months throughout Europe. Luther's last sermon at Wittenberg has gone down in history as a classic invective against reason, 'the Devil's Whore.' But it is by no means an isolated attack on philosophy.[113] Pope Leo X hoped the matter would die down of its own accord, because in 1518 he dismissed Luther as 'a drunken German.'

On June 15, 1520, the Pope warned Luther with the papal bull (edict) Exsurge Domine that he risked excommunication unless he recanted 41 sentences drawn from his writings, including the 95 Theses, within 60 days. But Luther, who had sent the pope a copy of *On the Freedom of a Christian* in October, publicly set fire to the bull at Wittenberg on December 10, 1520. As a consequence, Luther was excommunicated by Leo X on January 3, 1521, in the bull *Decet Romanum Pontificem*. Enforcement of the ban of the 41 sentences fell to secular authorities. Luther appeared, as ordered, on April 17, 1521, at the Diet of Worms before Emperor Charles V. The Emperor presented the final draft of the Edict of Worms on May 25, 1521, declaring Luther an outlaw, banning his literature and requiring his arrest: "We want him to be apprehended and punished as a notorious heretic." Luther secretly returned to Wittenberg on March 6, 1522.

Luther's Writings
Luther's writings circulated widely, reaching France, England and Italy as early as 1519, and students thronged to Wittenberg to hear him speak. He published a short commentary on Galatians and his *Work on the Psalms*. Three of his best-known works were published in 1520: 'To the Christian Nobility of the German Nation, Prelude on the Babylonian Captivity of the Church, and Freedom of a Christian.' In *On the Abrogation of the Private Mass*, in the summer of 1521, Luther widened his target from individual pieties like indulgences and pilgrimages to doctrines at the heart of Church practices. His essay *Concerning Confession* rejected the Roman Catholic Church's requirement of confession. In the introduction to his New Testament—published in September 1522 and selling 5,000 copies in two months—he explained that good works spring from faith; they do not produce it.

Luther's translation of the Bible into the vernacular, making it more accessible to ordinary people, had a tremendous political impact on the church and on German culture. The translation influenced the translation of the English King James Bible. His hymns inspired the development of congregational singing within Christianity. Luther is also known for his writings about the Jews, the nature and consequences of which are the subject of scholarly debate. During his stay at Wartburg, as an exile—'my Patmos', as he called it—Luther translated the New Testament from Greek into German and poured out doctrinal and polemical writings.

His Philosophy
Philosophy proved to be unsatisfying, offering assurance about the use of reason, but none about the importance of loving God. Reason could not lead men to God, he felt, and he developed as a love-hate relationship with Aristotle over the latter's emphasis on reason. Dr. Radhakrishnan wrote that Luther put the Bible in place of the infallible church and held it to be an unerring expression of God's relation to man.[114] For Luther, reason could be used to question men and institutions, but not God. Human beings could learn about God only through divine revelation and Scripture, therefore, became increasingly important to him.

For Luther there were three lights that illuminated human existence. There was the light of nature where a reason and common sense sufficed to solve many of the questions of everyday life. There was the light of grace by which the revelation in Scripture gave man knowledge of God, which was otherwise unattainable. And there was the light of glory that belonged to the future. For there were many questions that scripture left unresolved. Calvin's approach was set out less colourfully but more systematically than Luther's. But in essentials it was the same. Both could speak of a *twofold knowledge* of God. On the one hand, there is a general awareness of God that all men have. It is not a matter of scholastic proofs. It is a profound inner awareness of God over against us.

Justification by Faith
Luther came to understand justification as entirely the work of God. Against the teaching of his day that the righteous acts of believers are performed in co-operation with God, Luther wrote that Christians receive that righteousness entirely from outside themselves; that righteousness not only comes from Christ, it actually *is* the righteousness of Christ, imputed to us through faith. He explained his concept of 'justification' in the Smalcald Articles. He affirmed that this is necessary to believe. This cannot be otherwise acquired or grasped by any work, law or merit. Therefore, it is clear and certain that this faith alone justifies us. He wrote that faith is that which brings the Holy Spirit through the merits of Christ, and faith is a gift from God.

Catechism and the Eucharist
In 1528, Luther visited parishes and schools in Saxony to determine the quality of pastoral care and Christian education. He wrote in the preface to *The Small Catechism*: In response, he prepared the *Small Catechism* and *Large Catechism*, instructional and devotional material on confession and absolution. *The Small Catechism* was supposed to be read by the people themselves and the *Large Catechism* by the pastors; both remain popular instructional materials among Lutherans. Luther's *German Mass* of 1526 provided for weekday services and for catechetical instruction. He strongly objected to making a new law of the forms and urged the retention of other good liturgies. He saw in liturgical uniformity a fitting outward expression of unity in the faith, while in liturgical variation, an indication of possible doctrinal variation. He eliminated and condemned those parts of the Roman Catholic Mass that taught that the Eucharist was a propitiatory sacrifice and the body and blood of Christ

by transubstantiation but retained the use of historic liturgical forms and customs.

Luther's views on the Eucharist—the sacrament of the Lord's Supper—were put to the test in October 1529 at the Marburg Colloquy, an assembly of Protestant theologians. The theologians, including Zwingli, Andreas Karlstadt, Leo Jud and Johannes Oecolampadius, differed on the significance of the words spoken by Jesus at the Last Supper: 'This is my body which is for you,' 'This cup is the new covenant in my blood' (1 Cor. 11:23-26). Luther insisted on the Real Presence of the body and blood of Christ in the consecrated bread and wine, but the other theologians believed God to be only symbolically present.

Conclusion

Luther's nailing a copy of the *95 Theses* to the door of the Castle Church in Wittenberg is an event now seen as sparking the Protestant Reformation and celebrated every October 31 as Reformation Day. Luther came to understand justification as entirely the work of God. Against the teaching of his day that the righteous acts of believers are performed in co-operation with God, Luther wrote that Christians receive that righteousness entirely from outside themselves; that righteousness not only comes from Christ, it actually *is* the righteousness of Christ, imputed to us through faith. According to Luther, agreement in the faith was not necessary prior to entering political alliances. Nevertheless, interpretations of the Eucharist differ among Protestants to this day.

Zwingli

He was the founder of Swiss Protestantism and the first of the Reformed Scholars. He was a Swiss theologian and leader of the Reformation in Switzerland. He arrived at a Protestant position at about the same time as Luther. Zwingli was strongly influenced by the Humanism of Erasmus. In Switzerland, the Reformation was led by Zwingli at Zurich. He had come from backgrounds coloured by Renaissance Humanism but was convinced that Humanism alone was not enough.

Background

Ulrich Zwingli (1484-1531)[115] was born on January 1, 1484, in Wildhaus, Sankt Gallen. He was educated at the universities of Vienna and Basel. During his formative years, Zwingli was deeply influenced by the spirit of liberal humanism. In 1506, he was ordained and assigned to the town of Glarus as a parish priest. Glarus then was well known as a centre for recruiting mercenary soldiers for Europe's armies. On two occasions Zwingli served as chaplain with Glarus troops during bloody fighting on foreign soil, and these experiences led him to denounce the mercenary system publicly. In retaliation, certain town officials conspired to make his position at Glarus untenable. In 1516, he accepted an appointment at Einsiedeln, southeast of Zurich. Zwingli read widely and by this time he laid foundations for his Reformed beliefs. He came to realise the final and supreme role of the scripture.

During his ministry at Einsiedeln, Zwingli began to entertain doubts about certain church practices. In 1516, he read a Latin translation of the Greek New Testament published by the Dutch humanist Desiderius Erasmus, which he later transcribed into notebooks and memorised verbatim. Among the practices cited by Zwingli as unscriptural were the adoration of saints and relics, promises of miraculous cures and church abuses of the indulgence system. His forthright affirmations of scriptural authority won him wide popular repute, and on January 1, 1519, he was appointed priest at the Gross Munster (Great Cathedral) in Zurich.

After deliberation, the council upheld Zwingli by withdrawing the Zurich canton from the jurisdiction of the bishop of Constance; it also affirmed its previous ban against preaching not founded on the Scriptures. By taking these steps the council officially adopted the Reformation. In 1524, Zwingli marked his new status by marrying Anna Reinhard, a widow with whom he had lived openly. Meanwhile, Zwingli carried his crusade to cantons other than Zurich. In all, six cantons were converted to the Reformation. The remaining five, known as the Forest Cantons, remained staunchly Catholic. The antagonisms between Catholic and Protestant cantons created a serious split in the Swiss confederation. In 1529, the hostility between the cantons flared into open civil war. On October 10, 1531, Zwingli, acting as chaplain and standard-bearer for the Protestant forces, was wounded at Kappel am Albis and later put to death by the victorious troops of the Forest Cantons. After Zwingli's death, the Reformation made no further headway in Switzerland; the country is still half Catholic and half Protestant.

His Works
Zwingli quickly attracted large audiences to the cathedral by expounding the original Greek and Hebrew Scriptures chapter by chapter and book by book, beginning with the Gospel of Matthew. These oral translations of the original Scriptures broke sharply with church tradition. Previously,

priests had based their sermons on interpretations of the Vulgate and on the writings of the Fathers of the Church. In 1519, an admirer placed a printing press at the reformer's disposal and his bold new ideas spread far beyond the confines of Zurich. During the same year, Zwingli read for the first time the writings of his contemporary, Martin Luther. Heartened by Luther's stand against the German hierarchy, Zwingli in 1520 persuaded the Zurich council to forbid all religious teachings without foundation in the Scriptures.

Angered by Zwingli's behaviour, Pope Adrian VI, then forbade him the pulpit and asked the Zurich council to repudiate him as a heretic. In January 1523, Zwingli appeared before the council to defend himself. He asserted the supremacy of the Holy Writ over church dogma, attacked the worship of images, relics and saints and denounced the sacramental view of the Eucharist and enforced celibacy as well.

Zwingli's Philosophy

His first writing *The Clarity and Certainty of God's Word* was published in 1522. He propounded the fundamental Protestant Principle of the final authority of Scripture. For him, baptism is an outward sign of our faith. In 1525, he wrote *Baptism, Rebaptism and Baptism of Infants*. He set out his matured teaching on the Lord's Supper in a 'Confession of Faith' in 1530. Regarding the Lord's Table, he rejected Luther's idea of *real presence* and stated that the bread and wine are merely the symbols of Christ's body and blood and it is a thanksgiving memorial.[116] Zwingli's biblical studies led him to the conclusion that only what was specifically authorised by the Scriptures should be retained in church practice and doctrine. Lutheranism had kept many elements of the medieval liturgy, but Zwingli devised a very simple service, and in opposition to both Roman Catholicism and Lutheranism, he interpreted the Eucharist as a purely symbolic ceremony. Zwingli's reforms, adopted peacefully through votes of the Zurich town council, soon spread to other Swiss cities.

Like Luther, he was a scholar. But again like him, he found himself compelled by events to be practical men. One of the most striking things about the teaching of all the leading Reformers was its unanimity.[117] Luther and Zwingli were magisterial Reformers. They introduced reform in co-operation with the magistrates or rulers. They did not wish to break the link between the church and the state. Under the Reformation, Zurich became a theocracy ruled by Zwingli and a Christian magistrate. Sweeping reforms were instituted, among them the conversion of monasteries into hospitals, the removal of religious images and the elimination of Mass and confession. Eventually, Zwingli taught that devout Christians have need of neither the Pope nor the Church.

John Calvin

John Calvin (1509-1564 AD) was a French Protestant Christian Philosopher during the Protestant Reformation and was a central developer of the system of Christian theology called Calvinism or Reformed theology.[118] In Geneva, he rejected Papal authority, established a new scheme of civic and ecclesiastical governance and created a central hub from which Reformed theology was propagated. He is known for his teachings and writings.

Life and Works

Calvin was born with the name Jean Chauvin (Latin *Calvinus*) in Noyon, France, to Gerard Cauvin and Jeanne Lefranc. In 1523, Calvin's father, an attorney, sent his fourteen-year-old son to the University of Paris to study humanities and law. By 1532, he had attained a Doctor of Laws degree at Orleans. A close friend of Calvin's, Nicholas Cop, found it necessary to flee Paris after giving a customary discourse in the Church of the Mathurins. The speech has long been rumoured to be the work of Calvin himself. Calvin took flight within a few days. Calvin sheltered at Angouleme with a friend, Louis du Tillet. After 1534, he became firmly entrenched within a Reformist belief, beyond that of humanist thought. In 1536, as he was forced to choose an alternate route in the face of imperial and French forces, he passed by Geneva. The city council expelled Calvin and Farel. Farel travelled to Neuchatel, Calvin to Strasbourg. After being expelled from the city, he served as a pastor in Strasbourg from 1538 until 1541, before returning to Geneva, where he lived until his death in 1564.[119] After attaining his degree, John Calvin sought a wife in affirmation of his approval of marriage over clerical celibacy. In 1539, he married Idelette de Bure, a widow, who had a son and daughter from her previous marriage to an Anabaptist in Strasbourg. Calvin and Idelette had a son who died after only two weeks. Idelette died in 1549. John Calvin died in Geneva on May 27, 1564, at the age of 55. He was buried in the Cimetiere des Rois under a tombstone marked simply with the initials 'J.C', partially honouring his request that he be buried in an unknown place, without witnesses or ceremony.

Calvin's first published work was an edition of the Roman philosopher Seneca's *De Clementia*, accompanied by a commentary demonstrating a thorough knowledge of antiquity. His first theological work *Psychopannychia* (1534) demonstrates that Calvin was a 'theological Humanist' and a 'Biblicist.' At the age of twenty-six (1536), Calvin published the first edition of his *Institutes of the Christian Religion* in Basel. It is a seminal work in Christian theology that altered the course of Western history and is still read by theological students today. It was published in Latin in 1536 and in his native French in 1541. Calvin also produced many volumes of commentary on most of the books of the Bible. For the Old Testament, he published commentaries for all books except the histories after Joshua and the Wisdom literature other than the Book of Psalms. For the New Testament, he omitted only the brief second and third epistles of John and the Book of Revelation. These commentaries have proved to be of lasting value to students of the Bible. Calvin's body of letters has not received the wide readership of the *Institutes* and bible commentaries since his correspondence obviously addressed the particular needs and occasions of his day. B. B. Warfield even calls Calvin 'the great letter-writer of the Reformation age. His letters number some 4,000, and fill eleven of Calvin's fifty-nine volumes in the *Corpus Reformatorum*.

Calvin's Philosophy

Calvin was very familiar with the writings of the early Church Fathers and the great medieval schoolmen, and he was also in debt to earlier Reformers. Calvin was trained to be a lawyer. He studied under some of the best legal minds of the Renaissance in France. Part of that training involved the newer humanistic methods of exegesis. His legal and exegetical training was important for Calvin because, once convinced of the growing Protestant faith, he applied these exegetical methods to the Scripture. He self-consciously tried to mould his thinking along biblical lines and he laboured to preach and teach what he believed the Bible taught.

Calvin did not reject the Scholastics of the Middle Ages outright but rather made use of them and reformed their thoughts in accordance with his understanding of the Bible. Calvin compared Scripture with spectacles that put things into focus. The value and use of the spectacles could only be appreciated by using them. So it is with Scripture. Its value emerges in the light of its capacity to interpret human existence; recognising religious truth is like recognising colours. Calvin had a great commitment to the absolute sovereignty and holiness of God. Because of this, he is often associated with the doctrines of predestination and election, but it should be noted that he differed very little with the other magisterial

Reformers regarding these difficult doctrines. Calvin applied the methods of the humanistic scholarship to the Bible to find out the exact meaning of the words of a text and the circumstances of the history involved. His authority and integrity of the word made a critical approach to the text impossible. Though he allowed literal interpretation of a text, he mainly accepted allegorical method of interpretation.

On the doctrine of God, Calvin avoids discussion of the hidden essence of God and confines himself to biblical teaching on the nature of God. The Christian must not only be united to Christ but must live in conformity to Christ in his death and resurrection. Calvin followed Augustine for the teaching of sacraments as a visible sign of an invisible grace. Only baptism and the Lord's Supper were sacraments with dominical authority. He denounced the doctrine of substantiation.[120] Calvin sought to continue and complete the work begun by Luther and other Reformers. Calvinism bears his name and is a reflection of his thinking. While Calvin's philosophical contributions have had a wide influence, his legacy can also be seen in other areas. For example, he placed a high premium on education of the youth of Geneva, and in 1559, he founded the Academy of Geneva, which was a model for other academies around the world and which eventually became the University of Geneva. Calvin's thought in the area of church polity was seminal as well, giving rise to various Reformed and Presbyterian systems of church government. The Consistory of Geneva, with Calvin at its helm, was influential in sending out scores of missionaries, not only to France, but also to countries as far off as Brazil.

Reformational Philosophy
Vollenhoven's *Calvinism and the Reformation of Philosophy* (Dutch, 1933) launched a philosophical movement that, after the massive reinforcing effect of his brother-in-law Herman Dooyeweerd's first trilogy, *Philosophy of the Law-Idea* (1935-36), led to the formation of the Association for Calvinist Philosophy in 1936. For decades, Vollenhoven served as president of the aforementioned association, which has become the Association for Reformational Philosophy. Reformational philosophy is a movement pioneered by Herman Dooyeweerd and D. H. Th. Vollenhoven that seeks to develop philosophical thought in a radically Christian direction. Although Calvinistic in roots, Reformational philosophy has always been ecumenical in outlook. Dooyeweerd was Editor-in-Chief of *Philosophia Reformata*. He approached philosophy by way of investigating his own field of jurisprudence, penetrating to its foundations, which could be understood only in terms of a radically Christian-world-and-life view.

The great turning point of his thought came when he discovered that all thinking and indeed all of life have a religious root. He argued that science and philosophy can perform their respective tasks successfully only on a sound Christian foundation. Because of the intrinsic relation of philosophy and religion, his thought is fundamentally a critique of theoretical thought itself.[121]

Vollenhoven's *Calvinism and the Reformation of Philosophy* (Dutch, 1933) launched a philosophical movement that, after the massive re-enforcing effect of his brother-in-law Herman Dooyeweerd's first trilogy, *Philosophy of the Law-Idea* (1935-36), led to the formation of the Association for Calvinist Philosophy in 1936. For decades, Vollenhoven served as president of the aforementioned association. It has become the Association for Reformational Philosophy. It can be debated whether Vollenhoven, his colleague Herman Dooyeweerd and many among the subsequent generations of philosophers in the Reformational philosophy movement are best described as 'modern' or 'postmodern,' since they anticipated numerous themes that resurfaced in postmodernism, yet remain steadfastly and would-be distinctively Christian and non-Roman.

Reformational philosophy rejects the view that theoretical thought, including philosophical thought, is autonomous. The view that theoretical thinking is a purely rational activity has a purely rational ground or requires no pre-theoretical conditions or commitments, for its possibility cannot be sustained. Reformational philosophy has always been concerned that philosophy be fruitful for the special sciences; the theory of irreducible modal aspects has had the greatest influence in this respect. Although accounts differ, it is customary to distinguish fifteen modal aspects that evince the ways or modes in which we experience reality. These are: numerical, spatial, kinematic, physical, organic, psychical, logical, historical, linguistic, social, economic, aesthetic, jural, moral and political. Each mode expresses itself in all the other modes through analogies within the mode that either 'anticipates' later modes or 'retrocipate' earlier modes. Any non-reductionist account of reality must acknowledge the particular ways each entity, action or process function within all of the modal aspects or else fall, once again, into antinomies.

Conclusion
Luther and Zwingli did not wish to break the link between the church and the state. Zwingli laid the foundations for Swiss Protestantism and Reformed theology. Luther and Zwingli were magisterial Reformers whose

aim was not to found a new church, but to reform the old one. But the radical Reformers wanted to go further than the former.[122] Some of them were 'rationalists' who questioned the fundamental Christian doctrine and some were 'spiritualists' who disparaged the Bible and all outward forms. Some were known as 'revolutionaries' and others 'evangelicals.' While Reformers like Martin Luther may be seen as somewhat original thinkers that began a movement, Calvin was a great logician and systematiser of that movement, but not an innovator in doctrine. Calvin's publications spread his ideas of a properly reformed church to many parts of Europe and from there to the rest of the world. It is especially on account of his voluminous publications that he exerts such a lasting influence over Christianity and Western history.

As a result of Reformation, three major confessions—Roman Catholicism, Lutheranism and Calvinism—became increasingly preoccupied with a precise and intricate definition of their beliefs and their energies were largely expended in controversy within the different confessions. As an anti-protestant direction, the Roman Catholic Church introduced a programme of Catholic Reform. The Jesuits, founded by Ignatius Loyola, were the shock troops of the Catholic Reformation and spearheaded the counter-attack on Protestantism. As a result of Reformation, the Pietist movement pioneered by Spencer stressed the importance of practical Christian living in the seventeenth century and rationalism rose in the eighteenth century as a rival to Christian faith. Deism was seen as a religion of reason in opposition to the superstitions of traditional Christianity. Evangelical revival was the force in opposition to it. In due course, the English Reformation gave birth to Anglicanism, a distinct brand of Protestantism. The English Reformation has its own interesting features.

God is in search of church reformers. The Word of God is perfect, but the church is not perfect; the Lord wants the church to be perfect. We are trying every day to be perfect and to grow in the wisdom and knowledge of God. We should study God's Word to learn the perfect will of God in connection with the church. When the members of the church lack wisdom and forget the statues of God, God will raise somebody to reform the church. The Lord has some contribution in the history of His church every century and especially since the Reformation. God used the Reformation leaders in the sixteenth century to teach salvation and justification by faith. The church in the darkness came into the light of God. In the seventeenth century, the Lord used the Anabaptists to teach immersed baptism. John

Wesley and others were used by God in the eighteenth century to preach holiness. The Lord raised many missionary movements in the nineteenth century from Europe to many Asian and African countries. Tens of thousands of churches had been established. The Lord sent the Holy Spirit revival in the beginning of the twentieth century. The revival began in USA and spread all over the world. I still hope that the Lord will do something greater in the twenty-first century for His church. The Church in the modern period should learn something new from the Scripture in order to be perfect. Let us expect greater things from the Lord.

Helpful Questions
1. Is the Reformational philosophy of Erasmus justifiable?
2. How did Zwingli lead the Church to the Reformation?
3. Write short notes on Roman Catholicism, Lutheranism and Calvinism.

CHAPTER 7

Modern Christian Philosophy

This chapter focuses on rationalism, empiricism and idealism. It will help the reader to understand the history of modern philosophy. It will also give the reader an insight into the growth of the Christian philosophy of the seventeenth and eighteenth centuries.

While medieval philosophy found its guidance and inspiration in the Christian religion, modern philosophy (1600-1800 AD) turned its attention to the nature of the new science and its method. Two elements in the scientific method were identified: (1) The rational element, the use of mathematics and deductive reasoning; and (2) the empirical element, the rise of observation, experimentations and induction. Modern philosophy is usually considered to begin with the revival of skepticism and the genesis of modern physical science. Canonical figures include Descartes, Spinoza, Leibniz, Locke, Berkeley, Hume and Kant. Chronologically, this era spans the 17th and 18th centuries and is generally considered to end with Kant's systematic attempt to reconcile Newtonian mechanics with traditional metaphysical topics. Modern Christian thought has not been without its strong strains of rationalism.

The reformers of the sixteenth century were dominated by a concern for God. They took as their starting-point on God's action in Christ, as witnessed by the Scriptures. From there they proceeded to think about the world. The rationalists of the seventeenth century were absorbed not so much by God but by the world. Many of them were scientists who had made notable contributions to mathematics, especially to geometry. Their starting-point was logic, and their techniques were derived from mathematics. They were not irreligious men.[123] We think of modern thought, not because it is pure Christian philosophy, but it shows the necessity of linking Reformational philosophy to postmodern and contemporary Christian philosophy. Another major factor is that although modern Christian philosophical thought was highly influenced by science and rationalism, it was closely related to Christianity and most of them were Christians.

Rationalism

The seeds of rationalism have been firmly implanted in the Western world since at least the time of Plato. But the movement flowered in the modern triumvirate of Descartes, Spinoza, and Leibniz. Rationalism is characterised by its stress on the innate or a priori ability of human reason to know truth. Basically, rationalists hold that what is knowable or demonstrable by human reason is true. The heart of rationalism is the thesis that the rationally inescapable is the real. Different degrees of emphasis on this method or theory lead to a range of rationalist standpoints, from the moderate position that reason has precedence over other ways of acquiring knowledge to the radical position that reason is the unique path to knowledge. Lacey said that rationalism is any view appealing to reason as a source of knowledge or justification. In more technical terms, it is a method or a theory in which the criterion of truth is not sensory but intellectual and deductive. In various contexts, the appeal to reason is contrasted with revelation as in religion, or with emotion and feeling as in ethics. In philosophy, however, reason is more often contrasted with the senses, including introspection but not intuition. Colin Brown writes:[124]

> In everyday language rationalism has come to mean the attempt to judge everything in the light of reason. Bound up with this is the assumption that, when this is done, reason will have completely disposed of the supernatural, and that we are left with nothing but nature and hard facts. But in the more technical, philosophical sense of the term, rationalism denotes a more particular and certainly less atheistic approach. The rationalists of the seventeenth and eighteenth centuries differed widely among themselves in the way they worked out their different systems. But common to all was a belief in the rationality of the universe and the power of reason to grasp it.

Stuart Hackett, who advocated theistic Rationalism, entitles his view 'rational empiricism,' but it might with equal justice be called 'empirical rationalism' since he claims rational certainty for knowledge about God's existence and nature derived from sense experience. 'First of all, Scripture, the written words of the Bible, is the mind of God. What is said in Scripture is God's thought.' Rationalism is usually associated with the introduction of mathematical methods into philosophy—as in Descartes, Leibniz and Spinoza. This is commonly called continental rationalism.

Rene Descartes

Descartes, the Frenchman and the first of the rationalist philosophers, (1596–1650) is known as the 'father' of modern philosophy and a French mathematics genius-turned-philosopher. He inaugurated a method of intellectual enquiry whose procedure and results have commanded the attention of generations of successors.[125] His dates make him a contemporary of Charles I and Oliver Cromwell, Galileo and Harvey. His main contributions were made in the fields of geometry and philosophy. In the former, he invented co-ordinate geometry. In the latter, he pioneered rationalism and Cartesian doubt.

His two chief philosophical works were his *Discourse on Method* (1637) and his *Meditations* (1641). He thought that only knowledge of eternal truths—including the truths of mathematics and the epistemological and metaphysical foundations of the sciences—could be attained by reason alone. He also argued that although dreams appear as real as sense experience, these dreams cannot provide persons with knowledge. Also, since conscious sense experience can be the cause of illusion, sense experience itself can be doubtable.

Rationalism

Descartes wanted to overthrow the accumulation of life-long beliefs and use reason alone to establish solid and permanent truth. Mathematics must be the guide to clear the confusion and uncertainties of philosophy. Now mathematics consists of the use of two mental operations: (1) Intuition, the understanding of self-evident principles about which no doubts are possible; and (2) deduction, logical inference from self-evident proportions. Descartes therefore argued, as a result of his method, that reason alone determines knowledge and that this could be done independently of the senses.[126] This was, for Descartes, an irrefutable principle upon which to ground all forms of other knowledge.

As a result, Descartes deduced that a rational pursuit of truth should doubt every belief about reality. He elaborated these beliefs in such works as *Discourse on Method, Meditations on First Philosophy* and *Principles of Philosophy*. Descartes developed a method to attain truths. These truths are gained 'without any sensory experience', according to Descartes. Truths that are attained by reason are to be broken down into elements that intuition can grasp—this will result in clear truths about reality.

Methodical Doubt and Cogito

Descartes said: "Every time I doubt or think, I must exist to doubt or think. I cannot doubt that I am doubting, or thinking, therefore I exist. I think therefore I am." The *cogito* is the foundation of Cartesian philosophy. After that, through the method of deduction, Descartes inferred that god exists because the *cogito* reveals that our mind is full of 'innate' ideas among which is the idea of infinite perfection. That idea must exist (Descartes used the ontological argument) that the material world exists because the thinking man is not the cause of sense-perceptions and the truthful God cannot deceive man's perception of an external world.

Cartesian Dualism

Theologically, important consequences followed from another set of convictions, those pertaining to the relation of mind and body. Descartes was a dualist. To him a human being is composed of these two substantially distinct entities (mind or soul and body) characterised respectively by thought and extension.[127] By deduction Descartes concluded to the existence of a physical world is extension. Thus reality is made of two heterogeneous elements: mental, spiritual thinking substance and physical, spatial and extended substance. These are the two irreducible kinds of reality. This is called the Cartesian psycho-physical dualism. Reason, which for him led to the dual reality of the human essence, is a better guide than experience, which points at substantial unity and interaction. Descartes posited a metaphysical dualism, distinguishing between the substances of the human body and the mind or soul.

Critical Remarks

i. Descartes' glory and right to be labeled as the father of modern philosophy is because of his concept of the *cogito*. Every good thought must begin with the thinker himself, the truth of one's own existence as a conscious subject.

ii. Like the Medieval philosophers, he was interested in metaphysics. To the end of his life Descartes remained a nominal Catholic. But there is a sense in which Descartes represents a new departure. Descartes was interested in God.[128]

iii. The rationalism of Descartes was inspired by a fascination for the mathematical method and raised the problem of the respective roles of reason and experience in the philosophical project.

iv. Descartes was perhaps the last uncompromising advocate of anthropological dualism in western philosophy but the problem of the mind-body relationship or psycho-physical parallelism will never cease to stir up controversies.

v. His continental successors, pre-eminently Spinoza and Leibniz, have been labeled along with Descartes, rationalists to draw attention to the role of the mind apart from the senses in possessing and acquiring knowledge.

Gottfried Leibniz

G.W. Leibniz (1646-1716) was the last of the great Rationalists, who contributed heavily to other fields, such as mathematics. Descartes was a nominal catholic, and Leibniz was an eminent Protestant philosopher. Leibniz was a universal genius. He shares with Newton the honour of discovering the infinitesimal calculus. His original work on symbolic logic, lost for centuries, was brought to light again. He invented a calculating machine through which he earned the membership of the Royal Society. The Prussian Academy was largely his creation. He corresponded with and met many of the most eminent minds in Europe. His brief Monadology was published in 1720.

In Leibniz's view, there are infinitely many simple substances that he called 'monads.' Leibniz developed his theory of monads in response to both Descartes and Spinoza. In rejecting this response, he was forced to arrive at his own solution. Monads are the fundamental unit of reality, according to Leibniz, constituting both inanimate and animate things. These units of reality represent the universe, though they are not subject to the laws of causality or space. Colin Brown writes:[129]

> According to Leibniz, the universe is made up of an infinite number of monads or 'simple substances' without 'parts' and without 'windows' by which anything could come in or go out. They are indivisible and ever active. Each monad mirrors all existence. The monads form an ascending series from the lowest which is next to nothing to the highest which is God. By means of the ontological argument Leibniz deduced the existence of God, or Necessary Being, or 'the original simple substance, from which all monads, created and derived, are produced.

Leibniz broke up the world into a definitely large number of parts that move according to eternally existing laws and have neither the right nor the power to alter by a hair's breadth the order that is independent of them. Leibniz rejected Cartesian dualism and denied the existence of a material world. Leibniz introduced his principle of pre-established harmony in order to account for apparent causality in the world.

Valuable Strains in Rationalistic Thought
- One of the more basic contributions of rationalism is its stress on the inescapability of the basic laws of thought. Without this law, truth cannot be distinguished from falsity; all is equally true and false, which is to say nothing can be true.

- The second contribution is sometimes overlooked by overzealous empiricists, namely there must be an a priori dimension to knowledge. These need not be innate ideas but there must be at least some natural inclinations of the mind towards truth or towards the first principles of knowledge.

- Along with the first two contributions, we must list another, namely the rationalistic stress on the intelligibility and knowability of reality. The rationalists rightly preserve the truth that is intelligible.[130]

Inadequacy of Rationalistic Methodology
- It is based on an invalid move from thought to reality, from the possible to the actual.

- Contrary to the central claim of traditional rationalism, the rationally inescapable is not real. First of all, this claim *assumes* but does not prove.

- Even the weaker form of Christian rationalism represented by Gordon Clark is insufficient as a test for truth. Logic alone is at best a negative test for truth.

Conclusion
We have already seen that Descartes deduced that a rational pursuit of truth should doubt every belief about reality. He developed a method to attain truths, and these truths are gained 'without any sensory experience.' Gottfried Leibniz's attempt to grapple with the epistemological and metaphysical problems raised by Descartes led to the development of the fundamental approach of rationalism. Leibniz asserted that *in principle*, all knowledge, including scientific knowledge, could be gained through the use of reason alone, though they observed that this was not possible *in practice* for human beings except in specific areas, such as mathematics.

Descartes' *cognito*, Spinoza's *substance* and Hegel's *Being* are slightly different senses, which are the classical examples of the notion. Leibnitz called it 'the unthinkability of the opposite.'[131]

Gordon Clark stood for Revelational Rationalism. It is a kind of evangelical rationalism. It claims no rationally inescapable arguments. Having laid the ground for theism in his rational realism, Hackett turns his attention to proving the existence of God. Clark wrote that "since secular philosophy had failed to solve its problems, the alternative hypothesis of revelation, verbal communication, the Bible was proposed."

Empiricism

Empiricism is a theory of knowledge emphasising the role of experience, especially sensory perception, in the formation of ideas, while discounting the notion of innate ideas. It emphasises those aspects of scientific knowledge that are closely related to experience, especially as formed through deliberate experimental arrangements. The term "empiricism" has a dual etymology. It comes from the Greek word *empirismos*, the Latin translation of which is *experientia*, from which we derive the word "experience." It holds that all our knowledge is derived from our experience, usually our sense experience, of things and processes in space and time.[132] It also derives from a more specific classical Greek and Roman usage of *empiric*, referring to a physician whose skill derives from practical experience as opposed to instruction in theory. Philosophical empiricism is commonly contrasted with the philosophical school of thought known as rationalism which, in very broad terms, asserts that much knowledge is attributable to reason independently of the senses. Colin Brown writes:[133]

> In Britain the movement which philosophers today regard as being the most significant among the philosophical trends of that age was empiricism. Like rationalism, the term denotes not so much well-defined school of thought as general line of approach. In particular, the empiricists of the eighteenth century were especially concerned with the problems of knowledge. In contrast with the rationalists who tried to erect philosophical systems by means of reasoning on the basis of allegedly self-evident truths, the empiricists stressed the part played by experience in knowledge.

Empiricism is derived from the Greek word meaning "experience." In philosophy, it denotes roughly the point of view that holds that all our knowledge is derived from our experience, usually our sense-experience, of things and processes in space and time. The three leading eighteenth-century representatives were, in fact, an Englishman, an Irishman and a

Scotsman: Locke, Berkeley and Hume. Although Hume was a skeptic, Locke's theological writings show him to have been a man of sincere Christian faith; and Berkeley was an Anglican bishop. Even so, the movement is generally thought of as having made a great contribution to the general advance of modern agnosticism. For when Hume pushed empiricist techniques to their logical conclusions, he left no alternative to skepticism.

John Locke
John Locke (1632-1704) was the son of a small country land owner and lawyer. He went to Oxford when Puritanism was in its heyday. Among other things, Locke studied medicine and was eventually awarded an M.D. When he was in Holland, he had the time and leisure to complete his major philosophical treatise, *An Essay Concerning Human Understanding (1690)*, which proposed a new and ultimately very influential view wherein the *only* knowledge humans can have is a posteriori, i.e., based upon experience, and his first *Letter on Toleration* (1689). He subsequently published further letters on the same subject and treaties on education and civil government. *The Reasonableness of Christianity* (1695) was followed by the posthumous *Paraphrase and Notes on the Epistles of St. Paul* (1705-07) and *A Discourse on Miracles* (1706).

The *doctrine* of empiricism was first explicitly formulated by John Locke in the 17th century. Locke argued that the mind is a *tabula rasa* (clean slate or blank tablet) on which experiences leave their marks. Such empiricism denies that humans have innate ideas or that anything is knowable without reference to experience. According to Locke, our knowledge of things is a perception of ideas that are in accordance or discordance with each other, which is very different from the quest for certainty of Descartes.

Locke, for his part, held that some knowledge (e.g. knowledge of God's existence) could be arrived at through intuition and reasoning alone. For Locke, there are two sources of our ideas: sensation and reflection. In both cases, a distinction is made between simple and complex ideas. The former is unanalysable and broken down into primary and secondary qualities. Locke drew a distinction between faith and reason. He defined *Reason* as 'the discovery of the certainty or probability of such propositions or truths, which the mind arrives at by deduction made from such *ideas*, which it has got by the use of its natural faculties, viz by sensation or reflection. *Faith*, on the other side, is the assent to any proposition not thus made out by the deductions of reason, but upon the credit of the proposer, as coming from God, in some extraordinary way of communication. This way of discovering truths to men we call *Revelation*. Locke had laid down the further distinction between that which was according to reason, that which was above and that which was contrary to reason.[134] (a) According to reason, such propositions are consistent that by truth we can discover, by examining and tracing those ideas we have from sensation and reflection; and by natural deduction find to be true or probable. (b) Above reason, such propositions whose truth or probability we cannot by reason derive from those principles. (c) Contrary to reason, such propositions as are inconsistent with, or irreconcilable to, our clear and distinct ideas. Thus, the existence of one God is according to reason; the existence of more than one God is contrary to reason.

For Locke the miracles of Christianity are evidence for the Christian faith. Where the miracle is admitted, the doctrine cannot be rejected; it comes with the assurance of a divine attestation to him that allows the miracle, and he cannot question its truth. Today, Locke was chiefly remembered for pioneering the empiricist approach to knowledge. At Oxford, he was impressed by reading Descartes, but his own approach struck out in a very different direction. He rejected the rationalist idea that the mind had stamped on it from birth certain primary, self-evident notions.

Bishop George Berkeley

George Berkeley (1685-1753) was born in Ireland. He became a fellow of Trinity College, Dublin, when he was twenty-two, and Dean of Derry in 1724. Four years later, he made an abortive attempt to establish a missionary college in Bermuda for the evangelism of America. He subsequently became Bishop of Cloyne. Nearly all his major philosophical work was done by the time he was twenty-eight.[135] His chief works include *An Essay towards a New Theory of Vision* (1709), *A Treatise Concerning the Principles of Human Knowledge* (1710), *Three Dialogues between Hylas and Philonous* (1713) and *Alciphron or the Minute Philosopher* (1732).

George Berkeley determined that God fills in for humans by doing the perceiving whenever humans are not around to do it. In his text *Alciphron*, Berkeley maintained that any order humans may see in nature is the language or handwriting of God. As ideas of God, these will all have substantiality of our common sense, for God is omnipresent and omniscient.[136] Berkeley's approach to empiricism would later come to be called subjective idealism. Berkeley commented that Locke's view immediately opened a door that would lead to eventual atheism. In response to Locke, he put forth in his Treatise Concerning the Principles of Human Knowledge (1710) a different, very extreme form of empiricism in which things *only* exist either as a *result* of their being perceived, or by virtue of the fact that they are an entity doing the perceiving.

Conclusion

Berkeley or his immediate successors may not have seriously entertained such a possibility. Berkeley developed his empiricism in the direction of immaterialism and idealism. David Hume was pushed by it into thoroughgoing skepticism. For Locke, there are two sources of our ideas: sensation and reflection. In both cases, a distinction is made between simple and complex ideas. Berkeley introduced a different, very extreme form of empiricism in which things *only* exist either as a *result* of their being perceived, or by virtue of the fact that they are an entity doing the perceiving. Mill's formulation encounters difficulty when it describes what direct experience is by differentiating only between actual and possible sensations.

Idealism

Idealism is the epistemological doctrine that nothing can be directly known outside the minds of thinking beings. Or in an alternative stronger form, it is the metaphysical doctrine that nothing exists apart from minds and the contents of minds. The first prominent modern Western idealist in the metaphysical sense was George Berkeley. The term was first applied as a technical term in philosophy in the eighteenth century. And soon it was used to describe the teaching of Berkeley that nothing could be known to exist or did exist except ideas in the mind of the percipient. Berkeley himself preferred to call his philosophy *immaterialism*. But the term *idealism* stuck and was soon applied to other philosophies. Kant adopted it, carefully distinguishing his own teaching, which he called *Transcendental Idealism* from that of Descartes and Berkeley, which he called problematic and dogmatic idealism.[137] The word "idealism" has been used in a number of senses in different contexts and a quite a few of them are vague and loose. In philosophical parlour, it has some implications. It must be related, implicitly or explicitly, with ideas or thoughts, subjects or consciousness or the like; and it stands out in contrast with realism, materialism and naturalism.

Immanuel Kant

Immanuel Kant (1724-1804) was a German Philosopher from Konigsberg in East Prussia. He is regarded as one of the most influential thinkers of modern Europe and the last major philosopher of the Enlightenment. It is arguable whether Immanuel Kant should be placed in the eighteenth or nineteenth century. His dates (1724-1804) put him in both. And so does his thoughts. In some ways, it represents the climax of eighteenth-century rationalism and empiricism. In other ways, it is curiously modern. His skepticism cast a long shadow over the nineteenth century.

Life and Works

Immanuel Kant was born as the fourth of nine children. In his youth, Kant was a solid, albeit unspectacular student. He was raised in a Pietist household, a then-popular Lutheran reform movement that stressed intense religious devotion, personal humility and a literal reading of the Bible. Kant's health, long poor, took a turn for the worse and he died in 1804.

The publication of his first philosophical work, *Thoughts on the True Estimation of Living Forces*, took place on 1749. Kant published several more works on scientific topics, becoming a university lecturer in 1755. In the early 1760s, Kant produced a series of important works in philosophy. In 1770, at the age of 45, Kant was finally appointed Professor of Logic and Metaphysics at University of Konigsberg. At the age of 46, Kant was an established scholar and an increasingly influential philosopher. He also wrote a number of semi-popular essays on history, religion, politics and other topics. Kant wrote (1781) the *Critique of Pure Reason*.[138] Kant's reputation gradually rose through the 1780s, sparked by a series of important works: *Answer to the Questions: What is Enlightenment?* (1784), *Groundwork of the Metaphysics of Morals* (1785) and *Metaphysical Foundations of Natural Science* (1786). Kant continued to develop his moral philosophy notably in *Critique of Practical Reason* (1788) and *Metaphysics of Morals* (1797). The Critique of Judgment (1790) applied the Kantian system to aesthetics and teleology.

Moral Philosophy

With regard to morality, Kant argued that the source of the good lies not in anything outside the human subject, either in nature or given by God, but rather only the good will itself. A good will is the one that acts from duty in accordance with the universal moral law that the autonomous human being freely renders. The genuine moral life consists of man's repeated attempts to conform his will to the wholly Good Will. In the *Critique of Pure Reason* Kant distinguishes between the transcendental ideas of freedom, which as a psychological concept, is mainly empirical. The freedom of the will is for philosophy a real stumbling-block that has embarrassed speculative reason. Kant calls practical as 'everything that is possible through freedom', and the pure practical laws that are never given through sensuous conditions but are associated with either the cause or effect of our volition are moral laws. Reason can give us only the pragmatic laws of free action through the senses, but pure practical laws are given by reason *a priori*.

Kant was aware that the pursuit of virtue, the moral life, does not always lead to happiness, and that the pursuit of happiness does not necessarily lead to the achievement of virtue. Kant's moral concepts are merely luxurious and sophisticated extensions of morality of such a tenuous kind that they might conceivably be given up without noticeable loss or inconvenience. Kant's ethics might be transformed into a form of moral humanism. This view of God is re-echoed in *Religion within the Limits if Reason Alone*.[139] Morality does not need religion, but it points to it. It leads to the idea of the highest good in the world for whose possibility we must postulate a higher, moral, most holy and omnipotent *Being* that alone can unite the two elements of this highest good

Idea of God
Kant stated the practical necessity for a belief in God in his *Critique of Pure Reason*. For Kant, as an idea of pure reason, the idea of God cannot be separated from the relation of happiness with morality as the ideal of the supreme good. Later, he argued that the idea of God can only be proved through the moral law and only with practical intent so as, "to act as if there be a God." Kant's conclusion about the cosmological and teleological demonstrations of God's existence is that they must fail to convince to persuade; that they are invalid as proofs. James Richmond writes,[140]

> For Kant, God rounds off, completes and fulfils morality. He is clear that there is no possibility of combining our moral awareness of God with our scientific knowledge of the world into a metaphysical picture of a God-created and God-controlled cosmos. He distinguishes carefully between on the one hand, the knowledge gained by the empirical investigation of nature within space and time (which he calls 'theoretical knowledge'), and, on the other, the practical implications (which Kant calls 'postulates') of morality, namely freedom, immortality and God.

For Kant, we must believe in God and immortality, because in the struggle of the moral life there is a strongly felt need for assurance that we can attain to moral perfection, and that nature is such that we are not positively hindered from such attainment. The moral venture is that it requires something to bind together and reinforce our scattered moral inclinations, orienting them in the proper direction; and this something, for Kant, is God.

Aesthetic Philosophy

Kant's contribution to aesthetic theory is developed in his *Critique of Judgment*. In the first major division of the *Critique of Judgment*, Kant used the term "aesthetic." Prior to this, in *Critique of Pure Reason*, he noted the essential differences between judgments of taste, moral judgments and scientific judgments. Kant was one of the first philosophers to develop and integrate aesthetic theory into a unified and comprehensive philosophical system, utilising ideas that played an integral role throughout his philosophy. In the chapter "Analytic of the Beautiful" of *Critique of Judgment*, he stated that beauty is not a property of an artwork or natural phenomenon, but is instead a consciousness of the pleasure.

Kant also believed that a judgment of taste shares characteristics engaged in a moral judgment: both are disinterested, and we hold them to be universal. Kant had developed the distinction between an object of art as a material value subject to the conventions of society and the transcendental condition of the judgment of taste as a refined value in the propositions of his *Idea of a Universal History* (1784). A pure judgment of taste is in fact subjective insofar as it refers to the emotional response of the subject and is based upon nothing but esteem for an object itself: it is a *disinterested* pleasure, and we feel that pure judgments of taste, i.e. judgments of beauty, lay claim to universal validity.

Political Philosophy

In *Perceptual Peace: A Philosophical Sketch* (1795) Kant listed several conditions that he thought necessary for ending wars and creating a lasting peace. They included a world of constitutional republics. This was the first version of the democratic peace theory. The philosophical movement known as German Idealism developed from Kant's theoretical and practical writings. Kant distinguished his view from contemporary views of realism and idealism, but philosophers are not agreed upon what difference Kant draws. Strawson, Guyer and Allison, the three most well-known philosophical commentators, have made some interesting comments on this issue.

Transcendental Idealism

Transcendental idealism is a doctrine founded by Immanuel Kant. He presents it as the point of view that holds that our experience of things is about how they appear to us, not about those things as they are in and of themselves. It is occasionally identified with *formalistic idealism* on the basis of passages from Kant's Prolegomena to any future Metaphysics, although recent research has tended to dispute this identification. Once Kant wrote that the bounding of the understanding by something which is otherwise unknown to it, is still a cognition that remains to reason even at this standpoint, by which it is neither shut up within sensible nor does it stray without it but confines itself, as befits the knowledge of a boundary to the relatives between that which is without it and that which is contained.[141] Kant personifies modern man's confidence in the power of reason to grapple with material things and its incompetence to deal with anything beyond.[142] Rationalism (Descartes, Spinoza and Leibniz) believed in the absolute power of reason to solve metaphysical riddles such as the existence to God, etc. For Kant this stand was naive, uncritical and dogmatic. Pure, theoretical reason is powerless to reach transcendental realities.

Theory of Knowledge

The other terms that require definition are *a priori* and *posteriori*. *A priori* knowledge is knowledge that is absolutely of all experience. This contrasts with *posteriori* knowledge, which is empirical knowledge, knowledge that is possible only through experience. *Posteriori* knowledge—knowledge of people, places and things—depends upon experience.

To some extent, these pairs of concepts overlap. Analytic knowledge is also *a priori* knowledge. It is a matter of logical definition of terms and concepts. Synthetic knowledge is *posteriori*. It involves observation and experience through the senses. Kant believed that knowledge was also both *synthetic* and *priori*.[143]

Critical Remarks

- For Kant causality, though subjective, is a valid constituent of human knowledge. Science is the knowledge of the phenomena, it can never be the knowledge of the *noumenon*, that is, the things in themselves.

- Kant was right to stress the role played by subjectively in knowledge but he may have gone too far in his zeal to subjectivise knowledge to the point of regarding our knowing faculties as a screen or a veil that hides and prevents us from reaching the real. Kantian idealism is a reaction against the old realism, and its message is that we live in a world of our own making.

- The Kantian understanding of metaphysics closes the door to Transcendence. For Kant, while the reality of God cannot be demonstrated (by theoretical reason), it has to be believed (by practical reason). It is the foundation of moral life. In his *Dealing with the Problem of God*, Kant replaced reason by faith. He holds that 'Theoretical reason' is incapable of approaching the Transcendent; 'practical reason' posits the existence of God as a postulate of moral life.

- Kant's critical approach has helped to bring out the idea that the affirmation of God involves the commitment of the whole man, his free will as much as his intellect. In fact, Kant's understanding of God as a 'postulate' of practical reason has led some contemporary philosophers to develop the moral argument for the existence of God.

- Kant chose the shortest and latest embarrassing way of solving the 'mystery' by claiming that everything comes from the subject and nothing from the object. Knowledge is not vision by projection. The order of the universe is nothing to wonder at; it is the creation of the knower.

The two interconnected foundations of what Kant called his 'critical philosophy' were his epistemology of Transcendental Idealism and his moral philosophy. Kant had a decisive impact on the Romantic and German Idealist philosophies of the 19th century.

G. W. F. Hegel (1770-1831)

George Wilhelm Friedrich Hegel is regarded as the greatest and most difficult exponent of nineteenth-century philosophy—German Idealism. After a career as a private tutor, a newspaper editor and a head-master, Hegel accepted the chair of philosophy at Heidelberg in 1816 and succeeded Fichte at Berlin in 1818.

His collected works in German fill twenty volumes. They include *The Phenomenology of Mind* (1806), *A Science of Logic* (1812-16) and his

Encyclopedia of Philosophy (1817).[144] Hegel asserts that the twin aims of philosophy are to account for the contradictions apparent in human experience and simultaneously to resolve and preserve these contradictions by showing their compatibility at a higher level of examination. Absolute Idealism is generally linked with Hegel. It is generally taken to mean a system of thought that holds that there is one ultimate reality and it is of nature and spirit or idea and thought or knowledge.[145] Philosophers in the Hegelian tradition include Ludwig Andreas Feurback, Karl Marx, Friedrich Engels and the British Idealists, notably T. H. Green, J. M. E. Taggart and F. H. Bradley.

Immanence of the Absolute
Hegel introduced a new concept of the Absolute –no longer transcendent but immanent. The absolute dwells in the *finite* and not in 'another world.' More precisely, the Absolute is in the making in the finite, that is, the Absolute is not yet, but it will be. The finite world is in the process of becoming the Absolute. Hegelian metaphysics is thus: (a) pantheistic, as the Absolute does not transcend finite reality but dwells within it; and (b) idealistic, as the Absolute is in the process of gradual realisation within the finite.

Hegelian Dialects
To understand the movement of the historical reality in its progression towards the Absolute, Hegel uses the key-concept of dialectics. Dialectics, he said, is the synthesis of opposites. Contradiction is at the heart of dialectics. Progress in nature and mind occurs because of the opposition of one reality, one idea, with another. But in all cases, sooner or later, the conflict of opposites is overcome and surmounted by a superior term—"synthesis." Thus the dialectical movement involves three terms: the thesis, followed by the antithesis, its opposite, and finally the synthesis, which 'reconciles' thesis and antithesis not by compromise but in a superior harmony that combines the quality of the first two terms.

The positive side of the Hegelian dialectics must also be brought to light. It is often a useful method of resolving conflicting views. In the area of philosophical and religious 'truths', the mood of our time is more for dialogue than demonstrations. Dialectics is gaining momentum with the growing awareness of the 'intersubjectivity' of truth. In the field of education, it has been recorded that dialogues and discussions are a better learning process than the monologue of lectures. For Hegel, the concrete development of the dialectic depends upon the element of unreality or unknowability. This continuously results in contradictions and necessitates the synthesis.[146]

Hegelian Concept of Spirit

The basic idea in all Hegel's mature teaching is denoted by the German word *Geist*. The word may be translated as *Mind* (emphasising its rational aspect) or *Spirit* (emphasising the immaterial, or better, the supermaterial and religious -aspect of reality). Perhaps it is best to let Hegel state his meaning in his own words. At least it will enable the reader to capture some of the flavour of his writing. It is customary to describe Hegel's view of the outworking of Spirit as a Dialectic (which is simply another word for process or dynamic pattern) of Thesis, Antithesis and Synthesis. But it has been pointed out that Hegel made occasional use of these latter terms. In working out this all-embracing philosophy of Spirit, Hegel believed that he discovered the philosophy to end all philosophies. He had not only salvaged Christianity from modern attacks, but also found the key to its inner meaning.

Critical Remarks

- Kant had denounced the dogmatism of Rationalistic metaphysics wanting to replace it by critical metaphysics. But with Hegel dogmatism reappeared in full strength. Hegel was more a visionary with novel and revolutionary ideas than a critical thinker who took the pain of justifying his claims.

- The Hegelian concept of an immanent Absolute was the first step that led to contemporary atheistic humanism. Feuerbach simply substituted 'Humanity' for the Hegelian Absolute Spirit. With him Idealistic Pantheism became 'Anthropotheism.' Marx moved a step further and rejected the 'divinity' of man.[147]

- According to Kierkegaard, Hegelianism as "despite its good points, in its entirety, it proves to be an extreme form of dogmatic Rationalism, a philosophy of ideas and concepts, a system of essences and abstractions, a purely logical construction with no concern for man, self and existence."

- Philosophers before Hegel had not given any importance to history in their understanding of Reality. With Hegel the history of the World, which is the autobiography of the Absolute Spirit, is an integral part of philosophical reflection.

Conclusion

Modern Philosophy has been marked by a continuing interaction between systems of thought based on a mechanistic, materialistic interpretation of the universe and those founded on a belief in human thought as the only ultimate reality. This interaction has reflected the increasing effect of scientific discovery and political change on philosophical speculation. These great changes of the 15th and 16th centuries brought about three intellectual crises that profoundly affected Western civilisation. First, the decline of Aristotelian science was called into question of its methods and foundations of the sciences. This decline came about for a number of reasons, including the inability of Aristotelian principles to explain new observations in astronomy. Second, new attitudes towards religion undermined religious authority and gave agnostic and atheistic ideas a chance to be heard. Third, a challenge took place of what to choose either reason or experience as the means of acquiring knowledge; for which famous philosophers stood in two opposite poles.

In the seventeenth century, rationalism was usually associated with the introduction of mathematical methods into philosophy—as in Descartes and Leibniz. This is commonly called continental rationalism. Rationalism is often contrasted with empiricism. Taken very broadly, these views are not mutually exclusive, since a philosopher can be both rationalist and empiricist. Taken to extremes, the empiricist view holds that all ideas come to us through experience, either through the five external senses or through such inner sensations as pain and pleasure, and thus that knowledge is essentially based on or derived from experience. At issue is the fundamental source of human knowledge and the proper techniques for verifying what we think we know. The contrast between idealism and materialism is the question of whether the substance of the world is mental or physical—it has nothing to do with thinking that things should be idealised or with coveting goods.

Forms of idealism were prevalent in philosophy from the 18th to 19th centuries. Transcendental idealism as advocated by Immanuel Kant is the view that there are limits on what can be understood, since there is much that cannot be brought under the conditions of objective judgment. Subjective idealism is a theory in philosophy of perception. The theory describes a relationship between human experience of the external world and the world itself, in which objects are nothing more than collections of sense data in those who perceive them. Subjective Idealists and Phenomenologists hold that minds and their experiences constitute existence. Objective Idealists hold that all of reality is included in a Universal Thought or Experience (*Absolute Idealism*) or that the world is composed of mental realities.

Helpful Questions
1. What is Cartesian Rationalism?
2. What are the differences between the philosophies of Locke and Berkeley?
3. Describe Kantian Idealism.

CHAPTER 8

Postmodern Christian Philosophy

This chapter focuses on philosophical concepts such as Pragmatism, Existentialism and Analytical philosophy. It also presents the general understanding of Roman Catholic philosophy, Liberal Christian philosophy, Neo-Orthodox philosophy and Evangelical philosophy. Unlike other chapters, this chapter specially deals with the philosophical concepts used by the philosophers of Asia, Africa and the Western world. There was a tendency to forget African and Asian Christian philosophies knowingly or unknowingly, while the writers of the past dealt with philosophy. It is an irrefutable fact that philosophy is incomplete if Asian and African philosophies would be neglected. It seems that somebody knows only Western philosophy and they are ignorant of the philosophies of the other parts of the world. Otherwise it was caused by negligence towards third-world countries.

Postmodern philosophy (AD1800-2000) is usually considered to begin after the philosophy of Immanuel Kant at the beginning of the 19th century. For Kant the 'noumenon' (the unknowable object) was the reality behind the 'phenomenon' (the appearance which is known). The real is what the mind conceives, the rational, and vice versa the rational is real. Consequently, everything is perfectly logical and necessary. Nature and thought, matter and spirit are governed by the implacable laws of logic. Hegel's Idealism was absolute. Reason and existence coincide perfectly. Postmodern philosophy is often particularly skeptical about simple binary oppositions that pervade much of Western metaphysics and humanism, emphasising the problem of the philosopher, cleanly distinguishing knowledge from ignorance, social progress from reversion, dominance from submission and presence from absence.

Rejecting idealism, other philosophers, who were working from outside the university, initiated lines of thought that would occupy academic philosophy in the early and mid-20th century. In the late 19th century and early 20th century, several forms of pragmatic philosophy arose. The ideas of pragmatism developed mainly from the discussions that took place between philosophers like Charles Sanders Peirce and William James. Husserl initiated the school of phenomenology. Kierkegaard and Nietzsche laid the groundwork for existentialism. Frege's work in logic provided the tools for early analytical philosophy. Mill's utilitarianism and Marx and Engel's Marxism dominated discussions in political philosophy until Rawls' work, 'A Theory of Justice.'

Postmodern philosophy can be sub-divided into two categories: Early postmodern philosophy (1800-1900) and later postmodern philosophy (1900-2000). Early postmodern philosophy (nineteenth century) is usually considered to begin after the philosophy of Immanuel Kant, at the beginning of the 19th century. German idealists, such as Hegel, expanded on the work of Kant by maintaining that the world is entirely rational and its nature is fundamentally knowable. Much of the later postmodern philosophy (twentieth century) concerns itself with explaining the relation between the theories of the natural sciences and the ideas of the humanities or common sense. The second half of this chapter deals with philosophers from various fields like Roman Catholic, Liberal, Neo-Orthodoxy, Evangelical, etc. Contemporary philosophy began in the 21st century. We will look at it in a succeeding chapter.

Existentialism

Existentialism reacted against the then prevalent approaches and looked upon philosophy as a meditation on subjective existence. Existentialism is a multifaceted philosophical movement of the 20th century characterised by a deep concern for the meaning of individual subjective existence. The movement had its origins in the 19th century thought of Kierkegaard and Nietzsche and was prevalent in Continental philosophy. They were interested in people's concealment of the meaninglessness of life and the use of diversion to escape from boredom. Existentialism is a philosophical movement that claims that individual human beings have full responsibility for creating the meanings of their own lives. It is a reaction against more traditional philosophies, such as rationalism and empiricism. In 1670, Blaise Pascal's unfinished notes were published under the title *The Pensées (Thoughts)*. In this work, he described many fundamental themes of existentialism. Pascal argued that without a God, life would be meaningless and miserable. People would only be able to create obstacles and overcome them in an attempt to escape boredom. This was good enough reason not to choose to become an atheist, according to Pascal.

Gabriel Marcel pursued theological versions of existentialism, most notably Christian Existentialism. Other theological existentialists include Paul Tillich, Rudolf Bultmann, Thomas Hoar and Martin Buber. Theological existentialism, as advocated by philosophers and theologians mentioned above, shares many of the same tenets and themes that are central to theistic existentialism. Belief in God is a personal choice made on the basis of a *passion*, of faith, an observation or experience. Theistic existentialists can freely choose to believe in God and can, despite their doubt, have the faith that God exists and that God is good. A third type of existentialism is agnostic existentialism. It makes no claim to know, or not know, if there is a 'greater picture' in play; rather, he simply recognises that the greatest truth is that which he chooses to act upon. There are existentialists who profess Christianity. There are existentialists who deny that it is possible to work out a philosophical system, and there are those who do the opposite. Existentialists sprang up in Germany after the First World War; it flourished in France immediately after the second.[148]

Soren Kierkegaard
Son of a well-to-do, Lutheran businessman, Soren Aabye Kierkegaard (1813-55) was born at Copen-hagen. After a secluded and unhappy childhood, he became a student at University of Copenhagen and intended eventually to enter the ministry.[149] Kierkegaard is often hailed as the 'father of existentialism.' He was a Lutheran pastor from Copenhagen (Denmark), a passionate expounder of the Christian message and faith in God.

Kierkegaard also focused on the deep anxiety of human existence—the feeling that there is no purpose, indeed nothing, at its core. Finding a way to counter this nothingness by embracing existence is the fundamental theme of existentialism and the explanation for the philosophy's name. Kierkegaard saw rationality as a mechanism humans use to counter their existential anxiety, their fear of being in the world. The rejection of reason as the source of meaning is a common theme of existentialist thought.

Concept of God

For Kierkegaard, the irrational leap to God was the only way that can save. Kierkegaard preached that Christianity is not a doctrine to know or a creed to recite, but a message to live. Theologians err in wanting to demonstrate the 'truth' of Christianity. Being comes before knowing: the subjective thinker precedes the objective thinker. Existentialism is a meditation on subjective existence. Kierkegaard's view of truth is often discussed under the heading of *Subjectivity*. It is a term that he used frequently himself, as for example in his *Concluding Unscientific Postscript*, where he contrasts the objective approach with the subjective. But it is also vividly illustrated in the journals where he writes: "It is perfectly true, isolated subjectivity is, in the opinion of the age, evil; but 'objectivity' as a cure is not one better. The only salvation is subjectivity, i.e., God, as infinite compelling subjectivity."

His Existentialism

While someone who claims to believe in reality may be called a 'realist,' or someone who believes in a deity a 'theist,' someone who believes fundamentally only in existence and seeks to find meaning in his or her life solely by embracing existence is an existentialist. Emphasising action, freedom and decision as fundamental, existentialists oppose themselves to rationalism and positivism. That is, they argue against definitions of human beings as primarily rational. Rather, existentialists look at where people find meaning. Existentialism asserts that people actually make decisions based on what has meaning to them rather than what is rational.

For Kierkegaard the paradox of faith means that belief must be proportioned in inverse proportion to the evidence. The less evidence is the better. Faith and reason are mutually exclusive opposites. With Kierkegaard, what counts is not what you know, but how you react.[7] The end-product is not more factual knowledge but an enlarged understanding of oneself and human existence. This last point could be amply illustrated from works like *Christian Discourses* and *Works of Love*.[150] With Kierkegaard several important themes of existentialist philosophies clearly emerge. First, an exclusive focus on subjective existence and the individual self with no concern for nature, science, history and society. Second, the irrationality and even the absurdity of human existence, the sense of anguish caused by the devaluation of the intelligible, the awesome responsibility of man alone are before his destiny. Third, the theme of authentic existence, that is, the importance to be in the truth, to live one's subjective truth with little regard for what are commonly and universally accepted as moral standards by established traditions.

Rudolf Bultmann

Rudolf Bultmann argued that the Christian worldview, as expressed in the Bible, was outdated. In mythological terms, Bultmann argued, with references to a three-tiered universe, a heavenly city, a house of many mansions that included numerous thrones, and so forth, it depicted a cosmos alien to modern men and women. For him, the result was that many contemporary people tended to reject the Bible and the message of salvation inherent in its narrative. The solution was to recast the story of Christ's redemptive work in modern, philosophical, psychological and scientific language that would enable today's men and women to ascertain the truth that the mythological language no longer conveys. He viewed that biblical statements are to be translated completely and exhaustively into existential ones, so that the Bible becomes once again relevant for modern man.[151]

Tillich was quite impressed with Bultmann's call for the 'demythologization' of the Bible and undertook to replace the mythological expression of the Christian message with a new, existential interpretation. Agreement with that the Christian message needed to be 'demythologized,' arguing that the mythological terms in which the narrative is expressed are of a far richer and more multi-valiant character than Tillich's existential version.

Paul Tillich

Paul Johannes Tillich (1886-1965) was a German-American theologian and Christian existentialist philosopher. Tillich was, along with Karl Barth, one of the most influential Protestant theologians of the twentieth century. Rather than beginning his philosophical work with questions of God, Tillich began with a 'phenomenology of the Holy.' His basic thesis is that religion is *Ultimate Concern*. What a person is ultimately concerned with in regard to their ultimate meaning and *being* can be understood as religion because 'there is nobody to whom nothing is sacred because no one can rid themselves of their humanity no matter how desperately they may try.'[152]

His Life

Paul Tillich was born on August 20, 1886, in the province of Brandenburg in eastern Germany in the small village of Starzeddel. Paul's Prussian father was a Lutheran pastor. Tillich studied at a number of German universities including Berlin, Tubingen and Hale and joined the Christian fraternity Wingolf, finally obtaining his Ph.D. at Breslau in 1911. In 1912, he became an ordained minister in the Lutheran Church and soon took up a career as professor. Except for an interlude as chaplain in the German army during World War I, he taught in many universities throughout Germany over the next two decades. Tillich taught theology at the universities of Berlin, Marburg, Dresden and Leipzig, and philosophy at Frankfurt. However, in opposition to the Nazis, in 1933 he was replaced by philosopher Arnold Gehlen, who had joined the Nazi Party that year.

Tillich accepted an invitation from Reinhold Niebuhr to teach at the Union Theological Seminary in the United States, where he emigrated later that year. Tillich became a US citizen in 1940. It is at the Union Theological Seminary that Tillich earned his reputation, publishing a series of books that outlined his particular synthesis of Protestant Christian theology with existentialist philosophy. Between 1952 and 1954 Tillich gave the Gifford lectures at University of Aberdeen, which resulted in the comprehensive three-volume *Systematic Theology*. A book outlining many of his views on existentialism, *The Courage to Be* (1952), proved popular even outside philosophical and religious circles, earning him considerable acclaim and influence. These works led to a prestigious appointment at the Harvard Divinity School in 1954, where he wrote another popularly acclaimed book, *Dynamics of Faith* (1957). He was also a very important contributor to modern *Just War* thought. In 1962, he moved to the University of Chicago, where he continued until his death in 1965.

Culture and Faith

Tillich's approach was highly systematic. He sought to correlate culture and faith such that 'faith need not be unacceptable to contemporary culture and contemporary culture need not be unacceptable to faith.' Consequently, Tillich's orientation is apologetic, seeking to make concrete theological answers that are applicable to ordinary daily life. This contributed to his popularity because it made him easily accessible to lay readers. In a broader perspective, revelation is understood as the fountainhead of religion.

True religion is that which correctly reveals the infinite, but no religion can ever do so in any way other than through metaphor and symbol. Thus the whole of the Bible should be understood symbolically, and all spiritual and theological knowledge cannot be other than symbols. This idea is used by theologians as an effective counterpoint to religious fundamentalism. Tillich argued that symbols are immensely important to faith because 'faith is the state of being ultimately concerned.' Faith without symbols is a form of idolatry. It is faith in something finite, something that can be expressed without symbols, and something that is fundamentally less than the ultimate.

Concept of God
Tillich argued that anxiety of non-being is inherent in the experience of being itself. Put simply, people are afraid of their own death. Tillich says that in our most introspective moments, we face the terror of our own nothingness. That is, we realise our mortality—that we are finite beings. The question that naturally arises in the mind of one in this introspective mood is what causes us to 'be' in the first place. Tillich concludes that radically finite beings cannot be sustained or caused by another finite or existing being. What can sustain finite beings is *being* itself, or the 'ground of being.' Tillich identifies this as God.

Existence is that which is finite. Essence is the infinite. Since existence is being and essence is the ground of being, essence is the ground or source of existence. But because the one is infinite and the other not, then existence is fundamentally alienated from the essence. Man is alienated from God. This Tillich takes to be sin. To exist is to be alienated. He said that, "God does not exist. He is being itself beyond essence and existence. Therefore to argue that God exists is to deny him." Tillich's quotation summarises his conception of God. Here the term "existence" for Tillich is related to the temporary world and God is beyond this and He is invisible. God is above the existing things of the world.

Tillich sought to reconcile revelation and reason by arguing that revelation never runs counter to reason, but both poles of the subjective human experience are complementary. In his metaphysical approach, Tillich was a staunch existentialist, focusing on the nature of being. Nothingness is a major motif of existentialist philosophy that Tillich employed as a means of reifying being itself.

Christ, the 'New Being'
According to Tillich, Christ is the 'New Being', who rectifies in himself the alienation between essence and existence. Essence fully shows itself

within Christ, but Christ is also a finite man. This indicates, for Tillich, a revolution in the very nature of being. The gap is healed and essence can now be found within existence. Christ is not God *per se* in himself, but Christ is the revelation of God. Tillich believed that Christ was the emblem of the highest goal of man, what God wants men to become. Thus Christ is not different from other humans except insofar as he reveals God within his own finitude—something that, in principle, all humans can achieve.

Tillich became an outspoken socialist in Germany following World War I. Tillich raised not only a moral Christian demand for socialist policies, but analysed the very roots of both Christian and socialist thought to find their common and reinforcing foundations. Tillich was, among these, the leading scholar of religion and politics. He does not think of God as a being who exists in time and space, because that constrains God and makes God finite. Thus God is considered beyond being, above finitude and limitation, the power or essence of being itself. Here he goes beyond the boundary of a theologian.

Gabriel Marcel

Gabriel Marcel (1889-1973) was a convert to Christianity, a writer of plays, novels and diaries. He was a French Roman Catholic existentialist philosopher, dramatist and critic, who insisted that individuals can only be understood as embodied and involved in specific situations. Marcel's thought blows a breath of fresh air in the midst of otherwise negative, critical and pessimistic brands of philosophical views. In his first book, *Metaphysical Journal* (1927), Marcel argued for a concrete philosophy that recognised that one's incarnation in a body and one's historical situation essentially condition who one is.

Three Levels of Approaches

Marcel distinguished three levels of approaches: The first is the sensation level of unconscious involvement, or existence passively endured. The second is the reflection level of withdrawal from reality, thought, reason, logic, conceptualisation, objectification and philosophical systemisation into essences. The third is the level of recollection that operates a return to reality, a deeper conscious immersion in life, an ontological participation in being.

Marcel distinguished primary reflection, which deals with objects and abstractions and reaches its highest form in science and technology, from his own method, 'secondary reflection', which concerns those aspects of human existence, such as one's body and one's situation, in which one participates so completely that one cannot abstract oneself from them. Secondary reflection contemplates 'mysteries' and yields a kind of truth (philosophical, moral and religious) that cannot be scientifically verified but is confirmed insofar as it illuminates one's life. Marcel, unlike other existentialists, emphasised participation in a community, rather than human isolation. He expressed these ideas not only in his books, but also in his plays, which present complicated situations in which people find themselves trapped and which lead either to isolation and despair or to a fulfilling relation to other persons and to God.

Recollection, Mystery and Being
It can be explained in three words: recollection, mystery and being.[153] (a) Being: In daily life, there occurs the constant confusion of 'Being' (What we are) with 'Having' (what we possess). This situation prevents us from having access to Being—Our 'having' (possessions) determines our judgments of value. (b) Mystery: Being must be approached not as a problem, but as a mystery. A problem is something external to us, that confronts us and to which we can bring a 'solution.' A mystery is not something 'mysterious' (vague and unknowable) but a reality that cannot be approached from the outside (as problem can) because we are a part of it, i.e., it must be grasped in an experience of participation. (c) Recollection of meditation: Marcel distinguished three levels of approaches: The first is the sensation level of unconscious involvement, the second is the reflection level of withdrawal from reality and the third is the level of recollection that operates a return to reality.

Some criticised that his 'philosophy of communion' has been accused of being more an apology of Christianity than a genuine form of philosophical reflection. It is better that he was able to stand for a Christian philosophy. He disliked being classified as an Existentialist, a designation too closely associated with Sartre's thought, and called himself a "neo-Socratist'—one who invites and stimulates others to make a personal discovery of the truth within them.

Conclusion
Existentialism, philosophical movement or tendency, emphasising individual existence, freedom and choice, influenced many diverse writers in the 19th and 20th centuries. We studied that existentialism is a philosophical movement centred on individual existence, which denies that the universe has an intrinsic meaning or purpose. It requires people

to take responsibility for their own actions and shape their own destinies. There is a split among existentialists between those who, like Kierkegaard, conceive the fundamental existentialist question as man's relationship to God. Kierkegaard preached that man is bound to sink into despair unless he makes the leap of faith in God. Although there are certain common tendencies amongst existentialist thinkers, there are major differences and disagreements among them, and not all of them even accept the validity of the term "existentialism."

Pragmatism

Pragmatism is a different type of philosophical school that originated with Charles Sanders Peirce and came to fruition in the early twentieth-century philosophies of William James and John Dewey. It originated in North America in the second half of the nineteenth century and continued to dominate American philosophy until the 1930s. The term "pragmatism", derived from the Greek *pragma*, means 'acts', 'affairs', 'business'. It has come to be associated with such slogans as 'Truth is what works', 'The true is the expedient' and 'Faith in a fact helps create the fact.'[154] Most of the thinkers who describe themselves as *pragmatists* consider practical consequences or real effects to be vital components of both meaning and truth. Pragmatism regards philosophy as the servant of action. It is the American philosophy of men of action, successful businessmen.

Pragmatism holds that the truth of beliefs does not consist in their correspondence with reality, but in their usefulness and efficacy. S. P. Banerjee wrote that Pragmatism is not one neat, coherent system of thought developed by one philosopher. It is a name given to a number of different but allied trends of thought in modern western philosophy.[155] For the Pragmatist, to ascertain the value of the God-concept, one should consider the practical consequences that result from the belief in the life of individuals and societies. 'God' cannot be defined or proved in abstract; it must be judged by the concrete effects it has in the life of humanity.[156] Pragmatism differs from Empiricism. In the latter, truth depends on past experiences whereas, in Pragmatism, truth is also verified by future returns.

Charles Peirce

Charles Sanders Peirce (1839-1914) was highly influential in laying the groundwork for today's empirical scientific method.[157] Although Peirce severely criticised many elements of Descartes' peculiar brand of rationalism, he did not reject rationalism outright. Indeed, he concurred with the main ideas of rationalism, most importantly the idea that rational concepts can be meaningful and the idea that rational concepts necessarily go beyond the data given by empirical observation. In later years, he even emphasised the concept-driven side of the then ongoing debate between strict empiricism and strict rationalism. In order to counterbalance the excesses, some of his cohorts had taken pragmatism under the 'data-driven' strict-empiricist view.

Doctrine of Fallibilism

Peirce's approach presupposes that (a) the objects of knowledge are real things; (b) the characters (properties) of real things do not depend on our perceptions of them; and (c) everyone who has sufficient experience of real things will agree on the truth about them. According to Peirce's doctrine of fallibilism, the conclusions of science are always tentative. The rationality of the scientific method does not depend on the certainty of its conclusions but on its self-corrective character: by continued application of the method science can detect and correct its own mistakes and thus eventually lead to the discovery of truth.

Deductive and Inductive Reasoning

Peirce placed inductive reasoning and deductive reasoning in a complementary rather than competitive mode, the latter of which had been the primary trend among the educated since David Hume wrote a century before. To this, Peirce added the concept of adductive reasoning. The combined three forms of reasoning serve as a primary conceptual foundation for the empirically based scientific method today. In Harvard, in 'Lectures on Pragmatism' (1903), he observed that the link between sensory perception and intellectual conception is a two-way street. This in no way conflicts with the fallibility and revisability of scientific concepts, since it is only the immediate percept in its unique individuality. Scientific concepts are general in nature, and transient sensations do in another sense find correction within them. This notion of perception as abduction has received periodic revivals in artificial intelligence and cognitive science research.

William James
William James (1842 - 1910) is a famous American philosopher. Pragmatism is a philosophy 'made in USA', typical of a rising new culture of businessmen more concerned with the success of their enterprises than with the intellectual project of truth-seeking. The dictum 'Truth is in success' reflects the Pragmatist mentality. William James and John Dewey are the pioneers of the movement. Pragmatism is not concerned with 'barren' intellectual questions, abstract theories and ideas that do not offer

solutions to the concrete problems of men and societies. Knowledge must be at the service of life, action and behaviour. William James was drawing attention to an important aspect of religious belief when he stressed the element of choice. But the Christian faith is never a matter of blind choice. As we saw in discussing the Reformers, it is not a case of making an irrational choice in a situation where all the factors cancel each other out.

God and Truth

In his *The Will to Believe*, William James commented on the existence of God.[158] To him, the name of *hypothesis* to anything is that it may be proposed to our belief. A live hypothesis is one that appeals as a real possibility to him to whom it is proposed. The call to decision between hypotheses is an *option*. Options may be of several kinds. They may be living or dead, forced or avoidable, momentous or trivial. A living option is one in which both hypotheses are live ones. If we say, 'be an agnostic or be a Christian', trained as you are, each hypothesis makes some appeal, however small, to your belief. A forced option is one that arises when there is no standing outside the alternative hypotheses. For him, a momentous option is one that is presented when the opportunity is unique and the stake is significant, or when the decision is irreversible. William James viewed that our passional nature not only lawfully may decide an option between propositions, whenever it is a genuine option that cannot be decided on intellectual grounds.

God is the natural appellation for the supreme reality, so this higher part of the universe may best be called by the name of God. We and God have business with each other; and in opening ourselves to His influence, our deepest destiny is fulfilled. The universe, in those parts of it which our personal being constitutes, takes a turn genuinely for the worse or for the better in proportion as each one of us fulfills or evades God's demands. God's existence is the guarantee of an ideal order that shall be permanently preserved. This would indeed someday burn up or freeze up; but if it is part of His order, the old ideals are sure to be brought elsewhere to fruition, so that where God is, tragedy is only provisional and partial, and shipwreck and dissolution are not the absolutely final things. All this on the supposition that our passional nature may be prophetic and right: and that the religious hypothesis is a live hypothesis that may be true.

Truth is a property of certain of our ideas. It means their 'agreement', as falsity means their disagreement, with 'reality.' The popular notion is that a true idea must copy its reality. True ideas are those that we can assimilate, validate, corroborate and verify. False ideas are those that we cannot. That is the practical difference it makes to us to have true ideas; that, therefore, is the meaning of truth. The truth of an idea is not a stagnant property inherent in it. Truth happens to an idea. It becomes true, is made true by events. Its verity is in fact an event, a process, the process namely of its verifying itself, its verification. Its validity is the process of its validation. The importance to human life of having true beliefs about matters of fact is a thing too notorious. We live in a world of realities that can be infinitely useful or infinitely harmful. Ideas that tell us which of them to expect count as the true ideas in all this primary sphere of verification, and the pursuit of such ideas is a primary human duty. The possession of truth, so far from being here an end in itself, is only a preliminary means towards other vital satisfactions. The absolute truth will have to be made as a relation incidental to the growth of a mass of verification-experience, to which the half true ideas are all along contributing their quota. William James had already insisted on the fact that truth is made largely out of previous truths. Truth is the function of the beliefs that start and terminate among them.

Philosophy with Science and Religion
His view about philosophy is to be specially noted. Philosophy, etymologically meaning the love of wisdom, is the work of this class of minds, regarded with an indulgent relish. He further commented that philosophy is really the love of sophism. Philosophy is defined in the usual scholastic textbooks as 'the knowledge of things in general by the ultimate causes, so far as natural reason can attain to such knowledge.' Philosophy, in a sense, is only a compendious name for the spirit in education. Things can be taught in dry dogmatic ways or in a philosophic way. Philosophy is able to fancy everything different from what it is.

To William James, the sciences are branches of the tree of philosophy. Modern science began only after 1600, with Galileo. The men who began this work of emancipation were philosophers in the original sense of the word, universal sages. Galileo said that he had spent more years on philosophy than months on mathematics. Descartes was a universal philosopher in the fullest sense of the term. Philosophy has become a collective name for questions that have not yet been answered to the satisfaction of all by whom they have been asked. But to assume, therefore, that the only possible philosophy must be mechanical and mathematical and to disparage all enquiries into the other sorts of question is to forget the extreme diversity of aspects under which reality undoubtedly exists.

Philosophy is dogmatic and pretends to settle things by pure reason, whereas the only fruitful mode of getting at truth is to appeal to concrete experience. Science collects, classes and analyses facts, and thereby far outstrips philosophy. Philosophy must include the results of all the sciences and cannot be contrasted with the latter. In the more modern sense of something contrasted with the sciences, philosophy means 'metaphysics.' Metaphysics and religion may then again form a single body of wisdom and lend each other mutual support.

Science can only prove it by showing that such ascertainment and correction bring man all sorts of other goods that man's heart in turn declares desirable. Then he described the religious faith. For him, Science says that things are visible and morality says, some things are better than other things; and religion says that the best things are the more eternal things. For him, we are better off, if we believe the first affirmation to be true. And then logical elements of this situation are to be considered in case the religious hypothesis in both its branches is really true. Religion offers itself as a momentous option. We are supposed to gain, even now by our belief, and to lose by our non-belief, a certain vital good. Secondly, religion is a forced option so far as that vital good is concerned. We cannot escape the issue by remaining skeptical, because although we do avoid error in that way if religion be untrue, we lose the good, if it be true. The appeal of religion was made to our own active good will, as if evidence for its truth might be forever withheld from us unless we met the hypothesis halfway.

Other American Philosophers

John Dewey, the American educator and philosopher, viewed human experience as disconnected, fragmentary, full of beginnings without conclusions or as experiences deliberately manipulated as means to ends. The exceptional experiences that flow from their beginnings to consummations are aesthetic. Aesthetic experience is enjoyment for its own sake, complete and self-contained and terminal, not merely instrumental to other purposes. In America, the most famous contemporary philosopher is Richard Rorty. Originally an analytic philosopher, Rorty believed that combining Donald Davidson's criticism of the dualism between conceptual scheme and empirical content with William Van Orman's criticism of the analytic-synthetic distinction allowed for an abandonment of the view of the mind as a mirror of reality or external world. Contemporary American writer Chuck Palahniuk is often described as elements of distortion from the 'traditional' mode of narrative, which often try to grab and shock the readers and return to their present. This function, which comes through the form of their writing, has been described as a 'Metaphysics of Presence', in which, it is hoped, and the intentionality of consciousness will be diverted from its inauthentic state of care.

The other important American philosophers are Ronald Dworkin, Michael Sandel and John Rawls. Rawls is the author of *A Theory of Justice* (1971), considered to be the most significant work of political philosophy in the 20th century. In this book, he presents the idea of 'justice as fairness,' a principle that promotes the equal distribution of the benefits and burdens of society among individuals. Any advantages that society confers should benefit those who are most disadvantaged, Rawls believes. From this and other principles he has developed theories about political and social relations within liberal democracies and between those democracies and certain illiberal states. Rawls's ideas remain a major inspiration for much current work in political philosophy.

Positive Contributions of Pragmatism
It brings one back from the ivory tower of abstract possibilities to the concrete realities of life. In this regard, we may note several important contributions to the truth question.[159]

- Pragmatism provides a balance in the reaction against the purely formal and rationalistic approach. It stresses the practical vis-a-vis the purely theoretical. It is not content with seeking causes but also producing effects in lives.

- Truth, at least religious truth, is finally confirmed in personal experience. Any theory that offers itself as a world and life view must be applicable to life.

- Pragmatists also provide a helpful reminder of the tentative or probable nature of much of our knowledge. Perhaps no truth about reality can be known with rational inescapability.

- Finally, pragmatists, like existentialists, remind us again of the role of the personal and volitional in truth. The process of understanding and applying truth to one's life is more than purely rational. There must be a will to believe.

Criticisms of Pragmatic Theory

Many men have undertaken to criticise pragmatism from many perspectives. We summarise here only those observations that apply to pragmatism as a test for truth.

> The results or consequences of an action do not establish what is true but simply what happened to *work*. But success is not truth and failure is not necessarily falsity.

- Truth may be unrelated to results. The results may have been accidental.

- Truth is more than the expedient. At the heart of this criticism is the contention that we do mean more by truth than what works.

- James admits that it is impossible for us to know long-run consequences. On purely pragmatic grounds, there appears to be no other alternative for a finite person who cannot define the distant future.

- <u>A passional</u> and volitional basis alone for deciding truth is insufficient. Faith is certainly necessary for belief in God, but one must have some evidence or reason to believe.

- On purely pragmatic grounds opposing worldviews may work equally well. But they are opposing worldviews; both cannot be true at the same time and in the same sense. The pragmatic test for truth cannot rescue us from total relativism in this regard.[160]

Conclusion

American philosophy is marked with an approach to classical philosophy and pragmatism that is sympathetic to mainstream analytic philosophy and provides the most comprehensive programme for understanding the work of the philosophical giant Charles Peirce. Professional philosophers have tended either to shrug off American philosophy as negligible or derivative or to date American philosophy from the work of twentieth-century analytical positivists such as Quine. Russell Goodman expands on the revisionist position developed by Stanley Cavell—that the most interesting strain of American thought proceeds not from Puritan theology or from empirical science but from a peculiarly American kind of Romanticism. This insight leads Goodman, through Cavell, back to Emerson and Thoreau and thence to William James and John Dewey, as they assimilated to American circumstances and intellectual habits of the European thought from Kant to Wittgenstein.

There is a difference between a pragmatic *theory* of truth and a pragmatic *test* for truth. Christian apologists disavow the former but often employ the latter as part, if not all, of their test for the truth of Christianity. There are indeed some important insights provided by pragmatists that are not foreign to biblical Christianity. Of course, all truth must work, but not everything that works is necessarily true. Many differing views work for many different people. But results are often unrelated to truth. The Christian apologist believes that truth will work in the short run and the long run, but he cannot hold that what works is true, for many false and evil things have worked for many people for many years. And no finite can see the distant future. So, pragmatism fails as a sufficient test for truth in the present.

Analytical Philosophy

The term "analytic philosophy" roughly designates a group of philosophical methods that stress clarity of meaning above all other criteria. Analytic philosophy is a generic term for a style of philosophy that came to dominate English-speaking countries in the 20th century. In countries like United States, United Kingdom, Canada and Australia, the overwhelming majority of university philosophy departments self-identify as 'analytic' department. The historical roots of analytic philosophy can be summarily characterised thus: First, the positivist view that there are no specifically philosophical truths and that the object of philosophy is the logical clarification of thoughts. Second, the view is that the logical clarification of thoughts can only be achieved by analysis of the logical form of philosophical propositions. The logical form of a proposition is a way of representing it to display its similarity with all other propositions of the same type.

Bertrand Russell

Bertrand Arthur William Russell (1872-1970) was a British philosopher, logician, mathematician and advocate for social reform. He was a prolific writer, populariser of philosophy and a commentator on a large variety of topics. Russell was born at the height of Briton's economic and political ascendancy. Bertrand Russell was born on 18th May 1872 at Trellech, Monmouth shire, into an aristocratic family. Russell won a scholarship to read for the Mathematics Triops at Trinity College, Cambridge, and commenced his studies there in 1890. He became acquainted with the younger G. E. Moore and came under the influence of Alfred North Whittefield, who recommended him to the Cambridge Apostles. He quickly distinguished himself in mathematics and philosophy, graduating with a B.A. in the former subject in 1893 and adding a fellowship in the latter in 1895.

In 1896, he taught German social democracy at the London School of Economics, where he also lectured on the science of power in the autumn of 1937. He was also a member of the Coefficients dining club of social reformers set up in 1902. Russell became a fellow of the Royal Society in 1908. In 1920, Russell traveled to Russia as part of an official delegation sent by the British government to investigate the effects of the Russia Revolution. During the course of his visit, he met Lenin and had an hour-long conversation with him. Russell subsequently lectured in Beijing on philosophy for one year. He died of influenza at a time when the British Empire had all but vanished, its power dissipated by the two World Wars and the end of the imperial system. He died on 2nd February 1970 at his home in Merionethshire, Wales. As one of the world's best-known intellectuals, Russell's voice carried great moral authority, even into his death. Russell spent the 1950s and 1960s engaged in various political causes, primarily related to nuclear disarmament and opposing the U.S. invasion of Vietnam. In 1963 he became the inaugural recipient of the Jerusalem Prize, an award for writers concerned with the freedom of the individual in society. On 31st January 1970 he condemned the 'Israeli aggression' in the Middle East.'

His Writings
In 1950, Russell was made a Nobel Laureate in Literature, 'in recognition of his varied and significant writings in which he champions humanitarian ideals and freedom of thought.' Russell began his published work in 1896 with *German Social Democracy*, a study in politics that was an early indication of a lifelong interest in political and social theory. Russell's first mathematical book, *An Essay on the Foundations of Geometry*, was published in 1897. Perhaps Russell's most significant contribution to philosophy of language is his theory of descriptions, as presented in his seminal essay, *On Denoting*, first published in 1905 in the *Mind* philosophical journal, which the mathematician and philosopher Frank P. Ramsey described as 'a paradigm of philosophy.'

The first of three volumes of *Principia Mathematica* was published in 1910, which soon made Russell world famous in his field. Bertrand Russell published his three-volume autobiography in 1967, 1968 and 1969. He wrote a great many letters to world leaders during this period. Russell's last significant work in mathematics and logic, *Introduction to Mathematical Philosophy*, was written while he was in jail.

His Philosophy
Russell is generally recognised as one of the founders of analytic philosophy, even of its several branches. Russell saw formal logic and science as the principal tools of the philosopher. To him, the main task of the philosopher was to illuminate the most general propositions about the world and to eliminate confusion. Russell had great influence on modern mathematical logic. Russell frequently claimed that he was more convinced of his *method* of doing philosophy, the method of analysis, than of his philosophical conclusions. Science was one of the principal components of analysis, along with logic and mathematics. Russell was a believer in the scientific method that knowledge is derived from empirical research and for him this research should be verified through repeated testing. Russell's epistemology went through many phases. He remained a philosophical realist for the remainder of his life, believing that our direct experiences have primacy in the acquisition of knowledge. While some of his views have lost favour, his influence remains strong in the distinction between two ways in which we can be familiar with objects: 'Knowledge by acquaintance' and 'knowledge by description.'

Later, Russell subscribed to a kind of neutral monism, maintaining that the distinctions between the material and mental worlds, in the final analysis, were arbitrary, and that both can be reduced to a neutral property. In a set of lectures, "The Philosophy of Logical Atomism," which he gave in 1918, he described its central theme that the world consists of logically independent facts, a plurality of facts, and that our knowledge depends on the data of our direct experience of them. Russell developed a doctrine similar to that of the Logical Positivists, which he termed Logical Atomism. It is a doctrine that is introduced into a world of infinite, unchanging propositions that are eternally and absolutely true.[161] Bertrand Russell is a professed Humanist. But even the brief interview with Ved Mehta is sufficient to show that he is by no means confident of human progress. There was a time earlier in the century when Humanists could present a reasonably united front.[162] Russell's ethical outlook and his personal courage in facing controversies were certainly informed by his religious upbringing, principally by his paternal grandmother, who instructed him with the biblical injunction, 'Thou shalt not follow a multitude to do evil' (Exodus 23:2)—something, he says, that influenced him throughout his life.

Russell devised a technique for the analysis of definite descriptions, in which problematic expressions were eliminated in principle from discourse by rules of translation. By logical analysis, Russell splits up a general proposition into truth functional components of each of the terms used in the component-propositions.[163] Russell had a major influence on modern philosophy, especially in the English-speaking world. While others were also influential, notably Frege, Moore and Wittgenstein, Russell made analysis the dominant methodology of professional philosophy. The various analytic movements throughout the last century all owe something to Russell's earlier works.

Ludwig Wittgenstein

Another significant figure who, though an Austrian, was not directly associated with the group but who shared the same initial approach was Ludwig Wittgenstein (1889-1951). Today, he remains the most talked-about philosopher among English-speaking academicians.

Life and Works

Wittgenstein spent much of his life in England, first as a research student in aeronautics at Manchester and then as a Cambridge philosopher. In some ways, the movement is typified by the solitary figure of Wittgenstein at Cambridge, restlessly analysing the structure of thought, forever questioning. Wittgenstein's philosophy was a highly specialist discipline devoted to the analysis of language and thought.[164] His *Tractatus Logicophilosophicus* (1921) is regarded as one of the great seminal works of modern philosophy. Wittgenstein became professor at University of Cambridge and the chief spokesman of linguistic philosophy.

There were two stages in the development of his thought on the role of 'language and reality': the first is covered in his *Tractatus* and the second in a work printed posthumously and entitled *Philosophical Investigations*. In 1921, Ludwig Wittgenstein published his *Tractatus Logico-Philosophicus*, which gave a rigidly 'logical' account of linguistic and philosophical issues. At the time, he understood most of the problems of philosophy as mere puzzles of language, which could be solved by clear thought. Years later, he would reverse a number of the positions he had set out in *Tractatus*; for example, in his second major work, *Philosophical investigations* (1953). It encouraged the development of 'ordinary language philosophy', which was promoted by Gilbert Ryle, J. L. Austin and a few others.

His Linguistic Philosophy

Formerly Wittgenstein, in *Tractatus*, had dismissed words and propositions as meaningless if they did not conform to the criteria of picturing the facts. Later, Wittgenstein admitted that his picture theory was mistaken. For we do not use language only to picture facts but in many other ways: to tell stories, to worship, to play cricket or chess, etc. From this new view of language, Wittgenstein derived a new concept of meaning. In *Tractatus*, he contended that a proposition is meaningful when it is a picture of reality. He replaced this naive and narrow understanding of language by the view that words gain their meaning from how they are used in a language game. Wittgenstein assumed that there is a distinction between hidden apparent logical forms. The language disguises thought. There is much from the outward form of clothing, so it is impossible to infer the form of thought beneath it.[165] The task of philosophy must henceforth be to analyse language in order to unveil the many language games together with their respective rules. Philosophy is now analytic, descriptive of the language games. There have been several 'revolutions' in the history of Philosophy, and certainly Linguistic Philosophy is one of them for having shaken the very foundation of human thought. It has shown that one of the most important things about man is his language and even more importantly that there are many languages according to the cultures and forms of life of human societies. If the silent 'truth' is perhaps one and absolute, the spoken 'truths' are many and relative to the language used to express them. Linguistic philosophy gives a lesson in relativism and pluralism. It makes us aware of the limits of our human situation as users of language. For Wittgenstein it is not possible to break the veil of language; we are hopeless prisoners of our linguistic prejudices.

Wittgenstein was an influential figure of the concepts of language games. For him, the meaning of a proposition must be understood in its context, that is, in terms of the rules of the language game of which that proposition is a part. Philosophy, concluded Wittgenstein, is an attempt to resolve problems that arise as the result of linguistic confusion, and the key to the resolution of such problems is ordinary language analysis and the proper use of language.

Critical Remarks on Analytic Philosophy

- As a side-effect of the focus on logic and language in the early years of analytic philosophy, the tradition initially had little to say on the subject of ethics. The attitude was widespread among early analytics that these subjects were unsystematic and merely expressed personal attitudes about which philosophy could have little or nothing to say.

- As with the study of ethics, early analytic philosophy avoided the study of philosophy of religion, dismissing the subject as part of metaphysics and meaningless.

- The fact is that today there is a growing criticism of this philosophy that is out of touch with the vital matters of human life. If it has given an important tool for more correct and prudent thinking in both philosophical and theological circles, it has completely failed in achieving anything constructive.

- Analytic philosophy subsequently took various paths, including a rejection of formal analysis in favour of a close examination of natural language, inquiry into the logical underpinnings of languages and renewed interest in the ethical implications of the analytic method.

Roman Catholic Philosophy

There are few notable Roman Catholic philosophers in the postmodern world. We will look at some of the Roman Catholic philosophy of the postmodern world.

Teilhard De Chardin

One of the most interesting religious phenomena of the late 1950s and mid-1960s has been the post-humous popularity of the Jesuit scientist and mystic Fr. Teilhard de Chardin. Teilhard (1881-1955) was born near Clermont-Ferrand on May 1, 1881. Educated at Jesuit schools in France and England, he also studied at the Sorbonne in Paris, where he received a doctorate in Paleontology in 1922. Teilhard's teaching career at the Catholic Institute in Paris was terminated because his views were regarded as unorthodox by his religious superiors. He took a research position in China, where he remained, except for a few intervals, for almost 20 years, engaged in paleontological research and philosophical reflection. In 1952, he became associated with the Wenner Gren Foundation for Anthropological Research, located in New York City, where he died on

April 10, 1955. His major work, *The Phenomenon of Man* (1955), is an attempt to set forth a comprehensive evolutionary vision that speaks to both scientific and religious interests. Teilhard's other works include *Letters from a Traveller* (1956), *The Divine Milieu* (1957) and *The Future of Man* (1959). No account of the twentieth-century scene would be complete without some mention of Teilhard de Chardin.

The Law of Centro-Complexification
For Teilhard the world is a 'Cosmo-genesis', a progressive cosmic development from the first atom of matter to man. Now evolution occurs according to the law of convergence. Teilhard claims that sufficient scientific observations warrant what he calls the 'law of centro-complexification' according to which there is a constant progress in the sense of organised heterogeneity. The Cosmos does not evolve at random. It converges progressively towards a spiritual goal. Undoubtedly, Teilhard's synthesis amounts to a 'philosophy of Evolution' and therefore an interpretation of the world and man as scientific foundation. On the contrary, Teilhard's vision is based on science, but goes well beyond it in an effort to reach a harmonious and intelligible synthesis. His great aim was to reconcile Christian theology with the evolutionary theory in order to achieve a scientific view of the divine purpose and man's place in the universe. He was a French Jesuit priest and scientist (Paleontologist) who used science as a stepping stone for a vast philosophical and theological synthesis in which scientific facts and theories, philosophical reason and Christian faith are brought into one.

Noosphere: Meaning of Man
Teilhard's thought has a starting point on evolution. For him, "Evolution is a light illuminating all facts, a curve that all lines must follow." But evolution is not simply a way of understanding the past; it is our guide to understanding man's future development. People perceive the world as a dynamic totality, a progressive cosmic evolution with a purpose. This humanistic vision takes the shape of a 'Mystique' in which man realises that he is no longer an individual spectator of the cosmos but a responsible co-worker of the planetary future. His vocation is to build the earth.[166] Scientific evolutionary theory is the key to Teilhard's thought. He wrote that evolution is a general condition to which all theories must bow and which they must satisfy henceforward if they are to be thinkable and true.

With the emergence of the thinking man, evolution reaches a new phase, the 'noosphere'. The 'spiritualization' of evolution takes place.

Evolution becomes 'conscious' of itself, being now in the hand of free and conscious beings. Now that humanity itself is responsibility for evolution. At the mercy of human free will, evolution is exposed to failure. The noosphere passes through three stages of development. First, divergence and multiplication of social groups, institutions and races of nations; second, convergence, unification and genesis of the 'consciousnesses' of mankind; and third 'amortization' of evolution. He interpreted evolution as a purposive process in which the matter-energy of the universe has continually changed in the direction of increased complexity. With the emergence of humanity, he argued, evolutionary development entered a new dimension.

Spirituality and the Christic

Teilhard's synthesis includes elements of Christian theology. He was a scientist, a philosopher but also a believer. If the Omega Point, the personal pole of convergence, is, according to him, an ideal for human thought, it is reality for the Christian believer: the transcendent as well as the immanent reality of Christ. 'Christ is the alpha and the omega, the beginning and the end. Teilhardian Christology is a theology of incarnation and divine immanence with the Eucharistic presence as its central ritual expression. Christian theologians have pointedly remarked that Teilhard's silence on the essential redemptive role of Christ has resulted in a hazardous stage of traditional Christology.

Teilhard's spirituality shows the universal, cosmic dimension of every man's personal destiny, overlooked by the existentialist concept of one's 'subjectivity' as well as by the religious idea of salvation that focused on 'the souls and God.' The religious person can no longer be an isolated individual; he must have a sense of Evolution; he must feel bound to the immense task to 'build the earth.' From the biosphere (the layer of living things covering the earth) has emerged the noosphere (a mind layer surrounding the earth). This mind layer, or human consciousness, generates increasingly complex social arrangements that in turn give rise to a higher consciousness. Ultimately, the evolutionary process culminates in the convergence of the material and spiritual into a super consciousness that Teilhard called the Omega Point. By his love, this God-Omega attracts and thereby gives direction to the whole evolutionary process. Such love, for Teilhard, is most clearly evident in the universal Christ.

Karl Rahner

Karl Rahner (1904-1984), German theologian, leading Roman Catholic theologian of the 20th century, attended the local *Gymnasium* and entered the Jesuit order in 1922. He studied for the priesthood at seminaries in Feldkirch, Austria (1922-1925), Pullach, near Munich (1925-1927) and Valkenburg, Netherlands (1929-1933). He was ordained in 1932. At University of Freiburg, Rahner attended the German existentialist philosopher Martin Heidegger's seminar and was decisively influenced by him. Rahner took his doctorate in 1936 at University of Innsbruck. His teaching career, lasting until 1971, was spent at Innsbruck, Pullach, and the universities of Munich and Munster.[167] During World War II he did pastoral work in Vienna and in a Bavarian country parish.

His Works

Rahner's doctoral dissertation, a new interpretation on the thought of St. Thomas Aquinas, was published in 1939 as *Spirit in the World*. His major works include *Theological Investigations* (14 volumes), *Hearers of the Word* (1941), dealing with when and how humans are positively open to a divine revelation, and *Foundations of Christian Faith: An Introduction to the Idea of Christianity* (1978), which is a work on Systematic Theology.[168] In 1965, he was a founder of the journal *Concilium* and served as chief editor of the sourcebook of church documents, *Enchiridion Symbolorum*, from its 28th to 31st editions. He also edited several important theological reference works.

His Philosophy

The principal philosophical influences on Rahner were the 18th-century German philosopher Immanuel Kant, Heidegger and the Belgian Jesuit Joseph Marechal, founder of the school of transcendental Thomism, which affirms the insights of Aquinas but analyses human understanding in light of Kantian critical philosophy. Rahner's influence grew after his service (1960-1965) as an official papal theological expert before and during the Second Vatican Council.

His works combine historical investigation of actual human experience with reflection on the conditions of its possibilities. Characteristic of his theology is sensitivity to the modern philosophical concerns of evolution, existentialism and personalism. Rahner's intention was to place theological thought at the service of Christian faith and life by confronting problems posed by modern philosophy and science.

Anonymous Christianity

Karl Rahner is famous for his theory— 'Anonymous Christianity.' Anonymous Christian is one who accepts himself in a moral decision, even if that decision is not made in a 'religious' or 'theist' manner. 'Anonymous Christians' are saved not by their natural morality, but because they have experienced Jesus Christ's grace without realising it. Tony Lane writes: "The anonymous Christian' in our sense of the term is the pagan after the beginning of the Christian mission, who lives in the state of Christ's grace through faith, hope and love, yet who has no explicit knowledge of the fact that his life is orientated in grace-given salvation to Jesus Christ. There must be a Christian theory to account for the fact that every individual who does not in any absolute or ultimate sense act against his own conscience can say and does say in faith, hope and love, Abba, within his own spirit and is on these grounds in all truth a brother to Christians in God's sight."[169] The concept of the 'anonymous Christian' is very influential today, especially the idea that one can be an anonymous Christian without any sort of religious commitment.

Ken Gnanakan summarised Rahner's argument that Jesus is the only way, and yet there are claims to other ways.[170] A tension here Rahner offers is reconciliation. Christianity does not simply confront the member of extra-Christian religion as a mere non-Christian, but as someone who can and must already be regarded in this as an 'anonymous Christian.' One needs to grasp this clever argument. This argument is built on the fact of the universal availability of God's grace. They are already on their way to salvation through grace, even though they are outside of and ignorant of Christ. Therefore, the proclamation of the gospel does not simply turn someone from God, rather turns an anonymous Christian to God. Martin Goldsmith concluded that Rahner's thesis has been attacked both by Christians and the followers of other faiths. For Christians, this distorts the Christian message, for there seems to be no biblical base for the idea of anonymous Christians. The people of other religions accused Rahner of ecclesiastical imperialism. For them, it is presumptuous of a Christian to label Hindus as really being Christians.[171] However, Karl Rahner stands out among modern Christian philosophers not only for the quantity of output but for the universally recognised depth of his thought. Among the Roman Catholic theologians of the 20th century, he was the one who exercised the greatest influence on contemporary theologians. He died in Innsbruck on March 30, 1984.

Aloysius Pieris

Aloysius Pieris SJ is a leading Sri Lankan theologian and founder-director of Tulana Research Centre in Kelaniya, Sri Lanka. A theologian and an expert on Buddhist Philosophy, he is Professor of Pali Abhidhammika Literature. He has held Chairs of Theology in many universities and has been Guest Lecturer on many theology faculties. He is one of the most important Catholic theologians in Asia, a man who is most decidedly a liberation theologian himself and a Jesuit priest. He has been ignoring the efforts made by Rome to control him and his theological pioneering in Asia since he first took to heart a mandate that Pope Paul VI delivered to Asian bishops in the early 1970s.

Life and Works

Pieris is a diminutive person (5'2" feet). He was born in Sri Lanka, which became a British tea colony in 1818, dominated by the Portuguese and Dutch that dated back to the 16th century, when Pieris' ancestors became Catholic converts. Pieris is thankful for what they did; otherwise, he would never have received the education he did, in the Jesuit order, which he joined at the age of 19 at an international house of studies in India. He did his theology in Naples—close to the action at Vatican II during the early 1960s, when he and his classmates often entertained some of the Council's leading theologians, such as the German Jesuit Karl Rahner. Pieris remembers his last encounter with Karl Rahner and Rahner's exact words: "Vatican II is not an end, but a beginning. You have to take its liberating message out to your people, translate it for them, and help spell out its implications in the context of their lives."[172]

For the past many years, Pieris has been trying to do exactly that. After finishing his Jesuit training, he returned to Sri Lanka for doctoral studies in Buddhist philosophy at the University of Sri Lanka's Vidyodaya campus in Colombo, the first priest ever to win a doctorate there in Buddhist philosophy. At the time, in the late 1960s and early 1970s, revolution was in the air and Pieris studied with the rambunctious youth in Sri Lanka's cradle of revolution—the university campus—to watch them grow from the unthinking tools of others into adult actors in their own futures. Then the Jesuit general, Fr. Pedro Arrupe, snatched him up to teach Buddhism at the Jesuits' Gregorian University in Rome and, during the Roman summers, at another Jesuit training ground in Manila, the East Asian Pastoral Institute.

When Pieris returned to Sri Lanka two years later, he felt called to cross-fertilise the socialist concerns of his student friends with their own authentic Buddhist roots. In 1974, after two years of discernment and prayer and consultation with his superiors, he founded his Tulana Centre, "as a kind of laboratory where they could feel at home and deepen themselves in their own orientation." Pieris has continued to deepen his own knowledge about the sources of Buddhism. Working with its prime original texts in Pali and other Asian languages, Pieris has gone on to publish a number of learned commentaries on Buddhism, and his Buddhist library at the Tulana Centre is now a place where Buddhist scholars come to read, reflect and confer with him. But Pieris would not call himself a Buddhist. "I am critically loyal to the church," he says. "I have a deep faith in Jesus Christ."

Aloysius Pieris' famous book is *An Asian Theology of Liberation*. He collected materials from a number of journals, which deal with the interrelation between Asian poverty, religiosity and the development of an authentically Asian theology and faith. The book is classified into three parts. The first part examines the relationship between spirituality and secular action. The second part addresses the need for and method of developing an indigenous theology of Asia. The last part gives an outline of such a theology. Pieris says that all the church's formulas are culturally conditioned. As human constructs, they are relative, time-bound and culturally limited expressions of faith that cannot be used as absolute norms for measuring orthodoxy. For Pieris, dogmas are not divinely revealed at all but guiding statements that serve the believing community as practical aids to foster and fructify our faith and hope in God who is love.

Asian Church

For Pieris claimed that Asian theology is derived from the practice of religion. Spirituality, which should be intimately involved with the concerns of the culture, is not then the conclusion of theology but theology's starting point. In an Asian context, this requires a living involvement with Asian culture, one that creates a radical empathy with the central realities of Asian life, identified by Pieris as 'overwhelming poverty' and a 'multifaceted religiousness.' Paul F. Knitter commented that the local churches in Asia are strongly criticised by Pieris for failing to be local churches of Asia. Drawing on the example of Jesus in beginning his public ministry by humbly following John the Baptist, Pieris argues that the Asian church must immerse itself in the baptismal waters of Asian culture, losing itself in order to gain itself. So in asking Asian Christians to be immersed in the culture of Asia, Pieris is asking for nothing less than their immersion in non-Christian soteriologies, so that genuine Asian Christologies may be developed. Furthermore, and more controversially, his claim is that the soteriological nucleus of Asian religions is the only door for Christian kerugma. In support of such an uncompromising demand on Asian Christians, Pieris' choice of Jesus as precedent is deliberate. His is the only possible authority for the scope of what Pieris is demanding. Pieris claims that the Asian church cannot rely on the theological idiom and authority of Rome to gauge the orthodoxy of the theology it will develop.

Pieris is right to affirm that a liturgy separated from the day-to-day struggles of its members is a liturgy that has lost touch with the struggle and death of Christ and his kingdom of justice, which the sacraments in fact symbolise. He is also right to stress the importance—the 'vital nucleus'—of the liberation of the poor and oppressed in the Gospel, as the many references to Mammon and 'the poor' in the Gospels testify. But calling the story of Jesus 'preeminently' the story of a God acting for the poor is to swing the pendulum too far in the other direction. It contradicts his earlier, more balanced view of a mutual enveloping of liturgy, spirituality and secular action, arising from the realisation that each is a mode of perceiving the same mystery of redemption.

Asian Christ

The boundaries of this orthodoxy are pushed, but not crossed, in respect of the feature identified as central to an Asian consciousness—religiosity. Pieris has a progressive interpretation of Vatican II's position on Christ working within other religions. Pieris claims that inculturation in an Asian context must address and involve both poverty and religiosity. It is 'enreligionization' as well as 'inculturation.' This is because Asian religion is inseparably interfused with life and philosophy. Whereas Roman theology applied Greek philosophy but rejected Greek paganism, such a separation would be impossible in Asia. To ignore Asian religiosity in forming a local theology is described as colonial cultural arrogance. And to simply pluck out elements of Asian religion without regard for their soteriological matrix is identified as a subtle 'crypto-colonialism.'[173]

While recognising that religion can have an enslaving as well as a liberating side, Pieris points to the triune mystery of salvation at the heart of many religious cultures, i.e., the 'beyond' entering within the individual, salvific mediation and a human capacity for salvation. This religious urge inside all people, which for Pieris is equivalent to the urge to create a new humanity, must be given its own voice in its search for Christ—a voice not necessarily delimited by Western terminology. As an example, Christianity must make use of the psychological tools of introspection that Eastern sages have discovered. At this point, it is unclear what side of the somewhat greying borderline Pieris sits on inclusivism and acceptance of diverse idioms, or a pluralism of different essences. But despite the radicalism of the theological method Pieris is advocating, his aim, in his own words, is simply to allow Asians to express the Asian discovery of Christ.

Dogmas
Pieris goes right to the heart of the Ratzinger agenda with a gentle attack on the very notion of dogmatic definitions themselves, pieces of legalism that owe more to Roman law than to the loving words of Jesus and his followers in the early years of Christianity. "Faith", he writes, "began to be judged, and the deviants condemned, entirely on the basis of one's adherence to the formula of faith' as defined by church authorities. The result is a set of faith propositions that parallel a legal code and that seem to call for an efficient monitoring system that is run by a powerful clerical class armed with massive punitive powers.

The church, says Pieris, should have known better from its own history. "The history of the Christological dogmas is not an edifying story of an innocuous development of a teaching; it is a sad story of serious misunderstandings, punctuated by political intrigues and physical violence." He cites the Council of Chalcedon, which condemned the Patriarch of Alexandria in 451. Fifteen centuries later, Pope Pius XII revoked the condemnation in 1951 with an encyclical that admitted confusion over some vocabulary. Formulas, says Pieris, often do more harm than good, especially if those formulas are asserted as "coming from Divine Revelation." The reader cannot help being impressed by Pieris' attack on Mammon, acquisitiveness and a capitalism thriving on waste and want. Pieris critiques both Marxism and capitalism as failing the Asian culture. There is also a challenge to the Buddhist monastery, which, while advocating voluntary poverty, does so without the biblical co-requisite of giving to the poor. Although one may disagree with some aspects of the book, this is perhaps inevitable from a book that issues a powerful and prophetic challenge to both Western and other third-world theologies.

Ludovic Lado

Ludovic Lado SJ is from Cameroon, Africa. He entered the Society of Jesus in 1992 and was ordained priest in 2002. His training took him to several African countries and to the USA. He did doctoral study in social anthropology at Campion Hall, Oxford, with a focus on the anthropology of culture and religion. Ludovic Lado teaches in the Faculty of Social Sciences and Management of the Catholic University of Central Africa in Yaounde, Cameroon.

He wrote *Catholic Pentecostalism and the Paradoxes of Africanization* in 2009. Through an ethnographic study of localising processes in a Charismatic movement in Cameroon and Paris, the book critically explores the dialectics between 'Pentecostalization' and 'Africanization' within contemporary African Catholicism. It appears that both processes pursue, although for different purposes, the missionary policy of dismantling local cultures and religions: practices and discourses of Africanisation dissect them in search of 'authentic' African values; Charismatic ritual, on the other hand, features the dramatisation of the defeat of local deities and spirits by Christianity. The anthropological literature on religious innovation and resistance in African Christianity has tended to focus almost exclusively on what have come to be known as African Independent Churches. Very few anthropological studies have looked at similar processes within mission churches.

Inculturation

He says that some Portuguese pioneers in the sixteenth century reached sub-Saharan Africa during the 1800s. When they arrived, they were confronted with two major religious forces: African religions and Islam. But in the areas where they settled, the Islamic influence was not generally strong; it was African religions that were holding together the social and political fabric. Roman Catholics have been encouraged to think in positive terms about other religions since Vatican II, and in particular since the publication of *Nostra acetate*, the Council's 'Declaration on the Relation of the Church to non-Christian Religions ' In the African context, the effect has been to promote what is called 'inculturation': the attempt to discern the so-called 'authentic' African values or symbols and to assimilate these within the version of Christianity received from Western missionaries. For there is no clear demarcation between African cultures and African religions, the process of 'inculturation' should be essentially 'interreligious.' For him, early Christian missionary activity in Africa was both ethnocentric and iconoclastic in its attitudes towards African religion. Evangelisation was seen as liberation from a state of absolute awfulness, and the picture of unredeemed Africa was often painted in colours as gruesome as possible, the better to encourage missionary zeal at home. In historical context, such attitudes are all too easily understandable. Firstly, the missionaries were children of that particular age. Early travellers' accounts were 'based on inaccurate information and cultural prejudice.' The heroic commitment of Christian missionaries not only to the preaching of the gospel but also to the implantation of schools and hospitals was part of this general programme of elevating the 'primitive' African to the level of the 'civilized' Westerner.

Ludovic says that the 'positive values' of African religions are portrayed as 'semina Verbi', as 'preparation for the gospel.' And it is in this context that Ecclesia in Africa speaks of a version of inculturation. It is by looking at the mystery of the incarnation and of the redemption that the values and counter values of cultures are to be discerned. Just as the Word of God became like us in everything but sin, so too the inculturation of the good news takes on all authentic human values, purifying them from sin and restoring to them their full meaning. Despite all the ambiguities in the idea of inculturation and despite the ambivalence that the Church's teaching authority seems to show, some African theologians are making creative attempts to build bridges between African religions and Christianity. The gospel message does not change. Inculturation is indeed a difficult attempt to marry culture, which is always in motion, with the message of Christ ('Love God and love your neighbour'), which will never change. Given culture's susceptibility to change, the product of any attempt at inculturation is bound to be an unstable mixture. Jesus simply went around preaching the gospel and loving both Jews and non-Jews; we occasionally find him admiring the faith of the so-called pagans (Luke 7:9; Matthew 15:28).

African Religions
Ludovic Lado used the term "African religions" instead of the usual "African traditional religion." He says that the conventional term gives quite a wrong impression that we are dealing with something impervious to the upheavals of history, whereas African religions are in fact as dynamic as any other religion. Moreover, there are many forms of religion in Africa. Though there are some common factors, African religions vary according to whether it is farming, coastal or forest people who are practising them. Though there are similarities between these religions, it is wrong to lump them together disparagingly as 'fetishism' or 'animism.' Evolutionist

theories presented African religions as primitive, merely the first stage of the evolution of human religious history; and such ways of thinking remain influential long after they have become discredited among scholars. Christianity itself was being challenged and disrupted in the nineteenth century by rationalism and secularism. It was therefore on the defensive, and not in a position to be open to dialogue with religious 'otherness.' For him, the evangelisation of sub-Saharan Africa took place within the context of colonisation. For all the benefits it brought, it was essentially a violent enterprise. Missionary societies tended to work in areas where their home governments were directly involved. Indeed, in the nineteenth century, Christianity reached black Africa as part of the Western campaign of 'civilization' meant to 'redeem' the 'dark continent' from the claws of ignorance and devilish superstition.

African religions are certainly not dead. But they have been destabilised, first by colonial forces and more recently by globalisation; and they are desperately seeking new anchorages. In many places, what remains of them today are mere bits and pieces of beliefs and practices that have somehow survived into the postcolonial context. When African nations first became independent, there was much talk about restoring the 'authenticity' of African cultures disrupted by colonial forces. But the reality was more a matter of the political legitimation of bloody dictators, as violent as the colonial regimes they were replacing. There was little genuine concern about collective identities. It is very difficult to identify the real representatives of African religions, who could indeed act as partners in a dialogue with Christianity. In rural areas, they may have remained fairly influential, but in the cities, their credibility has been seriously undermined by money-minded charlatans commercialising bits and pieces of rituals in the name of African traditions.

Interreligious Dialogue
According to Ludovic Lado, equality, which is a presupposition of interreligious dialogue, refers to the equal personal dignity of the parties in dialogue, not to doctrinal content, nor even less to the position of Jesus Christ in relation to the founders of the other religions. To date, the most important document of the magisterium featuring a statement about dialogue between Catholicism and African. With regard to African traditional religion, a serene and prudent dialogue will be able, on the one hand, to protect Catholics from negative influences that condition the way of life of many of them and, on the other hand, to foster the assimilation of positive values such as belief in a Supreme Being who is

Eternal, Creator, Provident and Just Judge, values that are readily harmonised with the content of the faith. They can even be seen as a preparation for the Gospel, because they contain precious *semina Verbi* (seeds of the Word) that can lead, as already happened in the past, a great number of people 'to be open to the fullness of Revelation in Jesus Christ through the proclamation of the Gospel.' The adherents of African traditional religion should therefore be treated with great respect and esteem, and all inaccurate and disrespectful language should be avoided. For this purpose, suitable courses in African traditional religion should be given in houses of formation for priests and religious.

Here there is at least talk of respect, but it is still Christianity that is determining the conversation. Ludovic Lado says that the dialogue envisaged here has to be 'serene' and 'prudent' in order that Catholics be protected against 'negative influences' associated with African religions. The dialogue's aim is not so much to foster mutual understanding and mutual enrichment as to discern and assimilate the positive values of African religions; and 'positive' here means 'in harmony with Christianity.' Early Western missionaries in Africa struggled to learn the local languages that were without alphabets. Some developed an alphabet, and then the very first dictionaries of African languages appeared, all of which led to translations of the Bible and of catechisms and of hymnals. Because language is the home of culture, these translations blended not only different languages but also different cultures or cosmologies. Missionaries had to find African words suitable for the translation of Christian concepts such as God, Holy Spirit, Jesus Christ, angels and saints. Speculation in African religions makes it very difficult to envisage a genuine doctrinal dialogue between them and Catholicism. It is African theologians who are the ones dissecting these rituals and beliefs, and then making theories out of them for the purpose of developing an African Christian theology. The enterprise is surely highly questionable; it amounts to imposing on these religions an intellectualist attitude proper to Christianity. There is some danger that the current fashion for inculturation and assimilation may be masking just another disguised form of cultural violence. But perhaps there are other reasons why 'dialogue' is not a realistic term for describing Christianity's engagement with African religions and cultures today. In the current post-colonial context, it is quite difficult to identify who it is and with whom Christianity can undertake any dialogue. It is no easy matter to locate African religions today; moreover, postcolonial Africans have very complex attitudes towards them.

Conclusion

Roman Catholicism faced a lot of challenges down through the centuries from inside and outside the Catholic Church. Anyway, it deserves appreciation for famous Christian philosophers like St. Augustine, Thomas Aquinas and Anselm who had given valuable contributions to the field of Christian philosophy. Their thoughts seriously affected the theologians and philosophers of all ages after them. But these philosophers interpreted the Bible according to the prevalent Roman Catholic teaching and were not ready to correct the wrong teachings and practices of the Catholic Church. That is why famous Christian philosophers like Martin Luther protested against the evil practices of the Church. Roman Catholicism led the Church into darkness, and the church had its history of 'Dark Ages' from fourth century to fifteen century AD. Even after that period of time, the world was developed at all levels and the people in all spheres of life improved a lot. The Church went through the 'age of Enlightenment.' Science improved a lot. Human reason affected all fields of thoughts. People began to think and decided to develop in all respective areas. But still the Roman Catholic Church leads her adherents in the darkness by way of allowing them to worship the idols, pray to the saints, worship Mary and other saints, etc. Millions of innocent members in the Catholic Church are led astray and kept away from the real Christian faith of the Holy Bible.

Liberal Christian Philosophy

Liberalism is a thorough-going adaptation of Christian theology to the modern world. Liberals are prepared to sacrifice many elements of traditional Christian orthodoxy in their search for contemporary relevance. Although there were challenges, until the eighteenth century the theology of the churches remained predominantly orthodox. During the period from 1500 to 1800, theological debate took place mainly within different Confessions of the Church. This was the period of Confessional theology. But during the nineteenth and twentieth centuries, the picture has altered significantly. The Christian faith has faced a wide range of challenges, especially rationalism, science, historical criticism and secularisation. All of these changes have profoundly challenged Christian theology. Underlying them is the rejection of authority.

Schleiermacher

Friedrich Ernst Daniel Schleiermacher (1768-1834) was born on November 21, 1768, in Breslau, Lower Silesia (Poland). Despite his being the son of a reformed clergyman, Schleiermacher studied under the Moravian Brethren, gaining from them an appreciation for the Latin and Greek classics and a strong sense of religious life.

His Achievements

In 1787, he entered the University of Halle, where he studied the philosophies of Aristotle and Immanuel Kant. After his ordination in 1794, he accepted a position as a Reformed preacher in Berlin. There he mingled with German romantic philosophers, became a friend of Friedrich von Schlegel and began a translation of the works of Plato. He became a professor in the Humboldt University of Berlin.

James Richmond wrote that Schleiermacher was a German preacher and philosopher, who is regarded as a leading 19th-century theologian of the Protestant church. He is the first great protestant post-Kantian theologian. He lived in an age when there was danger of Christianity being dismissed by educated people as irrelevant and meaningless.[174] His book *Speeches to its cultural Despisers* (1799) speaks more of religion and *the Christian Faith* (1821) speaks more about systematic theology.[175] His other writings include *The Soliloquies* (1800), *Christmas Eve* (1806) and *Brief Outline of the Study of Theology* (1811).

His Philosophy

He endeavoured to analyse religious experience and extract from it the essence of religion. Having done this, he could then reinterpret the Christian faith in terms that were acceptable to modern man, whether he be inside or outside the church. Religion involves all kinds of things. There are religious acts like taking part in worship and doing good. There is also an element of knowledge that may be classified under the general heading of theology. Schleiermacher concluded that the essence of religion was neither activity nor knowledge but something common to both.[176] In other words, we are not to think of Jesus as the God man of Christian orthodoxy, the divine Word, who took human nature upon himself. For him, Jesus was a man who walked so closely with God that you could say that God dwelled in him. The redemptive work of Jesus was to assume 'believers into the power of His God-consciousness.' It was not to bear their sins on their behalf, but so to move men that 'His motive principle becomes ours also. Sin, for Schleiermacher, is that which disturbs our sense of absolute dependence, the desire to be free when we should be at one with God.[177] Schleiermacher is attempting to be empirical in his approach, rejecting abstract speculation in favour of analysis of religious experience. The difficulty is not that he was too empirical, but that he was not empirical enough.

All this raises the vital question of philosophical method. Schleiermacher approaches the Christian faith in the light of his general worldview, armed with certain rigid principles of interpretation. Karl Barth commented that Schleiermacher did not begin a school, rather an era. He is not only the founder of the liberal school of theology but of the whole of modern theology. This liberal optimism received a hard knock in the First World War, which gave birth to the neo-orthodox reaction of Barth and others. Karl Barth severely criticised Liberal Theology as it opposed the sound biblical teaching. Liberal theologians like Schleiermacher applied human wisdom to interpret wrongly the word of God, instead of dividing the word of God rightly. They do not believe in the miracles, virgin birth and the biblical concept of the sacrificial death of Jesus Christ.

Albrecht Ritschl

Albrecht Ritschl (1822-1889) was born in Berlin as the son of a Lutheran pastor, who later became a Bishop. He was a German Protestant philosopher who founded one of the most influential schools of modern theology.

His Background

Born in Berlin, Ritschl studied philosophy and theology at the universities of Bonn, Halle, Heidelberg and Tubingen. He was professor of theology at Bonn (1846-1864) and at the University of Gottingen from 1864 until his death. His major work was *The Christian Doctrine of Justification and Reconciliation* (1870-74) and three volumes of *History of Pietism* (1880-86), a movement of which he disapproved. He followed in the Liberal Tradition pioneered by Schleiermacher.[178]

Ritschlian Philosophy

Ritschl's Christian philosophy was characterised by an emphasis on history and a rejection of metaphysics. He was highly influenced by the 18th-century German philosopher Immanuel Kant. Ritschl associated religious faith and doctrines with judgments of value rather than of fact. The crucial Christian doctrines for Ritschl were those of redemption, or the atonement, and the kingdom of God, which he understood in ethical terms as the fellowship of human beings realised through mutual love. Ritschl accordingly stressed the ethical Christian life, which can be attained only within the community of faith founded by Christ. Ritschl had based his concepts on Christian experience. For him, Christian theology is to be based in God's revelation in Jesus Christ, recorded in the New Testament. Ritschl's opposition to individualism and subjectivism also emerges in his stress on the communal side of Christianity. Ritschl stresses that Christian salvation is experienced only in the fellowship of the church, because Christianity can be experienced only within a living community. One cannot be a Christian in solitary isolation. He was against Greek Philosophy and its adaptation by the Church Fathers. Ritschl commented that the early Church Fathers had corrupted Christianity by importing Greek Philosophy into it and turned the God of the Bible into the absolute of the philosophers, and the Jesus of the Gospels into the 'eternal Word' (logos) of Greek Platonism.[179] Ritschl denied the doctrine of the original sin and commented that it is possible to lead a life without sin. For him, there is no wrath of God against sin and the reconciliation brought by Jesus Christ is essentially a change in our attitude to God, not vice versa. While speaking on Jesus deity, he meant that Jesus had a perfect humanity.

Ritschl was deeply concerned about ethics and his whole thought has a moral way of thinking. He interpreted the kingdom of God largely in terms of a moral unification of the human race through love. His teaching on the kingdom of God stimulated the rise of the 'Social Gospel.' He was the most influential of the nineteenth century Liberals, and the Ritschlian School was very strong in the latter part of the century and in the beginning of the next.

Ritschl became infamous for his claim that theological statements are value judgments, rather than theoretical judgments. Also, it specially noted that he was against the works of the Church Fathers who tried to similarise Christianity with the Greek philosophy. Ritschl, as a Liberal theologian, was a critical thinker and most of his teachings are against the biblical teaching.

M. M. Thomas

Madathilparampil Mammen Thomas (1916-1996) was a renowned Indian Christian theologian, social thinker and activist. He is known as the spokesman of the liberal theology of the Eastern world. He also served as the Chairperson of the Central Committee of World Council of Churches (1968-1975). He was conferred with the honorary doctorate degree by the University of Uppsala in 1978. M. M. Thomas is a crucial theologian in his own right. He is not only the most experienced among the liberal Indian thinkers but also the one who has read most and written most. His ecumenical activities took him all over the globe. His understanding of society, revolution and ideology was stabilised mainly in connection with his preparation for and contribution in this conference.

Background

Thomas was born on May 15, 1916, at Kozhencherry, Kerala, India. Thomas was the eldest of the nine children to his parents. He had a Christian upbringing at home and maintained strong Christian convictions and ideals. It was this Christocentric upbringing confronted with the demands of a pluralistic society and secular politics that produced M. M. Thomas. Soon after obtaining his degree in 1935, he accepted the post of teacher at Ashramam High School, a school run by the Mar Thoma Church. In 1937, instead of taking a lucrative job, he went to Trivandrum, the capital of Kerala, and started an orphanage there. He was influenced by Indian Independence and the Marxist movement.

The vehicle of his ministry was the ecumenical movement in India and abroad. M. M. Thomas was the first full time Organizing Secretary of Yuvajana Sakhyam (the youth wing of the Mar Thoma Church from 1945-47. By self-education he became a theologian and was later involved in the ecumenical movement. He became the Student Christian Movement secretary in Madras and Youth Secretary of the Mar Thoma Church. In 1941, he was instrumental in defining the social creed for the Mar Thoma Students' Organisation, which also became the social manifesto of the church. From 1947 to 1952, he served on the staff of the World Student Christian Federation in Geneva, with special emphasis on Christian political witness. Returning from Geneva in 1952, he threw himself into social work and joined with India's leading theologian, P. D. Devanandan from 1957 in the Christian Institute for the Study of Religion and Society, which he served first as Associate Director and then, upon Devanandan's death, as Director until his retirement in 1976. He took part in the First Assembly of the World Council of Churches in 1948 and in the formation of the Council's Department of Church and Society, of which he became an active member and chairman from 1961 to 1968. In this capacity, he also chaired the World Conference on Church and Society at Geneva in 1966. From 1968 to 1975, he served as Chairman of the Central Committee of the World Council of Churches itself, guiding it through some of the stormiest years of its history. Between 1980 and 1987, M. M. Thomas served as guest professor of Ethics, Mission, and Ecumenics at Princeton Theological Seminary.

His Major Works

His theological output, as already mentioned, is unbelievably great. Besides nearly 1,000 articles, he has written several books and contributed or edited many more. All of his books highly influenced the theological circle of the past and even today. Here is a list of his important books: (1) The acknowledged Christ of the Indian Renaissance (1969), (2) Risking Christ for Christ's Sake, (3) Nagas towards 2000, (4) My Ecumenical Journey—1947-75 (1990), (5) Response to Tyranny, (6) Man and the Universe of Faiths, (7) The Christian in the World's Struggle, (8) Salvation and Humanization, (9) The Christian Response to the Asian Revolution, (10) Christian Participation in Nation Building, (11) Secularism in India and the Secular Meaning of Christ and (12) Towards a Theology of Contemporary Ecumenism.

He produced a large and diverse literature of his own, in his native Malayalam and English, on themes as diverse as *Man in the Universe of Faiths, Secular Ideologies and the Secular Meaning of Christ, The Christian Response to the Asian Revolution; Meditations of the Realization of the Cross*, and a series of Bible studies for the church in Kerala. It also did not prevent him from opposing, at serious risk of arrest and imprisonment, Indira Gandhi's suspension of democracy in 1976. This led indirectly to his appointment as governor of the largely Christian state of Nagaland in North East India in 1991, a state with a large number of Christians. Due to his disagreement with the Government of India he resigned in 1993. He lived at Manjadi, Tiruvalla. He died on December 3, 1996.

Philosophy of M. M. Thomas

He rejected both evangelism and the exclusive claims of Christianity, arguing that 'love is at the heart of universe' and in love we need not pressurise one another to change one's convictions. This impossible attempt of Thomas to reconcile the spirit of Christ to the Marxist-Leninist ideology has remained the most dominant characteristic of his life and thought throughout. The theology of M. M. Thomas, a leading non-Dalit Indian Christian philosopher of the twentieth century, offered significant signposts for the emergence and development of the Dalit Christian community. While it is clear that he could not construct a Dalit theology, this thesis argues that Thomas's philosophical reflections in the midst of a rapidly changing and pluralistic religio-secular Indian context brought to the fore of theological debate essential questions relating to the concept of salvation, humanisation and justice relevant to the emergence of Dalit Christian philosophy. Seeking to relate Christology to the Indian context dynamically, M. M. Thomas sought a theology that could be 'challengingly relevant' to the people of India in the post-Independent search for a just and equal society.

It is necessary to have a look at his method. With an astounding consistency, Thomas starts with the world. He looks at the world, analyses what is happening in it and tries to understand what the Christian solution can be. Thus the first step in his ideology is what can be called a contextual or situational approach. Since it speaks only to those issues that are relevant, that becomes a selective theology, and since the human situation is the starting point, his theology asks for pluralistic answers. Apparently, this sounds as if his theology lacks the power of conviction. One also gets that feeling that his theology is not only empirical, but also quite fragmentary, which he himself admits. His theology is action-oriented. Like the liberation theologians of Latin America, he places praxis before orthodoxy. He finds the basis for this in the New Testament: as 'faith working through love.' It is for this reason that Boyd labels Thomas' theology as 'The Way of Action.'

Christ-centred Syncretism

Continuing on the revolutions, Thomas says there must be a fundamental change in our understanding of human spirituality. He is not so much concerned about human nature or person or spirit but spirituality, which he defines as 'the way in which man, in the freedom of his self-transcendence, seeks a structure of ultimate meaning and sacredness', the goal being self-realisation through involvement in history. His contention is that for our age of revolutions an adequacy must be sought in open secularism. The goal of such ideology, as of revolutions, is a responsible world society; in other words, either the kingdom of God or the Marxian classless society. Since religion is a most potent source for strife in the world it does not help towards a classless society. So there must be a need for inter-religious dialogue. And so he comes up with his famous 'Christ-centred syncretism', which means conversion not of individuals but of the whole religious systems to Christ. And so, ultimately, all religions and ideologies will be found in Christ. In talking of Christ's incarnation, Thomas is concerned not so much about God becoming man but rather about two aspects—since Jesus is a man born in particular time in history, for him the incarnation means the validation of man as the method of God and history as the arena of God's action. M. M. Thomas interprets salvation in terms of humanisation by which man finds his true humanness, which has been oppressed by social injustice, war and poverty.

His view of salvation is very much horizontal-oriented towards humanity at the expense of the vertical relationship with God.[180]

In 'Revolution as Revelation: A Study of M. M. Thomas's Theology' (1984) by Sunand Sumithra, we see few comments on Thomas' ideology.[181] Sumithra commented that M. M. Thomas attempted to reconcile a philosophy of continuous dynamic evolution, Marxist-Leninist ideology and Hindu spirituality, on the one hand, with the biblical revelation, on the other, tends ultimately to deprive God of his holiness, Jesus Christ of his lordship and man of his faith, primarily because Thomas neglects the unique character of the Bible.' Thomas wrote that when the Christian Church speaks of the 'original sin' it means that this self-centricity is a fact for all men in all conditions of society, so that self-interest and self-righteousness are perennially present in man's life. According to Sumithra, the original sin, for Thomas, means universality of sin, not that every single individual is a sinner. When Thomas wrote that Paul sees in the risen Christ 'the first fruits' of the re-creation of humanity, the inauguration of a movement through which Christ establishes his reign over all rule and authority. Thomas writes: "God must be worshipped through Jesus Christ as an essential part of the community life." Sumithra made comments again: "Thus, Jesus being God-for-man in Thomas's thinking, he takes a place similar to that of a demiurge."

Church and Mission
The Church's mission is primarily one of humanisation and not of salvation. Salvation or redemption is only one aspect of humanisation, catering to the inward or to the spiritual aspects of mankind. The recipients of Christian mission are not individuals anymore but structures such as cultures, religions and ideologies. The method is no more proclamation, but now it is participation or as he calls it the confession of participation. The bearers are no more the called and sent missionaries, but rather organisations or the churches that do the work. He has enough to say why the verbal communication of the gospel is utterly inadequate for our time. So he comes to the conclusion that evangelism in our time equals service. Unless the church exercises its prophetic ministry of constructive criticism, the priestly ministry of the suffering servant, it has lost its salt. Following from here he goes on to give details of the task the church has in several areas of national and international life—the political, the economic, the cultural, the social, the religious, etc.

Critical Remarks

- Evidently, the ideology, we have outlined thus far, is very much a political or sociological history of man. This is to the credit of Thomas, for he does not see the spiritual aspect of man isolated but in its integral relations with all other aspects. Thomas has tried to reconcile the biblical revelation with three systems: Marxist ideology, Hindu spirituality and process philosophy, but he has failed in bringing this reconciliation.

- He has so failed because the character of the biblical revelation is entirely different from the other three systems. Since he has attempted this impossible amalgamation, his theology ultimately ends up in one or all of the following results: Either God's holiness as given in the Bible will be rejected, or the personal lordship of Christ will be rejected, or faith as the connection between God and man will be rejected.

- Following from such an understanding of God, Christ, man and the world, Thomas' philosophy inevitably leads to political action.

- There is a basic lack in his approach to the scriptural revelation—he has tried to find revelation in the revolutions. Thomas has done very little exegesis in all his theological writings. His writings are more philosophical, sociological, ideological or political, but almost never have biblical support. Raising history and scientific expertise to the level of the scriptures in authority he has diluted the scriptures radically.

John Mbiti

John Samuel Mbiti was born in Kenya on 30 November 1931. He is a Christian religious philosopher. His field of studies and his close contact with ecumenism made him one of the famous Liberal Christian philosophers. He is an ordained Anglican priest, and as of 2005, a canon. Mbiti studied in Uganda and the United States, taking his doctorate in 1963 at University of Cambridge, UK. John Mbiti taught Theology and Religion for many years at Makerere University in Uganda. After that he served as Director of the Ecumenical Institute Bossey, of the World Council of Churches near Geneva, Switzerland. He has been Visiting Professor at many universities in Europe, America, Canada and Australia and has travelled widely in many countries. Professor Mbiti has published over 400 articles, reviews and books on theology, religion, philosophy, African oral traditions and literature. Mbiti is Emeritus Professor at University of Bern and Parish Minister to the town of Burgdorf, Switzerland.

His Works

Mbiti's research interests include theology in Africa and Asia and ecumenism. He has also collaborated on a book of African proverbs, collected from across the continent. Mbiti's seminal book, *African Religions and Philosophy* (1969), was the first work to significantly challenge Christian assumptions that traditional African religious ideas were 'demonic and anti-Christian.' African Religions and Philosophy is a systematic study of the attitudes of mind and belief that have evolved in the many societies of Africa. In this second edition, Dr. Mbiti has updated his material to include the involvement of women in religion and the potential unity to be found in what was once thought to be a mass of quite separate religions. Mbiti's *African Religions and Philosophy* is a great addition to Philosophy.

He wrote many books and hundreds of articles. A list of the books is given below: *The Akamba Stories* (1966), *Poems of Nature and Faith* (1969), *African Religions and Philosophy* (1969), *Concepts of God in Africa* (1970), *New Testament Eschatology in an African Background* (1971), *Love and Marriage in Africa* (1973), *Introduction to African Religion* (1991), *The Prayers of African Religion* (1975), *Bible and Theology in African Christianity* (1987) and *African Proverbs* (1997).

African Religion

Without the African religion, Christianity would not have made impact on religious landscape of Africa. African religious systems are a complete system. There is no section of African life that is not touched by religion. People practice differently in different places, but there is enough commonality to call it singular. Religion is found in all areas of human life. It has dominated the thinking of African peoples to such an extent that it has shaped their cultures, their social life, their political organisations and economic activities. We can say, therefore, that religion is closely bound up with the traditional way of African life, while at the same time, this way of life has shaped religion as well.[182] Mbiti's *Introduction to African Religion* provides an excellent overview of the native religion in Africa. It also offers a useful and up-to-date list of books for more advanced reading, questions for each chapter and a collection of wise sayings to illustrate the oral tradition. The comprehensiveness of the treatment of where the African religion is found, the discussion of its god, spirits and cosmology and of how human life is related to the religion make this book especially helpful to those familiar only with religions having sacred scriptures. The African religion dominated the religious scene from ancient times. No religious vacuum existed when Christianity arrived. Thus, African belief in God existed before the arrival of missionaries. *Missionaries did not bring God to Africa, rather it was God who brought the missionaries here.* African religiosity was very receptive to the Christian message and enabled the message to make sense, to sink into spiritual soil. The new element was the naming of Jesus Christ as messenger of God in whom Africans believed already.

People pay attention to Jesus as the Messenger and Son of the same God. So, they can claim Jesus Christ to be on their side since he reveals the God they already knew. Jesus is the radical person or element that merges biblical revelation with insights from the African religion. Jesus Christ introduces a radical new dimension. According to Mbiti, Africans can claim Jesus to be on their side, since he reveals a God that they knew all along. It is with that knowledge from the African religion that people can appropriate, sing and dance a Christian message. Even though he is not mentioned in African Traditional Religion, he is known and embraced. Jesus Christ finds a home among them, because he is a messenger of the same God their forefathers and mothers believed in. One thing is clear—African Christians have fallen in love with Christ.

Dialogue in the African World
The process is going on from the very first proclamation of Gospel in African languages through Bible translation. The Gospel found receptive and fertile spiritual soil in Africa; it germinated, grew and began to bear fruit. Through Bible translations, the African world entered the biblical world and vice-versa. The African world interprets the biblical world through its own terms, values and needs. The Bible was enormously translated into 718 African languages by 2008. For Mbiti, the use of religious vocabulary in translation, the Bible was made an African Bible and an African book. The Bible found a home in Africa and Africa found a home in the Bible. Using God's name in translations is immediate declaration of dialogue between the biblical world and the African religion. People identify themselves in the Bible. Further, they see the same God that they have been worshipping all along. Mbiti had collected some 1,700 names of God in African languages to use them in translating and teaching Christian signals and endorsing spontaneous dialogue. This means, *interalia*, the God in whom Africans believe from ancient times is the same God described in the Bible. Mbiti states that the Bible encounter is a

dialogue. Various translations of the Bible helped a lot for that dialogue. For Mbiti, prayer is an encounter and a dialogue. Christian spirituality is deeply shaped by spirituality of African religion. Praying merges the two worlds at a spiritual level, with the African religion asserting the strongest impact on Christianity. Prayer is offered with elements of adoration, praise, thanksgiving, dedication and confession of faith. Prayer is an encounter, a dialogue. People are simply standing before God with prayer.

Jesus Christ is signified as the Focus of Dialogue and Encounter. Jesus is a unique and crucial element that has landed on the African world through Christian Faith. He is not named as such in the African religion, but some of his teachings and activities are present in African life. Jesus of the Gospels is very 'visible and tangible': walking in the countryside, healing, exorcising, using parables drawn from daily life (family, sowing, sheep, etc.). Jesus is not a stranger. The Africans respond to him with a hearty welcome, endearment, respect and love. Christianity in Africa is built upon Person and Work of Jesus Christ. It is very Christological. African Christianity has put Jesus at both the centre and the peripherals. It has embraced classical and traditional Christology, but has added its own understanding of who Jesus Christ is. It is inevitable that most of the dialogue takes place around Jesus. Evangelisation is an exercise in dialogue. This happens both privately within the individual and publicly. It is in that way that Jesus Christ becomes a living reality. **Jesus Christ is the subject, African religiosity is the verb and the Gospel is the object.** Most of it is expressed orally and is not written down. It takes place in prayer. Some African theologians publish on Christology, now one of the most popular subjects.

Mbiti had collected a list of 165 Christological titles; although not every Christian uses these titles, they attempt to contextualise. These are spiritual and mental aids for identifying with Jesus Christ employed in songs, counseling, slogans and sermons in their homes and workplaces and in mass media. And in so naming, they establish a personal and living relationship with him. Many of these Christological symbols are symbolic and figurative. For the most part, lay people articulate these titles as they talk about the faith. They produce oral theology. Thus, this can be considered as public Christology.

Concept of God
In one case the thinking and experience of the people produced a written record of God's dealings with the Jewish people in particular. In the other

case, no such written record exists. But God's dealings with the African people are recorded; nevertheless, in living form—oral communication, rituals, symbols, ceremonies and community faith. The God, as described in the Bible, is none other than the God who is already known in the framework of our traditional African religiosity. The missionaries who introduced the gospel to Africa in the past 200 years did not bring God to our continent. Instead, God brought them. They proclaimed the name of Jesus Christ. But they used the names of the God who was and is already known by African peoples—such as Mungu, Mulungu, Katonda, Ngai, Olodumare, Asis, Ruwa, Ruhanga, Jok, Modimo, Unkulunkulu and many more. These were not empty names. They were names of one and the same God, the creator of the world, the father of our Lord Jesus Christ. One African theologian, Gabriel Setiloane, has even argued that the concept of God that the missionaries presented to the Sotho-Tswana peoples was a devaluation of the traditional currency of Modimo (God) among the Sotho-Tswana.

The basic truth seems to be that God's revelation is not confined to the biblical record. One important task is to see the nature, method and implications of God's revelation among African peoples, in the light of the biblical record of the same revelation. Revelation is given not in a vacuum but within particular historical experiences and reflections. When we identify the God of the Bible as the same God who is known through the African religion, we must also take it that God has had a historical relationship with African peoples. God is not insensitive to the history of peoples other than Israel. Their history has a theological meaning. His interpretation of Israel's history demands a new look at the history of African peoples, among whom this same God of Abraham, Isaac and Jacob has indeed been at work. In this case, the so-called 'salvation history' must widen its outreach in order to embrace the horizons of other peoples' histories.

African Church

It is in this complex of religiosity that the preaching of the gospel makes sense; it is this preparedness that has undergirded the spreading of the gospel like wildfire among African societies, which had hitherto followed and practiced traditional religion. Consequently, people are discovering that the biblical faith is not harmful to their religious sensibilities. A close geographical correlation exists between the location of the African religion and the rapid expansion of the Christian faith. This is not an empty coincidence. It is the southern two-thirds of Africa, which we can rightly call Christian Africa.

This rapid spreading of the Christian faith, where people have been predominantly followers of the African religion, provokes interesting questions. That which had been seen as the enemy of the gospel turns out to be indeed a very welcoming friend. The African religion has equipped people to listen to the gospel to discover meaningful passages in the Bible and to avoid unhealthy religious conflict.

African Theology
Theological development in Africa must inevitably grow within this religious setting. For this reason, some African theologians take African religiosity to be one of the sources of theological reflection. A conference of mainly African theologians, held in Ghana in December 1977, said in its final communique: "The God of history speaks to all peoples in particular ways. In Africa, the traditional religions are a major source for the study of the African experience of God. The beliefs and practices of the traditional religions in Africa can enrich Christian theology and spirituality.' These statements await further exploration by African theologians. Their culture, history, worldviews and spiritual aspirations of people who come out of the African religious background cannot be taken away from them. These impinge upon their daily life and experience of the Christian faith. So the Church that exists on the African scene bears the marks of its people's backgrounds.

According to Mbiti, no viable theology can grow in Africa without addressing itself to the interreligious phenomenon at work there. We should feel deeply the value of biblical studies in this exercise and the contribution of biblical insights in this development. Mbiti concentrated these comments on the role of African background in his theological reflection. There are other areas of exploration in which he continued to be engaged. There is no room to describe them, and he mentioned only two or three of them briefly. His doctoral studies in New Testament eschatology led him also to the field of Christology. Mbiti says that consequences for theological and ecclesiological developments are yet to be faced.

Conclusion
In liberal Christian teaching, which is not Christian at all, man's reason is stressed and is treated as the final authority. Liberal theologians seek

to reconcile Christianity with secular science and modern thinking. In doing so, they treat science as all-knowing and the Bible as fable-laden and false. The very idea of a revelation has been radically questioned—not just by unbelievers, but by theologians within the mainstream churches. In a sense, liberal theology became a threat to biblical Christianity. As a result of the reasoning by liberal theologians, the following doctrines are taught by liberal quasi-Christian theologians: (1) The Bible is not 'God-breathed and has errors. Belief that the Bible is inspired by God is neglected. This directly contradicts 2 Timothy 3:16-17. (2) The virgin birth of Christ is a mythological false teaching. This directly contradicts Isaiah 7:14 and Luke 2 ch. Jesus did not rise again from the grave in bodily form. This contradicts the resurrection accounts in all four Gospels and the entire New Testament. (3) No sacrificial death by Christ is necessary since a loving God would not send a person to such a place as hell and since man is not born in sin. This contradicts Jesus Himself, who declared himself to be the Way to God, through His atoning death (John 14:6). There are many pronouncements of Scripture against those who would deny the deity of Christ, (2 Peter 2:1; Gal. 1:8), which liberal Christianity does.

Neo-Orthodox Philosophy
Although British Evangelicals gave philosophy a wide berth, a number of independent thinkers on the Continent and in the United States were alive to the situation. The philosophy and faith in the twentieth century should be evaluated by looking at three important philosophers: Cornelius Van Til, Karl Barth and Francis Schaeffer. All are agreed that natural theology is a blind alley. It is wrong in both its conclusions and methods. They agree that the proper starting-point for thinking about God is God himself and his revelation. They differ, however, in the way that they work this out. Cornelius Van Til stands in the conservative tradition of Dutch Reformed theology. Van Til argued that natural theology leads to the idea of an impersonal first cause that falls far short of the living God of the Bible and experience. From Aristotle onwards secular philosophers and Christian philosophers who adopted their arguments have begun with the latter. The result is that, whether they are for or against God, they have been debating a figment of the human imagination. Christian thought must begin with the living, triune God who is perfect and self-contained.[183] Francis Schaeffer presents his philosophy as a belief-system. He does not demonstrate every single part of it, e.g. that there is a life after death. Such items of belief are unverified. Although clues to their meaningfulness may be picked up in this life, in the last analysis, they are accepted on the

Karl Barth

Karl Barth (1886-1968) was a Swiss Christian philosopher; he wrote the massive *Church Dogmatics*—unfinished at about six million words by his death in 1968. In 1921, Barth accepted a call to teach theo-logy at Gottingen. His book, *Commentary on Romans* (1919), was the best among all of his publications.[184] Barth emphasised the distinction between human thought and divine reality and that while humans may attempt to understand the divine, our concepts of the divine are never precisely aligned to the divine reality itself, although God reveals his reality in part through human language and culture. Barth strenuously disavowed being a philosopher; he considered himself a dogmatician of the Church and a preacher. Karl Barth was the most significant theologian of the twentieth century. His multivolume *Church Dogmatics* constitutes the weightiest contribution to Protestant theology.[185]

Knowledge of God

In terms of his account of the knowledge of God, Barth's confidence in the self-evidence of the object of theology leads him into a fideism, which refuses to offer any sort of bridges between the knowledge of revelation and knowledge of the human world. Barth sees God as utterly transcendent. He is not to be identified directly with anything in the World, not even with the words of Scripture. Revelation comes to men in the same way as a vertical line intersects a horizontal plane, or as a tangent touches a circle. For Barth, the knowledge of God is not something separate from the gospel of Jesus Christ. It is not something that man can arrive at just as he wishes by following certain subtle philosophical arguments. Knowledge of God is the result of encounter with God, which in turn is the result of encounter with Christ, for Christ is the revealing Word of God to man.[186]

Dialectical Theology

From 1921 to 1930, he taught in Gottingen and Munster, played a leading role in the so-called 'dialectical theology' movement and wrote prolifically. He also wrote an abortive prolegomena volume entitled, *Christian Dogmatics*.[187] Dialectical Theology certainly had something. It brought with it a vivid awareness of God and of man's inadequacy. But in the 1920s and 1930s, Barth came to realise that it was not the whole story.

Knowledge of God arises out of encounter with God. It is mediated by the Son. But according to the New Testament, there can be no knowledge of God without the illuminating work of the Holy Spirit.[188] Moreover, to make progress in the knowledge of God, it is not a matter of intellectual acuteness. The knowledge of God operates, as it were, on a different plane. Faith, love, humility and prayer matter the most.

Revelation
In the case of theology, encounter with God through revelation of the Word is primary. And in this sense, Barth argues, theology is a science. (a) Like all other so-called sciences, it is a human effort after a definite object of knowledge. (b) Like all other sciences, it follows a definite, self-consistent path of knowledge. (c) Like all other sciences, it is in the position of being accountable for this path to itself and to everyone. Reality is not shaped by our private likes and dislikes. Any philosophy worthy of the name must take into account things as they in fact are and not things as the private individual may like them to be. Barth became increasingly dismayed with the resource of his liberal theological education, and his gradual rediscovery of scripture as revelation eventually led to his explosive commentary on Romans.[189]

In response to the questions on how do we know God and what objective proof do we have, Barth replies that in the very nature of the case, there can be no 'objective' proof in the sense of external evidence from outside our encounter with the Word of God. The old-fashioned proofs of God's existence do not really lead to the living God. Natural theology is a futile enterprise. It is like trying to 'cook' a theorem in geometry by digging up proofs that do not really work. Encounter with God brings its own proof. Dismayed with the moral weakness of liberal theology, Barth plunged into a study of the Bible, especially Paul's Epistle to the Romans, to see what insights it could offer. It rocked the theological community. Liberal theologians gasped in horror and attacked Barth furiously, for in this and later works, he assaulted their easy optimism. In response to their amiable view of humankind, Barth wrote, "Men have never been good, they are not good, they will never be good." His theology came to be known as 'dialectical theology,' or 'the theology of crisis'; it blossomed into a school of theology known as neo-orthodoxy.

Dietrich Bonhoeffer
Dietrich Bonhoeffer (1906-1945) was born in Breslau (now in Poland) in 1906. He was a German Lutheran theologian. His life and thought had an

increasing influence on the church until his death. Bonhoeffer received his theological education at the universities of Tubingen and Berlin.[190]

His Works
After serving (1928-1929) as an assistant pastor in a German-speaking congregation in Barcelona, Spain, and a further year of study at Union Theological Seminary in New York City, he became a lecturer in theology in Berlin in the fall of 1931. Bonhoeffer joined the Confessing Church, which resisted the Nazi attempt to impose anti-Semitism on the church and society and became an outspoken opponent of Adolf Hitler and the Nazi regime on their rise to power in 1933. He left Berlin in protest and spent two years (1933-1935) as pastor of German-speaking congregations in London. Again Bonhoeffer became director of a seminary of the Confessing Church at Finkenwald, Pomerania, Germany, in 1935. This 'illegal' enterprise was eventually closed by the Gestapo in 1937. Many restrictions were imposed upon Bonhoeffer: He was forbidden to lecture in Berlin, to preach and finally, in 1941, to write or publish.[191] His most influential books have been *The Cost of Discipleship* (1937), *Life Together* (1939) and the posthumously edited *Letters and Papers from Prison* (1951). After the start of World War II, Bonhoeffer joined in the political resistance to Hitler that led to his imprisonment in April 1943 in Berlin and his death by hanging at the Nazi concentration camp at Flossenburg on April 9, 1945.

His Philosophy
Bonhoeffer is important for his ecumenism, his efforts towards world peace and his firm belief in the need for a reinterpretation of Christianity for the modern secular world. Bonhoeffer's proposal is a 'religionless Christianity'—that we should see Jesus Christ as the 'Lord of the religionless.' For him, the Christian today must learn to speak of God in a secular way. The believer must live a 'secular life' and thereby share in God's sufferings. It is not the religious act that makes the Christian, but participation in the sufferings of God in the secular life. In opposing religion, Bonhoeffer was following Barth, who greatly influenced him. He took Barth's negative approach of religion. In advocating a religionless Christianity, Bonhoeffer wishes to see Christianity purged of certain facets of bourgeois religiosity.[192]

Bonhoeffer commented that religion has taken God's transcendence and made him abstract and remote. Salvation then comes to be seen as escape to another world and as a result, this world is devalued and neglected. Bonhoeffer recognised the need for an individual, personal faith; but religion emphasises this to the detriment of the church and the world. He wanted to bring God and the church back into the secular world. God is to be seen at the centre of life.[193] The Christian must learn to live his Christianity and speak of God in a secular way. The church is not to be preoccupied with its own religious concerns, but to serve the world. The church must follow the pattern of Jesus, 'the man for others.' Bonhoeffer stressed that there must be a secular interpretation of Christianity and the church.

Conclusion

The New Orthodoxy was used by God as an instrument to beat the surpassing challenges of the Liberal theology against the true Christian faith. Karl Barth and all his colleagues by all means spoke and wrote against the conceptual onslaughts of liberal theology. It is always correct to say that God uses somebody in the history of Christianity to fight against the unsound teachings and to prove what the teaching of pure Christianity is. It is true that Karl Barth was a true believer and kept his faith until the last. But when we think of the philosophy of New Orthodoxy, it stands between Orthodoxy and liberal theology.

Neo-orthodoxy is a broad term, but it is mostly used in the sense of 'modern or contemporary theology.' Fundamentally, neo-orthodoxy differs from orthodoxy with its approach to the 'doctrine of the word.' The orthodox view holds that the Bible is the revealed Word of God, which was given by inspiration of God. Neo-orthodoxy denies this orthodox approach of inerrancy and inspiration, saying that inspiration was not given verbally, but that the author interpreted the events or word of God, thus writing his own interpretation. This denies what God has revealed to us in the above passages, among others. Scripture in its original manuscripts is the very words of God in the words of men. But neo-orthodoxy drifts even further away from the orthodox view by denying other elements of the doctrine of the Word, which is alarming and worth looking at. In orthodox circles, the Bible is regarded as the complete and sufficient revelation of God (2 Timothy 3:16-17; Jude 3v). Neo-orthodoxy believes that the Bible is a medium of revelation (while orthodoxy believes it as revelation). To the believers in neo-orthodoxy, revelation is therefore dependent on the experience of each individual, making truth a mystical experience, rather than a concrete fact. Neo-orthodoxy would make a distinction between the 'word of God' and the 'revealed Word of God.'

Evangelical Philosophy

Evangelicalism is a movement that emphasises personal commitment to Christ and the authority of the Bible. It is represented in most Protestant denominations. Evangelicals believe that each individual has a need for spiritual rebirth and personal commitment to Jesus Christ as saviour through faith in his atoning death on the cross. They emphasise strict orthodoxy on cardinal doctrines, morals and especially on the authority of the Bible. Many Evangelicals follow a traditional, precritical interpretation of the Bible and insist on its inerrancy. Many Evangelicals today describe themselves as 'born-again Christians', meaning that they have made a new and passionate commitment to Jesus Christ and the Christian faith. In the general sense, the term *evangelical* means simply pertaining to the Gospel. The word identified the early leaders of the Reformation, who emphasised the biblical message and rejected the official interpretation of dogma by the Roman Catholic Church. Thus, *evangelical* often simply means Protestant in continental Europe and in the names of churches elsewhere.

The evangelical label began to be applied to interdenominational efforts at outreach and the establishment of foreign missions. Revivalism was typified by camp meetings and the itinerant ministries of such evangelists as Charles G. Finney and Dwight L. Moody. Their outstanding 20th-century successor is Billy Graham, a leading figure in evangelicalism since World War II.

Peter Forsyth

Peter Taylor Forsyth, who is also known as P. T. Forsyth (1848-1921), was a Scottish theologian. He was born at Aberdeen as the son of a postman. Forsyth studied at the University of Aberdeen and then in Gottingen, supposedly under Albrecht Ritschl. He was ordained into the congregational ministry and served churches as pastor at Bradford, Manchester, Leicester and Cambridge before becoming Principal of Hackney College, London, in 1901.

His Works

His theology and his attack on liberal Christianity can be found in his most famous work, *The Person and Place of Christ* (1909), which anticipated much of the neo-orthodox theology of the next generation. He has often lazily been coined the 'Barthian before Barth', but this fails to account for many areas of divergence with the Swiss theologian's thought. In his textbook *Christian Theology: An Introduction*, Alister E. McGrath makes note of Forsyth's *Justification of God* (1916). McGrath says this book "represents an impassioned plea to allow the notion of the 'justice of God' to be rediscovered." Forsyth wrote many books, including *The Centrality of the Cross, Gospel and Authority, Positive Preaching and Modern Mind* and *The Work of Christ*.

His Doctrinal Position
At first, he stood at the liberal tradition, but during his last pastorate, he underwent an evangelical conversion. But he did not turn to the old orthodoxy. An early interest in critical theology made him suspect to some 'orthodox' Christians. However, he increasingly came to the conclusion that liberal theology failed to account adequately for the moral problem of the guilty conscience. This led him to a moral crisis that he found resolved in the atoning work of Christ. Although Forsyth rejected many of his earlier liberal leanings, he retained many of Adolf von Harnack's criticisms of Chalcedonian Christology. This led him to expound a kenotic doctrine of the incarnation. Where he differed from other kenotic theologies of the atonement was the claim that Christ did not give up his divine attributes but condensed them; i.e., the incarnation was the expression of God's omnipotence rather than its negation. P.T. Forsyth's position was then called 'believing criticism', which is a combination of biblical criticism and acceptance of the doctrines of the gospel.[194]

Forsyth's Philosophy
Forsyth is less concerned than Anselm for the legal and juridical aspects of the cross; his interest centres on the manner in which the cross is inextricably linked with 'the whole moral fabric and movement of the universe.' The doctrine of the atonement is inseparable from 'the rightness of things.' For Forsyth, God's supreme revelation is Jesus Christ and especially on the cross. Authority in Christian theology lies in the gospel, which is recorded in the Bible. The Bible is authoritative as the supreme witness to Jesus Christ. He saw the cross, like the New Testament, as the centre of Christian faith. He was against liberalism, saying that although liberalism taught the love of God, it denied the God's holy wrath against sin. This ended up with a sentimental concept of love. Forsyth rediscovered God's holiness and wrath against sin.

Forsyth was known for his interpretation of the incarnation of Jesus Christ. He sought to modify the prevalent liberal traditional theories in connection with the incarnation of Jesus and was prepared enough to face all challenges and criticisms of the day. Forsyth admits that God cannot lose his attributes; instead they can become latent or potential. In the incarnation Jesus voluntarily limited himself. He reduced or retracted his divine attributes so as to make them potential rather than actual. This is the kenosis or self-emptying. For him, there is also a reverse process of plerosis or self-fulfillment. In his earthly life, Jesus regained the divine attributes by a gradual moral reconquest. The Godhead that freely made man was never so free as in becoming man.[195] While many of Forsyth's most significant insights have largely gone ignored, not a few consider him to be among the greatest of English-speaking theologians of the early twentieth century. His theology was based on the Bible, but he accepted fully the methods and results of biblical criticism.

Francis Schaeffer

Francis August Schaeffer (1912-1984) was an American Evangelical Christian philosopher and Presbyterian pastor. Schaeffer was born on January 30, 1912, in Germantown, Pennsylvania to Franz A. Schaeffer III and Bessie Williamson. Schaeffer promoted a more historic Protestant faith and a presuppositional approach to Christian apologetics, which he believed would answer the questions of the age. A number of Christian leaders, authors and evangelists were highly influenced by Schaeffer.

His Background

In 1935, Schaeffer graduated from Hampden-Sydney College. The same year he married Edith Seville. Schaeffer then enrolled at Westminster Theological Seminary in the fall and studied under Cornelius Van Til and J. Gresham Machen. In 1937, Schaeffer transferred to Faith Theological Seminary and was graduated in 1938. In 1954, Schaeffer was awarded the honorary Doctor of Divinity degree from Highland College in Long Beach, California. In 1971, Schaeffer received the honorary Doctor of Letters degree from Gordon College in Wenham, Massachusetts. In 1982, John Warwick Montgomery nominated Schaeffer for an honorary Doctor of Laws degree, which was conferred in 1983 by the Simon Greenleaf School of Law, Anaheim, California, in recognition of his apologetic writings and ministry.

Schaeffer was the first student to graduate and the first to be ordained in the Bible Presbyterian Church. He served pastorates in Pennsylvania and St. Louis, Missouri, for ten years from 1938 to 1948.[196] He later left the BPC and joined the Reformed Presbyterian Church, Evangelical Synod, a forerunner of the Presbyterian Church in America, an evangelical denomination. In 1948, the Schaeffer family moved to Switzerland and in 1955 established the community called L'Abri (French for 'the shelter').

Serving as both a philosophy seminar and a spiritual community, L'Abri attracted thousands of young people, and was later expanded into Sweden, France, the Netherlands, the United Kingdom and the United States. Schaeffer died of lymphoma on May 15, 1984, in Rochester, Minnesota.

Schaeffer's Writings

Schaeffer wrote twenty-two books, which cover a range of spiritual issues. They can be roughly split into five sections, as in the edition of his *Complete Works*:

i. A Christian View of Philosophy and Culture: The first three books in this block are known as Schaeffer's 'trilogy,' laying down the apologetical, philosophical, epistemological and theological foundation for all his work. (a) The God Who Is There; (b) Escape from Reason; (c) He Is There and He Is Not Silent.

ii. Christian View of the Bible as Truth: (a) Genesis in Space and Time; (b) No Final Conflict; (c) Joshua and the Flow of Biblical History; (d) Basic Bible Studies; (e) Art and the Bible.

iii. A Christian View of Spirituality: (a) No Little People; (b) True Spirituality; (c) The New Super-Spirituality; (d) Two Contents, Two Realities.

iv. A Christian View of the Church: (a) The Church at the End of the Twentieth Century; (b) The Church Before the Watching World; (c) The Mark of the Christian; (d) Death in the City; (e) The Great Evangelical Disaster.

v. A Christian View of the West: (a) Pollution and the Death of Man; (b) How Should We Then Live? (c) The Rise and Decline of Western Thought and Culture; (d) Whatever Happened to the Human Race? (e) A Christian Manifesto.

Apologetics

Schaeffer's approach to Christian apologetics was primarily influenced by Herman Dooyeweerd, Edward John Carnell and Cornelius Van Til, but he was not known to be a strict presuppositionalist in the Van Tillian tradition. In a 1948 article in *The Bible Today*, Schaeffer explained his own apologetics and how he walked a middle path between evidentialism and presuppositionalism

Schaeffer came to use this *middle path* as the basis for his method of evangelism, which he called *Taking the roof off*. An example of *taking the roof off* in written form can be found in Schaeffer's work entitled *Death in the City*. Schaeffer explains it in his other two books, *Escape from Reason* and *The God Who Is There*, in this way: the history of the two-story division of knowledge, often referred to as the fact-value split. He also describes his apologetic method, which combined elements of both evidentialism and presuppositionalism.

Political Activism
Francis Schaeffer is credited with helping spark a return to political activism among Protestant evangelicals and fundamentalists in the late 1970s and early 1980s, especially in relation to the issue of abortion. In his memoir *Crazy for God*, Schaeffer's son Frank takes credit for pressing his father to take on the abortion issue, which Schaeffer initially considered 'too political.' Schaeffer called for a challenge to what he saw as the increasing influence of secular humanism. Schaeffer's views were expressed in two works: his book entitled, *A Christian Manifesto*, and the book and film series, *Whatever Happened to the Human Race? A Christian Manifesto*, which is intended to position its thesis as a Christian answer to *The Communist Manifesto* of 1848 and the *Humanist Manifesto* documents of 1933 and 1973. Schaeffer's diagnosis is that the decline of Western Civilization is due to society having become increasingly pluralistic, resulting in a shift 'away from a world view that was at least vaguely Christian in people's memory toward something completely different.' Schaeffer argues that there is a philosophical struggle between the people of God and secular humanists.

History of Western Culture
Francis Schaeffer has provided us with the most interesting survey of the history of western culture in his book entitled, *How Should We Then Live?* He sees decline and renewal as being directly related to the way people have treated God and especially related to the attitude people have had towards the authority of the Bible.[197] Right at the start of his book, he emphasises the key role of deliberate thought about the meaning of life. There is a flow to history and culture. This flow is rooted and has its wellspring in the thoughts of people. People are unique in the inner life of the mind—what they are in their thought world determines how they act. This is true of their value systems and it is true of their creativity. It is true of their corporate actions, such as political decisions, and it is true

of their personal lives. The results of their thought world flow through their fingers or from their tongues into the external world. By presuppositions we mean the basic way an individual looks at life, his basic worldview, the grid through which he sees the world. Presuppositions rest upon that which a person considers to be the truth of what exists. People's presuppositions lay a grid for all they bring forth into the external world. Their presuppositions also provide the basis for their values and therefore the basis for their decisions. His analysis of the history of modern western culture lays a strong emphasis on the reformation and rise of modern science. He tries to make clear the way that modern philosophy and much of modern theology have helped to remove the real influence of Christ from the modern world. The effects of this departure from God are illustrated from many areas of life and thought in the modern world. He believes that living with a strong faith in God and in obedience to the Bible is the key to a healthy future, just as he sees failure in these matters to be the main reasons for problems in the past. Much of the second half of the book is taken up also with describing the rise of secular humanism in the West, and with the serious effects this is having, increasingly, in our society.

Some evangelicals want to follow a different philosophical path from the one Schaeffer tried to follow. Whatever the strengths and weaknesses of his philosophical views, he has had a salutary Christian influence in the intellectual world where he has moved, and has reflected in the most valuable way upon the key problems of today. Schaeffer was successful in presenting the true faith of Christianity to the world of philosophy. Although he had his own way of interpreting the philosophical systems, as all other philosophers do, he was able to contribute a lot in the field of Evangelical Christian philosophy.

Bolaji Idowu

Bolaji Idowu (1913-1993) was the third native-born leader of the Methodist Church Nigeria, serving from 1972 to 1984. He is also well known for his ethnographic and theological studies of the Yoruba people. As he was the one from the African background, he was able to formulate a people-oriented African theology. His conversion to Christianity influenced his way of thinking, especially as a church leader.

His Life

Idowu was born on 28 September 1913 in Ikorodu, Lagos State, Nigeria. His early education was at the Anglican and Methodist schools in Ikorodu.

There, he met the Rev. A. T. Ola Olude and was converted to Christianity. After finishing at Wesley College in Ibadan, he became headmaster at the primary school in Remo, Ogun State. He was ordained in 1942. From 1945 to 1948, he continued his studies at Wesley House, Cambridge. From 1957 to 1958, he was posted in Germany in an effort to resolve some of the problems that were facing African and Asian students there. In 1958, he joined the staff of the Department of Religious Studies at University of Ibadan and served as its head from 1963 to 1976.

In 1972, he was elected president of the Methodist Church, Nigeria. He immediately initiated a reform of the church's constitution, emphasising the need for autonomy and indigenisation. The new constitution was ratified in 1976, whereupon Idowu became the church's patriarch. Church members held him in such high esteem that the items he had touched during his services were believed to have healing powers. He retired in 1984 and died in 1993. A cathedral in Ikorodu was named in his honour.

Publications
Idowu wrote many books. In spite of his busy schedule as a church leader, he was able to contribute a lot in the field of publication. His writings were mainly in connection with the African religion and its traditions. Some of his important books are as follows: *Olodumare: God in Yoruba Belief* (1994), *African Traditional Religion: A Definition*, (1973), *Olodumare: God in Yoruba Belief* (1982) and *Towards an Indigenous Church* (1965).

Ethno-theology
In the process of preparing a doctoral thesis for University of London (1955), Idowu discovered that all the available material on the African religion appeared to be inaccurate, condescending or simply ridiculous. (For example: Leo Frobenius' belief that the Yoruba religion came from Plato's Atlantis by way of Egypt.) As a result, he set out to describe the religious beliefs of his own Yoruba people according to universal theological concerns, such as the nature of the deity, morality and ultimate destiny of mankind. His writings on the subject are among the first examples of the African religion seen from the viewpoint of an African. His main concepts are based on his own community and the issues he touched are community-oriented. He placed great stress on the indigenisation the African church; he suggested that the African church must be indigenised in the African perspective. The church in Africa must formulate a theology for its own people.

Bong Rin Ro

Dr. Bong Rin Ro is a famous Asian evangelical scholar. Bong Rin Ro served as General Secretary of Asia Theological Association for twenty years prior to his professorship at TTGU. He is the Korean Director of Hawaii Theological Seminary in Honolulu. He served for 30 years as an OMF missionary in Singapore (1970-74), Taiwan (1975-89) and Korea (1990-2000). From 1970 to 1990, he was the Executive Secretary of Asia Theological Association (ATA) and International Director of the Theological Commission (World Evangelical Alliance) from 1990 to 1996.

His Works

Bong Rin Ro edited many books and wrote on very important topics. The important books for which he was editor or writer include *The Bible and Theology in Asian Contexts: An Evangelical Perspective on Asian Theology* (1984), *The Voice of the Church in Asia* (1975), *Korean Church Growth Explosion: Vol. 1* (1983), *Christian Alternatives in Ancestor Practices* (1985), *God in Asian Contexts* (1988) and *Urban Ministry in Asia* (1988).

Contextualisation

Bong Rin Ro stated that contextualisation should be the focal concern because through it alone will come reform and renewal. Contextualisation of the Gospel is a missiological necessity. But there are dangers, one of which in the Third World is that such contextualisation may not take place in response to the really urgent issues of its own context, in its own time and in its own place, but in those times and places that are out of date and out of place in the Third World. He further says that there are two preliminary remarks that need to be considered before dealing with the historical approach to universalism in Asian contexts.[198] First, universalism throughout the history of the church has been dealt with from its own cultural context and theological trends of the time. The second important factor is the deep influence of the Western theological thought on Asian theology either through Western missionaries or Asian theologians who have been trained in the West.

According to Bong Rin Ro, we must pay attention to three areas in our attempt to contextualise theology. First, the essential biblical doctrines, such as the uniqueness and finality of Jesus Christ and the unique revelation in the Bible, cannot be compromised. Second, the priority of the biblical exegesis must be emphasised to make adequate application to different contexts. Third, we must pay careful attention to the historic creeds to find out how God worked in the lives of Christians in centuries past.[199] The concept of indigenisation was taken one step further by applying it in the area of mission, theological approach and educational method and structure. Contextualisation takes into account the processes of secularity, technology and the struggles for human justice which characterises the history of nations in Asia. Asian theologians have used the concepts of indigenisation and contextualisation to justify the development of Asian theologies. The key issue in the whole argument around developing an Asian theology is whether in the process of contextualisation the biblical and historical doctrines of the Christian church can be preserved without compromise. Asian Christians must listen to, evaluate and be open minded to different Asian theological views on contextualisation and yet, without compromise, be faithful to the gospel and proclaim it in love, as the apostle Paul exhorts: "Be on the alert, stand firm in the faith, act like men, be strong. Let all that you do be done in love' (1 Cor. 16:13 - 14).

Asian Theology
Bong Rin Ro says that some recent efforts have attempted to first understand Eastern culture and belief systems. With this foundation, it has been possible to develop deeper communication with the residents there which has allowed mutual understanding. In order to understand Asian theology, one must examine distinctions between Eastern and Western cultures. In the period of post-colonialism, Asian theologians have been seeking liberation from Western theologies in order to make the gospel more relevant to their own life situations. Historically, the development of Asian theology is closely related to the development of indigenisation in the early twentieth century and to the recent development of the concept of contextualisation in missions. In order to understand Asian theology, one must examine distinctions between Eastern and Western cultures. Bong Rin Ro says that biblically-oriented Asian theology must set up certain propositions and circumscribed limits in order to avoid theological confusion and thus promote evangelical harmony and co-operation.[200] He says that the gospel must also be translated today into the particular forms of Asian cultures, and consequently numerous Asian theologies claim to represent Asian cultural forms: pain of God theology (Japan), water buffalo theology (Thailand), third-eye theology (for the Chinese), minjung theology (Korea), theology of change (Taiwan) and a score of other national theologies, such as Indian theology, Burmese theology and Sri Lankan theology.

Dr. Ro says that there is a need for biblically-oriented Asian theology. Theology in Asia has been taught by Western missionaries. The West has its own theological formulations derived out of its own cultural background, Calvinism, Armenianism, etc. Yet in Asia the circumstances facing Christians differ from the West. Asian Christians must make their theologies relevant to their living situations in Asia. Some of the main issues that Christians in Asia are facing today are communism, poverty, suffering, war, idolatry, demon possession, bribery and cheating. Most evangelical theologians see the value of Asian theology in allowing Asians to express their theological thoughts within their own contexts. Nevertheless, they are also very apprehensive of the danger of syncretism and of minimising fundamental scriptural teachings during the process of contextualisation. The major proponents of Asian theology have been liberal theologians of mainline denominational seminaries. An increasing number of evangelical theologians have sharply reacted against the concept of Asian theology. Other evangelicals are insisting on the necessity of it. Due to the existence of very divergent religious cultures in Asia, the content of Asian theology is also diversified. It can be classified in four main areas: (1) syncretistic theology, (2) accommodation theology, (3) situational theology, and (4) biblical theology that is relevant to Asian needs.

Doctrine of Salvation
Bong Ring Ro says that the biblical and historical doctrine of salvation is possible through the only incarnate Son of God. The doctrines of salvation by grace through faith and the eternal condemnation to those who reject the Christ had been taught consistently from the early church. This concept had not been challenged until the eighteenth-century ecumenical leaders and many liberal Roman Catholic theologians taught universalism and religious pluralism. It is so sad that even some evangelical church leaders have been also influenced by the prevailing universalistic thinking. Evangelical theologians and Christian philosophers in Asia must take their initiative in the formulation of the doctrine of salvation from the Scripture according to their particular Asian contexts.[201] We are reminded to be faithful to the teachings of the Scripture and at the same time, be sensitive to our own cultural context in such a way that we may be able to communicate the gospel more effectively to our people.

The doctrine of salvation in the Bible depends on the historicity of the incarnation, the cross and the resurrection of Jesus Christ. Asian Christians must approach the doctrine of salvation in their own contexts where their Christian faith meets constant challenges from living religions. Bong Rin

Ro is correct in pointing out the necessity of Asian Christians and especially evangelical scholars to be loyal to the Lord and His Scripture and keep our faith on the basis of the biblical mandate and to observe and evaluate the situations in the Asian context.

Conclusion

In the last hundred years, philosophy has increasingly become an activity practiced within modern research universities, and accordingly it has grown more specialised and more distinct from the natural sciences. Much philosophy in this period concerns itself with explaining the relation between the theories of the natural sciences. Herman Dooyeweerd, Immanuel Kant, Soren Kierkegaard, John D. Caputo, Jacques Ellul, Knud Ejler Logstrup, Bernard Lonergan, Gabriel Marcel, Jacques Maritain, John Henry Newman, Melville Y. Stewart, Peter van Inwagen and Cornelius van Til are the famous Christian philosophers in the modern and post-modern periods. Postmodern philosophy is an eclectic and elusive movement characterised by its criticism of the conventions of Western philosophy. Beginning as a critique of Continental Philosophy it was heavily influenced by phenomenology, Structuralism and Existentialism, including writings of both Soren Kierkegaard and Martin Heidegger.

The purpose of the book does not allow the author to look at all philosophers in this book. This book mainly presents Christian philosophical views; although few philosophers are very famous in the field of philosophy, they are not enlisted in this book, because their teaching may not be Christian or they may not believe in God. Christian philosophy from the West, Africa and Asia are dealt with in this chapter, especially in the field of Roman Catholic philosophy, Liberal Christian philosophy and Evangelical Christian Philosophy. There should have been a universal framework for Christian Philosophy from the beginning. Most of the Christian philosophical writers were from the West and they had concentrated only on Western Christian philosophy, and other philosophers from the East and Africa were knowingly or unknowingly neglected. We should have a Christian philosophy that is wider enough to accept Christian philosophers from all corners of the world. Christian philosophy should be formulated on the basis of Christian faith and not on the basis of colour or race. Christian philosophy should be based on the biblical mandate, and all unbiblical teachings and philosophies must be cancelled out.

Helpful Questions
1. Write short notes on Existentialism, Pragmatism and Asian Liberation theology.
2. Describe Russell's analytical philosophy.
3. How did Thomas and Mbiti teach ecumenism?
4. Evaluate Asian evangelical philosophy.

CHAPTER 9

Contemporary Christian Philosophy

This chapter will focus on the origin and nature of contemporary philosophy and the contributions of a few contemporary philosophers.

Origin and Nature

The philosophic community needs to respond to the dangers coming ahead in a thoughtful and proactive way. In the 20th century, philosophy abandoned its Socratic heritage in favour of a disciplinary model of practice. Rather than engaging citizens in all walks of life on the issues they faced, philosophers spoke mainly to one another about the problems of their own invention. It was a model that became self-justifying by defining its own goals and standards, and the demand for philosophy was decreasing. Christian philosophers must come down to the grassroots level to make the public understand the purpose of their self and their Creator, instead of creating now theories year after year. The twenty-first-century Christian philosophy must deal with the crucial issues of life, especially our faith in God. It is time to reclaim the public role of philosophy. The philosophising lies in the asking rather than the answering, an asking that goes on without end and at the same time standing strictly within the prescribed Scriptural boundary. Here we will learn about the origin and nature of contemporary Christian philosophy.

The Period

We have already studied that modern philosophy covers a period of AD1600-1800 and postmodern philosophy AD1800-2000. And I prefer signifying contemporary Christian philosophy as of the twenty-first and twenty-second centuries (2000-2200). If the world will exist as such for two centuries, the period of contemporary philosophy can be classified again into two: Early contemporary philosophy (2000-2100) and post-contemporary philosophy (2100-2200). Some philosophers already classified contemporary philosophy from 1960 to the present. This is not an easy classification. The term "to the present" does not give an exact period of time. Another factor is that all the previous periods of philosophy are classified as per the centuries; this will also be periodically separated for a century (2000- 2100). The 'twenty-first century' is the best method of separation of the period of contemporary Christian philosophy from postmodern philosophy. Contemporary Christian philosophy is a growing philosophy and it is supposed to have a long way to go. Contemporary Christian philosophers may have been born in the twentieth century or even they may have lived for many years in the previous century. Even then, if they wrote books or if their books were published in the twenty-first century, they can be considered as contemporary Christian philosophers.

Modern and Postmodern Philosophies
We have already seen that postmodern philosophy can be subdivided into two categories: Early postmodern philosophy (1800-1900) and later postmodern philosophy (1900-2000). Early postmodern philosophy (nineteenth century) is usually considered to begin after the philosophy of Immanuel Kant at the beginning of the 19th century. German idealists, such as Hegel, expanded on the work of Kant by maintaining that the world is entirely rational and its nature is fundamentally knowable. For Kant the 'noumenon' (the unknowable object) was the reality behind the 'phenomenon' (the appearance which is known). The real is, what the mind conceives, the rational, and vice versa the rational is real. Consequently, everything is perfectly logical and necessary. Nature and thought, matter and spirit are governed by the implacable laws of logic. Hegel's idealism was absolute. Reason and existence coincide perfectly. Much of the later postmodern philosophy (twentieth century) concerns itself with explaining the relation between the theories of the natural sciences and the ideas of the humanities or common sense. Postmodern philosophy is often particularly skeptical about simple binary oppositions that pervade much of Western metaphysics and humanism, emphasising the problem of the philosopher, cleanly distinguishing knowledge from ignorance, social progress from reversion, dominance from submission and presence from absence.

We have already seen that modern philosophy turned its attention to the nature of the new science and its method. Two elements in the scientific method were identified: The rational element, the use of mathematics and deductive reasoning, and the empirical element, the rise of observation, experimentations and induction. The ideas of pragmatism, in its various forms, developed mainly from the discussions that took place among philosophers like Charles Sanders Peirce and William James. Husserl initiated the school of phenomenology. Kierkegaard and Nietzsche laid the groundwork for existentialism. Frege's work in logic provided the tools for early analytical philosophy. Mill's utilitarianism and Marx and Engel's Marxism dominated discussions in political philosophy.

Emergence of Contemporary Christian Philosophy

As we have shown our interest to philosophy, we want the field to survive and prosper. Philosophy has been facing a crisis since the last quarter of the twentieth century. Research consisted in talking about applied ethics rather than actually applying, or better, integrating philosophic insights with problems on the ground. Normally, we write a paper on the subject; rather than sharing our insights with policy makers or the concerned public, we publish our work in an academic journal, one that relevant decision makers are probably not even aware of. Really, what we need is the Socratic task of public philosophising; but unfortunately it remains undone. Christian philosophers should work within the needy field of thought on the basis of the need of the Christian world of philosophy. The current institutional dimensions of philosophy—training, teaching, promotion and tenure—need to be thought afresh. We need to train future philosophers so they can recognise philosophical disputes happening in the world and insert themselves artfully into public spheres. We should develop new, more interactive models of rigour that take account of the need for timeliness, sensitivity to context and rhetorical skill in communicating with multiple audiences. We need to learn how to identify and create opportunities for integrating philosophy outside the discipline. Philosophers have broad social responsibilities that require directly engaging in social problems.

Practical philosophy, interactional philosophy, Diological philosophy, Field philosophy, public philosophy, experimental philosophy, etc., are all expressions of a growing world of philosophy. We seek to promote this change in a new phase with a new perspective. We view modern philosophy as an aberration—academically challenging work that forgot half of philosophy's task. It is time to strike out in new, intellectually exciting and socially useful directions. Moreover, contemporary philosophy of the twenty-first century is the philosophy, back to God. It is religious philosophy. The postmodern man already realised the vacuum and urgency of faith in God. It is the need of the hour for the reconsideration of faith in God and re-emphasis should be given to religious philosophy. In a more detailed way of thinking from my point of view is that it is the age of Christian philosophy. The younger generation who are going astray must come back to the God of the Bible in order to have self-realisation and God-realisation.

Nature of Contemporary Christian Philosophy

Contemporary philosophy began by the twenty-first century. It does not mean the philosophers who were born in the twentieth century will not be included in the list of twenty-first century philosophers. By the term "twenty-first" we mean that philosophical books were written or published in the twenty-first century. The term "contemporary Christian philosopher" refers not just to figures who are alive, but also those who died in the recent past, in the twenty-first century. As contemporary philosophy represents the period of twenty-first and twenty-second centuries, we should have a new outlook on philosophy in this new era. It is definitely true that our philosophical foundation has already been laid and we should never forget the later developments in the field of philosophy; but at the same time, we should frame a new philosophy that should appropriate to the life-situation of the people who live in the twenty-first century.

There are of course undeniable differences within and between these philosophical concepts. Philosophy was always intended to clear up ontological, epistemological and ethical questions relatively independent of the respective cultural and religious environment they developed. The specific problem of contemporary philosophy comes from the situation that one of the cultural settings of the past has been more successful than others in establishing itself on a global scale as being non-traditional but scientific.[202] Contemporary philosophy is a growing field of thought, and there is plenty of time to reach into its perfect stage, when it will reach at 2100. Although most contemporary philosophy is highly technical and inaccessible to non-specialists, some contemporary philosophers concern themselves with practical questions and strive to influence today's culture. Nowhere have philosophers more enthusiastically embraced practical relevance than in contemporary applied ethics. Most of the questions applied ethicists raise concern the general theme 'How should we live and die?'

Contemporary Christian Philosophers

Few contemporary Christian philosophers are dealt with in this part of the book. As in all the ages of Christian philosophy, there are many Christian philosophers in the contemporary world of Christian philosophy. A representation has been given for important continents like Asia, Africa and the Western world.

Kwesi Dickson

Kwesi Abotsia Dickson (July 1929-October 2005) was priest, theologian, author and academic. He was the 7th President of the Methodist Church, Ghana, and professor, University of Ghana, Legon.

Early Life and Education

Kwesi Dickson was born at Saltpond, central region of Ghana. He was educated at Mfantsipim School, Cape Coast. He completed his basic ministerial training at Trinity Theological Seminary (then Trinity College in Kumasi) in 1951. He then attended the University of Ghana, then University College of the Gold Coast. Next, he went to the United Kingdom, where his post-graduate education was at Mansfield College, Oxford at Oxford University.

His Career

Dickson was ordained into the ministry of the Methodist Church of Ghana at the British Methodist Conference of 1957. He served in various capacities at University of Ghana over three decades until 1989. He was Head, Department for the Study of Religions; Dean, Faculty of Arts; Master of Commonwealth Hall; first Dean of Students and Director, Institute of African Studies. At various times, he served as adjunct professor of Old Testament and Hebrew at Trinity Theological Seminary, Legon. He was also a fellow of the Ghana Academy of Arts and Sciences. He was its president on two occasions. He also worked at the University of Swaziland as a visiting professor. In 1989, he was elected as President, the Methodist Church Ghana. He served two consecutive four-year terms ending in 1997. He has served as Chairman, Christian Council of Ghana, and President, All African Council of Churches.

He loved music and was a good pianist. Dickson died at Korle Bu Teaching Hospital, Accra, after a brief illness. His funeral and burial were attended by many notable Ghanaian citizens including John Agyekum Kufuor, who was President of Ghana at the time, and John Atta Mills, who was a colleague at University of Ghana and was to become the next Ghanaian president.

Publications
Kwesi Dickson has many publications to his name. He has authoritative works such as Theology in Africa and others on religious exclusivism. Some of his texts were also used for GCE Ordinary Level and GCE Advanced Level curricula. His works include the following: *Akan Religion and the Christian Faith* (1965); *Aspects of Religion and Life in Africa* (1977); *Prohibitions; Religions of the World; Human Dimensions in Theological Quest* (1976); *Uncompleted Mission: Christianity and Exclusivism* (1991); *Theology in Africa* (1984); *Story of the Early Church Found in the Acts of the Apostles* (1976), etc. Although he lived and worked more in the last century, most of his books were published or republished in the twenty-first century.

Dickson's Philosophical Teachings
Dickson wrote authoritatively on African religion and he compared it with religious exclusivism. He made a comparative study of Christianity and the Akan religion of Africa. He had a major role in the formation of African theology. His contribution in the fields of theology, religion and Mission are commendable. He concentrated on the formation of an African Christian philosophy that is based on African cultural values and heritage. Exclusivism is his major area. For him, religion is to be meaningful, because it is part of life. Religion is inseparable from life. Especially in Africa, religion has an important role in human life.

Alvin Plantinga
Alvin Carl Plantinga (born November 15, 1932) is an American analytic philosopher, the Professor of Philosophy at University of Notre Dame and the inaugural holder of the Jellema Chair in Philosophy at Calvin College. Alvin Plantinga is famous for his Reformed Epistemology.

Education and Career
At the end of 11th grade, as per father's decision, Plantinga skipped his last year of high school and immediately enrolled in college. In 1949, a few months before his 17th birthday, he enrolled in Jamestown College, Jamestown, North Dakota. In January 1950, Plantinga moved to Grand Rapids with his family and enrolled in Calvin College. During his first semester at Calvin, Plantinga was awarded a scholarship to attend Harvard University. Beginning in the fall of 1950, Plantinga spent two semesters

at Harvard. In 1954, Plantinga began his graduate studies at the University of Michigan where he studied under William Alston, William Frankena and Richard Cartwright. A year later, in 1955, he transferred to Yale University, where he received his Ph.D. in 1958.

Plantinga began his career as an instructor in the philosophy department at Yale in 1957, and then in 1958 he became a professor of philosophy at Wayne State University. In 1963, he accepted a teaching job at Calvin College, where he replaced the retiring Jellema. He then spent the next 19 years at Calvin before moving to the University of Notre Dame in 1982. He retired from University of Notre Dame in 2010 and returned to Calvin College, where he serves as the first holder of the William Harry Jellema Chair in Philosophy. In 2006, the University of Notre Dame's Center for Philosophy of Religion renamed its Distinguished Scholar Fellowship as the Alvin Plantinga Fellowship. The fellowship includes an annual lecture by the current Plantinga Fellow.

He is the author of numerous books, such as *Warranted Christian Belief* (2000); *Warrant and Proper Function* (1993); *Warrant: the Current Debate* (1993); *Does God Have a Nature?* (1980); *God, Freedom and Evil* (1974); *The Nature of Necessity* (1974); and *God and Other Minds* (1967).[203] He has delivered the prestigious Gifford Lectures three times and was described by *Time Magazine* as "America's leading orthodox Protestant philosopher of God." Plantinga is widely known for his work in philosophy of religion, epistemology, metaphysics and Christian apologetics. More recently, Nicholas Wolterstorff commented regarding Plantinga's contributions to contemporary philosophy: "But as for the philosophy of religion and the central main philosophical disciplines of epistemology and metaphysics, his fingerprints are indeed everywhere."

Problem of Evil
Plantinga posited a 'free will defense' in Max Black in 1965, which attempts to refute the logical problem of evil, the argument that the existence of evil is logically incompatible with the existence of an omnipotent, omniscient, wholly good God. Plantinga's argument is that "it is possible that God, even being omnipotent, could not create a world with free creatures that never choose evil. Furthermore, it is possible that God, even being omnibenevolent, would desire to create a world which contains evil if moral goodness requires free moral creatures." Plantinga's defense has received wide acceptance among contemporary philosophers when addressing the problem of evil.[204] However, the argument fails to address

natural evil, and it presupposes an incompatible view of free will. J. L. Mackie has argued that Plantiga's free will defense is incoherent.

Reformed Epistemology

Plantinga's contributions to epistemology include an argument that he calls 'Reformed epistemology.' According to Reformed epistemology, belief in God can be rational and justified even without arguments or evidence for the existence of God. More specifically, Plantinga argues that belief in God is properly basic, and due to a religious externalist epistemology, he claims belief in God could be justified independently of evidence. His externalist epistemology, called 'Proper functionalism', is a form of epistemological reliabilism. Plantinga discusses his view of Reformed epistemology and Proper functionalism in a three volume series. In the first book of the trilogy, *Warrant: The Current Debate*, Plantinga introduces, analyses, and criticises 20th century developments in analytic epistemology. In the second book, *Warrant and Proper Function*, he introduces the notion of warrant as an alternative to justification and discusses topics like self-knowledge, memories, perception and probability. Plantinga explains his argument for proper function with reference to a *design plan*, as well as an environment in which one's cognitive equipment is optimal for use. Plantinga seeks to defend this view of proper function against alternative views of proper function proposed by other philosophers.

Plantinga has argued that some people can know that God exists as a basic belief, requiring no argument. He has developed this argument in two different fashions: firstly, in *God and Other Minds*, by drawing equivalence between the teleological argument and the commonsense view that people have of other minds existing by analogy with their own minds. Plantinga has also developed a more comprehensive epistemological account of the nature of warrant that allows for the existence of God as a basic belief. Plantinga has also argued that there is no logical inconsistency between the existence of evil and the existence of an all-powerful, all-knowing, wholly good God.

Evolution and Christianity

In Plantinga's evolutionary argument against naturalism, he argues that the truth of evolution is an epistemic defeater for naturalism. His basic argument is that if evolution and naturalism are true, human cognitive faculties, which are evolved to produce beliefs with survival value, will not necessarily produce true beliefs. Thus, since human cognitive faculties are tuned to survival rather than truth in the naturalism-evolution model, there is reason to doubt the veracity of the products of those same faculties, including naturalism and evolution themselves. On the other hand, if God created man 'in his image' by way of an evolutionary process, then Plantinga argues our faculties would probably be reliable.

In the past, Plantinga has lent support to the intelligent design movement. In a March 2010 article in the Chronicle of Higher Education, philosopher of science Michael Ruse claims that Plantinga is an "open enthusiast of intelligent design." In a letter to the editor, Plantinga has the following response: Like any Christian, I believe that the world has been created by God, and hence 'intelligently designed.'

Ken Gnanakan

Ken Gnanakan, who was born in October 15, 1940, is India's well-known educator, environmentalist and theologian. He is an Asian Christian philosopher and one of the famous contemporary Christian philosophers. Ken Gnanakan is based in Bangalore, India. After his studies in chemical engineering in India, Gnanakan completed his Ph.D. in philosophy at King's College, London. Returning to India in 1979, he established the ACTS Institute, a vocational training school, which also imparted practical skills and spiritual values to young people. The author of the book studied under him 'Theology of Religion, Theology of Mission and Philosophy and Religion'. I was able to do my 'Mater of Theology (M.Th.) in Religion and Philosophy and Doctor of Philosophy (Ph.D.) in Religious Philosophy in the Acts Academy of Higher Education, headed by Dr. Ken Gnanakan. As a famous resource person, he has been extensively travelling all over the world and teaching the thousands in the academic world as a 'philosopher of religion and a theologian.'

His Career

Gnanakan heads up the ACTS Group of Institutions, which includes primary and secondary schools, colleges and a private university. William Carey University is a unique model being set up in North East India. Soon the Acts Institute became a large network of education, health and environmental projects all over India under the banner of ACTS. He himself teaches in universities in India and in other parts of the world on varied subjects, such as management, environment, education, theology and philosophies.

Gnanakan is also an accomplished musician and used to be part of the *Trojans*. The band is known as 'the Indian Beatles' for mainly Bangalore, Calcutta and Bombay. He continues to sing regularly with various professionals from Bangalore in the Bangalore Music Group. He has produced many CDs of his Christian spiritual compositions. He has written an environmental theme song sung by children all over the country. He worked for many years as General Secretary, Asia Theological Association. Ken Gnanakan is widely connected to all over the world with academic and social programmes. He is President, International Council for Higher Education (Switzerland), and Member, International Association for Promotion of Christian Higher Education, USA. He is a board member of International Ecological Engineering Society, Switzerland.

His Works

Ken Gnanakan wrote many books, which highly influenced the theological, philosophical and educational circle; he also worked as editor for a few books. Gnanakan's works include the following: *Kingdom Concerns* (1989); *The Pluralistic Predicament, Biblical Theology in Asia* (Editor, 1995); *Still Learning, Trees: Poems on the Environment; Managing Yourself, Proclaiming Christ in a Pluralistic Context* (2000); *God's Word: A Theology of the Environment* (1999); *Responsible Stewardship of God's Creation* (2004); *Learning in an Integrated Environment* (2004); and *Integrated Learning*(2012).

Ken Gnanakan has written extensively on various issues. At present, he propagates the concept of 'in Africa and Asia' through workshops based on his books and articles. He has written an introductory certificate course in health and environment as well as several courses on NGO Management for Indira Gandhi National Open University (IGNOU), headquartered in New Delhi. His textbooks on Theology and Philosophy are being used in various parts of the world. Gnanakan has initiated the Programme for Environmental Awareness at schools, a nationwide network aimed at motivating students into action. His book entitled, *Trees*—a collection of poems on environmental issues—is being used at various schools. He edits the quarterly *PEAS* Magazine, India's first environmental magazine for schools reaching thousands of students.

Inclusivistic Exclusivism

In *Proclaiming Christ in a Pluralistic Context*, Ken Gnanakan pointed out the weaknesses of exclusivism.[205] There are some questions and issues the exclusivist must address. First, in asserting the absolute claims of the Bible there is sometimes an absolutist and judgmental position that the individual takes in relation to others. The main problem has to do with the concept of the 'Absoluteness' of God. The question is: How does our acceptance of God's absoluteness differ from the philosophical concept of the Absolute, or even the Hindu concept of an inanimate ultimate, totally remote from the reality of this world? The unreachable and unknowable concept of God is not the same as the personal Yahweh of the Old Testament or the incarnate Lord Jesus Christ. Second, the term 'exclusivism' does not fully project the biblical Christ-like attitude. The word *exclusive* itself is problematic as it implies bigotry. Gnanakan says, in fact, Jesus severely attacked this attitude, which was so characteristic of the Jew in his time. Third, exclusivism must address its idea of discontinuity between Christianity and other religions. Barth and Kraemer wanted to show the absoluteness of God in revelation in Jesus Christ. This prerogative meant that religion that was purely a human phenomenon had no relation to revelation. Fourth, the exclusivist position will need to consider the totality of biblical teaching of salvation through Jesus Christ. The Bible clearly asserts that there is no other name through which we can be saved. But those holding to the exclusivist position cannot continue to state this without realising the sensitivity of our present religious, social and political situation.

Ken Gnanakan went further to support pluralism. He says that while exclusivism is far too restricted and inclusivism did not go far enough, there are calls to consider the position referred to as Pluralism. Rather than claiming any biblical validity for their viewpoint, pluralists plead for an understanding and acceptance of other beliefs despite the diversities. In a world that is threatened to be torn apart by various forces, including that of religious fanaticism, a united stand is being called for. Like exclusivism and inclusivism, there are varied versions of pluralism.[206] Again, he says, the exclusivist position does not take this fact seriously. However, the inclusivist position could be problematic. The far too positive evaluation of religion and the not so strong emphasis on the nature and mission of the church, the worshipping and witnessing people of God, could easily lead to pluralism.[207] For him, the strength of the pluralistic position is its forceful reminder of the urgent need for us to become an integral part of the global community. The exclusivistic arrogance and its absolutised pronouncements on the positions of other religions have caused sufficient havoc that calls for a humble change of mind. On the other hand, the subtle takeover of all religions in the name of 'inclusivism' is as imperialistic as colonial Christianity. The pluralist's reminder is for us to correct our approach, reassess our message and become part of the world of people within which we are integrally located.[208]

Although Ken Gnanakan dealt with various religious perspectives, such as exclusivism, inclusivism, syncretism and pluralism, he suggests that the better method for the evangelicals to adapt is *inclusivistic exclusivism*. He writes in his *Proclaiming Christ in a Pluralistic Context*[209]:

> The finality of God's revelation in Jesus Christ is carefully maintained, while a sincere attempt is made to allow some justification for the existence of religious beliefs all around us. Rather than merely condemning shortcomings, a more positive relationship is sought. Perhaps with a little more cautious openness to other religions and a much clearer underlining of the finality of Jesus Christ, inclusivism, perhaps an "inclusivistic-exclusivism" may be a justifiable position for even evangelicals to consider.

Most of the traditional Church has stood by an exclusive position, as it takes the Bible seriously. The New Testament is interpreted in its clear call to an acceptance of Jesus Christ as the ultimate revelation of God in history. For many centuries the exclusive claim went unchallenged within the Church. The Church proclaimed salvation in Jesus and denied truth in other religions. Until the 19th century most Protestant and Roman Catholic churches would have accepted that they were 'exclusivists' believing this to be the historical tradition of the early church as recorded in the Bible.

Missiological Philosophy

Dr. Ken Gnanakan wrote *Kingdom Concerns*, which is a textbook on Theology of Mission. It is widely accepted by many theological schools and seminaries. His philosophical concept of missiology is clearly seen in this book. He writes: "Mission in any context today brings us face to face with varying and contrasting concepts of God, divine beings and divinity. Teachers and teachings confuse millions by their claims. And this makes it important for the Church to get a clearer grasp of the God of the Bible. There are two factors we will constantly encounter. First, the God of the Bible is a personal God. Second, he has revealed himself historically. The task of mission is to present this kind of God as convincingly as possible."[210] God, who desires his people to be holy, is basically involved in a mission of bringing them back into a holy relationship. He says that holiness is not a static property that God appropriates for himself. It is something he desires to impart to his people. The dynamic personality of God based on his holiness arouses fear, reverence and a consciousness of human unholiness. In his grace, he makes Israel holy, separating her for his purposes and imparting to her a holiness that is a result of her holy relationship to God. That is the motivation for Israel to continue to seek God's holiness: "You shall be holy, for I the Lord your God am holy" (Lev. 19:2). Religious pluralism is bringing the God of the Bible into a direct encounter with the gods of other religions. Dialogue is helpful, but only in making us sensitive to the context. The Old Testament believer was hardly in touch with adherents of other faiths. Any compromise was rejected. We note, for instance, that in revealing the Decalogue to Moses, God refers to himself as a "Jealous God" (Exod. 20:5) As with the concept of God's wrath, we need to understand the jealousy of God in its context. This attribute of God causes him to claim the totality of Israel's commitment in a personal and exclusive bond just as in marriage. God will not share his people with any other so-called gods.

Ken Gnanakan noted down the attributes of God in closer connection with mission. God's mission without God's love would be no mission at all. It is this covenant love that strengthens our mission in today's world. It proclaims a tangible relationship in contrast to experiences offered by "religions" that adapt to the demands of the commercialised world. God's righteousness is on those who had already entered into a righteous relationship with God. Social righteousness cannot be demanded without first challenging people to a right relationship with God. The one-sided stress on social justice without an adequate stress on a prior relationship with God is untenable. The overemphasis on mission in terms of justice needs to be challenged on biblical grounds. The primary thrust of mission is therefore the presenting of the God of justice, rather than the justice of God. In our great concern for justice and righteousness, we may forget that it is God's doing. His Messianic mission will make right the wrongs in his world, as righteousness will characterise his Messianic rule. The Messiah is "The Righteous One" (Isa. 53:11) who will ultimately demonstrate God's righteousness. But this does not exempt the Church as God's people from demonstrating messianic justice here and now. The Church must be the model and agent of God's right relationships in the world today. The Lord of the Church is the Lord of Righteousness.[211]

Ken Gnanakan goes further in exploring the relation of mission with the Church. He says that mission is an inescapable reality of the church and this must be recovered. We outline three major concerns. First, the Church must discover its missiological essence, not something from outside, but that which essentially belongs to its very nature. Second, the church must underline the uniqueness of its message. Only when we are convinced of the uniqueness of the revelation of Jesus Christ, we will be convinced of the necessity of our mission. Third, the church needs to discover the totality of God's mission. The church without mission, ecclesiology without missiology, is a static symbol of what God wants from his living body in witness to the world today. Despite great attempts to establish the true nature of the Church in its Christo-centricity and its relationship to the preached word, sadly, the Reformers failed to get to the heart of God's concern for mission. The undergirding of the Church with its missiological foundation must be accompanied by the affirmation of the uniqueness of the Christian message. Fervour in mission will be directly proportionate to the Church's commitment to the uniqueness of the revelation of Jesus Christ and the accompanying conviction that this is the message for the world. The dilution we see in the content of mission, on the one hand, and the decline in the commitment to mission, on the other, are related to the lack of clear recognition of the unique message of salvation in Jesus Christ.[212]

Gnanakan concluded that our operation should be from a purely New Testament perspective without the Old Testament background of the overall plan of Jesus Christ's mission. We do not mean that we have totally confined our studies to the New Testament. Some Old Testament themes have been included, but our studies have missed their true missiological potential. Even missiology has been only one section of our theology. The challenge is to see theology totally as missiological, rather than to merely attempt to give to missiology a theological touch up. Even our casual glance at the Bible, depicting the outworking of God in the world, has revealed a missionary God fulfilling missionary purposes. Our missiology will make our theology dynamic and contextual.

Integrated Learning
Ken Gnanakan's contribution on the educational philosophy is commendable. In his book entitled, *Integrated Learning*, he argues that education is more than just classrooms; it is a lifelong process of learning and evolution. Presenting a holistic picture of education is a means to personal development and social transformation, for a spontaneous learning environment within real-life contexts. It differs strongly from existing classroom perspectives on education, analysing its variegated forms within the broadest possible imperatives—integrating experience and learning. Exploring the ideas and teachings of Indian and Western educational thinkers—Plato, Dewey, Tagore and Gandhi among others—

this book draws out the essence of good education and its impact on the social order. It emphasises creativity in classrooms, focusing on interdisciplinary approaches and positive teacher-student interaction, and advocates the applications of learning in real-world situations. Through comparative theoretical analysis, this volume argues for a well-integrated educational set-up in which schools and colleges produce people who naturally merge into society at large, thus upholding the real essence of learning.

The objectives of *Integrated Learning* are to promote an integrated approach to teaching and learning, survey the teachings of Indian and Western educational thinkers, advocate creative classroom activity and positive student-teacher interaction and stress integration of personal and social growth of individuals with clearly balanced arguments and explanations.

This book upholds the idea of learning and education as a means to individual development and social empowerment. It presents a holistic picture, looking at learning as an integral part of one's social and physical life. Strongly differing from existing classroom perspectives, the book analyses integrated learning at its broadest possible imperative—arguing for a spontaneous learning environment within real-life contexts. The book broadly covers creativity in classroom education with a focus on interdisciplinary approach and positive teacher-student interaction. It also focuses on the essence of good education with a deep concern for the impact on social order with the application of learning to real-world situations

Conclusion

We have learnt about many Christian philosophical concepts in a historical perspective. The progress of Christian philosophy in history divides itself into six main periods: (1) *Early (ancient)* from the first century AD to the third century AD; (2) *medieval*, from the fourth century to the fifteenth century; (3) *Reformational*, in the sixteenth century; (4) *modern*, in the seventeenth and eighteenth centuries; (5) *Postmodern* philosophy in the nineteen and twenty centuries; and (6) *Contemporary*, in the twenty-first century onwards.

We also learnt that early Christian philosophy covers the period from the first century to the third century. This period gave us glimpses of the philosophical teachings of Jesus Christ, Paul and the Hellenistic Christian philosophers. There is no Christian philosophy without Christ. Apostle

Paul elaborated the Christian philosophy that was established by Jesus Christ. Paul realised his Hebrew message to the gentiles in the Greek language and adapted the content of the gospel to a new philosophical context. We have learned that medieval philosophy is 'Christian' philosophy. The philosophy of the medieval period is influenced by Christianity and sometimes 'used' to serve it. Philosophy is an autonomous discipline but at times, especially in the past, it has been strongly influenced by a religious context. The Middle Ages are commonly dated from the fourth century to the fifteenth century. Martin Luther, Erasmus, John Calvin and Zwingli were the Reformation Christian philosophers. It covered the history of Christian philosophy from 1500-1600 AD. The reformers of the sixteenth century were dominated by a concern for God. They took as their starting-point God's action in Christ, as witnessed by the Scriptures. From there they proceeded to think about the world.

We have realised the fact that while medieval philosophy found its guide and inspiration in the Christian religion, modern philosophy (1600-1800 AD) turned its attention to the nature of the new science and its method. Modern philosophy is usually considered to begin with the revival of skepticism and the genesis of modern physical science. Modern Christian thought has not been without its strong strains of rationalism. The rationalists of the seventeenth century were absorbed not so much in God but in the world. Many of them were scientists. Their starting-point was logic, and their techniques were derived from mathematics. But they were not irreligious men. Later modern philosophers of the eighteenth century contributed much in touch with empiricism and idealism.

Postmodern philosophy (AD1800-2000) is usually considered to begin after the philosophy of Immanuel Kant, at the beginning of the nineteenth century. Postmodern philosophy can be sub-divided into two categories: Early postmodern philosophy (1800-1900) and later postmodern philosophy (1900-2000). Early postmodern philosophy (nineteenth century) is usually considered to begin after the philosophy of Immanuel Kant, at the beginning of the nineteenth century. The second half of the chapter dealt with philosophers of various fields, such as Roman Catholic, Liberal, Neo-Orthodoxy and Evangelical. Contemporary philosophy is dealt with at the end. This period began in the twenty-first century. Contemporary philosophy has just begun and has a long way to go.

Helpful Questions
1. Briefly describe contemporary philosophy.
2. List the contributions of Ken Gnanakan to Christian Philosophy.
3. What do you know about Plantinga's Reformed Epistemology?

CHAPTER 10
Christian Philosophy

This chapter tries to make the reader understand that Christian philosophy is helpful in conceptualising and pursuing the absolute ultimate of perfection. It will give the reader a glimpse into Christian philosophy and Christian philosophers. In addition, this chapter will help the reader to understand the arguments about the existence of God and different views on the theory of knowledge.

Philosophy is not absolutely condemned in the Holy Bible. But there is a warning always for God's people to be cautioned against the manifestation and in its inherent tendency towards humanistic and cosmological perspectives. Christian philosophy strives for 'wholism' that Christianity has a distinctive perspective on all facets of reality. Christian philosophy should be Christo-centric and biblical. Philosophy that begins only with the temporal horizons and self-deduced wisdom can never know the eternal and infinite God (Col. 1:21). Christian philosophy originated with Jesus Christ and was developed by the Hellenistic philosophers, but it flourished under the medieval Christian philosophers. It faced many challenges during the days of modern Christian philosophers. During the Middle Ages, medieval Christian philosophers attempted to demonstrate to the religious authorities that Greek philosophy and Christian faith used, in fact, compatible methods for arriving at divine truth.

What Is Christian Philosophy?
'Christian philosophy' is Medieval philosophy (from 300 AD to 1500 AD); but not in the sense that philosophy or science or geography can be Christian, Hindu or Muslim but because the philosophy of the medieval

period is influenced by Christianity and sometimes 'used' to serve it. Philosophy is an autonomous discipline but at times, especially in the past, it has been strongly influenced by a religious context.[213] It is not right to think that Western Medieval philosophy jumps from Plotinus to Descartes and ignores 1,200 years of 'Christian' thought. In the Medieval period, Christian philosophy was mixed with pagan philosophy. The church had a monopoly of learning and most medieval philosophers were clerics. They were amateurs in the sense that they were non-professionals, and in the sense that they did it because they loved it. The church has inherited from its past Scriptures (New Testament) and writers (Augustine). From them it learned and thought doctrines of God, creation and salvation. But it also inherited a good deal of Greek philosophy. And many of its best minds were concerned to bring the church up to date and produce a synthesis of the two.[214]

Greek philosophers believed that ideas existed only as they were expressed in individual objects. They were also interested in the different kinds of causes that produced things. For the world as a whole, Aristotle believed that there was a First cause who is the Unmoved Mover of all things. Aristotle was also deeply interested in ethics and logic, and his writings on both subjects deeply influenced posterity. Greek thought left its mark not only upon the content but also upon the form of Medieval Christian writing. Whereas Augustine was direct, personal and biblical, later medieval writing was often logical but formal, thorough and thoroughly dry. This is true in varying degrees of the two medieval thinkers who count for most in theological philosophy today: Anselm of Canterbury and Thomas Aquinas. Platonism permeated the teaching of the Christian theologians of Alexandria, Clement and Origen. In third century AD, Plotinus developed what came to be known as Neo-Platonism. It was a belief in the ultimate One that lies behind all experience. In the One, all distinctions between thought and reality are overcome. The One is known by a method of abstraction—by saying what it is not like. By this Way of Negation, all non-essentials are removed. The One is known by profound, inner, mystical experience.

Definition

Philosophy is the systematic enquiry of man and his relation to the universe. Christian Philosophy is the systematic enquiry of God with His relation to man and his universe. The scripture portions, Col. 2:8 and 1 Cor. 1:18-25, can be said of the usual evangelical tirade against philosophy based on Paul's statement. There may not be more popular description in the Holy Bible. Here the cultural context is very important and necessarily applicable to the interpretation. Paul mainly dealt with in this part of the epistle against Gnostic-type movement within the church at Colossae (Col. 2:16-23). He gave them warning against a specific heresy that threatened to carry them off from real biblical Christianity. There is a Christian philosophy, an outlook upon life as well as a way to live. This outlook is discovered not by man, but given to man. It is God-initiated through historical and propositional revelation, culminating in the revelation or uncovering of God Himself in Jesus Christ. The centre of Christian philosophy is Christ and His cross. It is of course a stumbling block to the Jews and outright foolishness to the Greeks (1 Cor. 1:18-25). It is clearly revealed when we look at the dominant philosophies of the first century—Epicureanism and Stoicism (Acts 17:18), which always stood against pure Christian philosophy.

Christian philosophy is a term to describe the fusion of various fields of philosophy, historically derived from the philosophical traditions of Western thinkers such as Plato and Aristotle, with the theological doctrines of Christianity. Christian philosophy originated during the Middle Ages as medieval theologians attempted to demonstrate to the religious authorities that Greek philosophy and Christian faith were, in fact, compatible methods for arriving at divine truth. Augustine developed classical Christian philosophy, largely by synthesising Hebrew and Greek thought. He drew particularly from the Greek pagan thinker Plato, Neo-Platonism and stoicism, which he altered and refined in light of divine revelation of Christian teaching and the Bible. We have to develop a Christian philosophy that must support the biblical teaching and stand contradictory to the unsound teachings of the heretics and the secular philosophy. The secular philosophy or philosophy in general cannot be accepted as it is. It is the role of the Christian philosopher to reveal pure Christianity and stand against the non-Christian teachings of philosophy. The Christian philosopher has the responsibility to distinguish between Christ-centred philosophy and the other. Christian philosophy is the philosophy that reveals pure Christianity to the non-Christian world.

Important Christian Philosophers
We have already seen that in the early church, there were those such as Justin Martyr and Clement of Alexandria who assured their readers that many a pagan had been led to true religion through philosophy and that philosophy was to ancient Greeks what the Old Testament was to the Jews. The Greek-speaking father Justin Martyr, wearing the pallium, the

philosopher's cloak, proclaimed that the Christian faith was the 'only reliable and profitable philosophy.' He argued that the divine *Logos* (Word or Reason) had enlightened thinkers like Socrates to see the errors of paganism. The logical conclusion of such enlightenment was Christianity. But such suggestions were swept aside by writers such as the Latin writer Tertullian who rejected their arguments, pointed out that philosophy was often the root of heresy and that worldly wisdom without faith could never bring men to the knowledge of Christ. Philosophy is an intellectual discipline that is concerned with the nature of reality and the investigation of the general principles of knowledge and existence. In the early church, there was a kind of love-hate relationship with secular philosophy. Some denounced philosophy as the root of all heresy and insisted that worldly wisdom without faith was vain. Also, we saw that the Alexandrian fathers, Clement and Origen, who went even beyond Justin, had their respect for classical philosophy. Origen used Platonic ideas to reinterpret the whole range of Christian teaching on God, Christ and salvation.[215]

Later, in the medieval period, Christian philosophers such as St. Augustine of Hippo (354-430), St. Anselm of Canterbury (1033-1109), St. Thomas Aquinas (1225-74), Martin Luther, John Calvin and Rene Descartes (1596-1650) were convinced that man could attain some knowledge of that divine, supernatural framework within which Christian doctrine made sense. We cannot forget these Christian philosophers and their valuable contributions to Christian philosophic thought. The scholastics were not interested so much in reaching new and original conclusions as in devising logical arguments, supporting and explaining the doctrine of the faith. The age was mainly concerned with the rationalisation of the creed. All these prominent Christian philosophers tried to rationalise and harmonise the Christian doctrine with the Greek philosophy. Their chief interest was the transcendental world and their thought was fixed not so much on things that are seen in this world. The essence of things is prior to the existence of things.

Questions Asked in Christian Philosophy
However, Christian philosophy has concerned itself with more than just metaphysical questions. In fact, the subject has long involved important questions in areas such as epistemology, philosophy of language, philosophical logic and moral philosophy. Christianity is concerned not only with eternity, but with time; not only with evangelism, but ethics; and not only with proper worship, but with vocational choices as well. They predominantly consider the existence of God as axiomatic or self-

evident. Most theological treatises seek to justify or support religious claims by two primary epistemic means: rationalisation or intuitive metaphors. A Christian philosopher examines and critiques the epistemological, logical, aesthetic and ethical foundations inherent in the claims of a religion. They could elaborate metaphysically on the nature of God either rationally or experientially, a·Christian philosopher is more interested in asking what may be knowable and opinable with regards to religions' claims.

A Christian philosopher does not ask what God is, for such a question assumes the existence of God and that God has a knowable nature. Instead, a Christian philosopher asks whether there are sound reasons to think that God does or does not exist. Still, there are other questions usually being asked in Christian philosophy. For example, What would give us good reason to believe that a miracle has occurred? What is the relationship between faith and reason? What is the relationship between morality and religion? What is the status of religious language? Does petitionary prayer make sense? Some of them raised a question that if a theology is based partly upon the Christian revelation and partly upon alien philosophical ideas, what will be the result? At best the end product is a mixture containing ideas that cancel each other out. At worst the alien philosophy has been so allowed to crowd out and transform that the result is scarcely recognisable as Christianity at all. The early phases of this process can be seen in Aquinas.[216]

Nature of Christian Philosophy

Religion is a pathway to Christian philosophy. 'Isms' are in distance with Christian Philosophy. Atheism is in far distance. Christian philosophy seeks to prove the existence of God and assumes it as an ultimate out of which it forms its specific logic and interest; and it will reflect on the God-provided creational structures of existence in their diachronic processes of change over time.

Reconciling Christianity with Philosophy

For some, as with any fusion of religion and philosophy, the attempt to reconcile the two is difficult. Classical philosophers start with no preconditions for which conclusions they must reach in their investigation. Classical religious believers have a set of religious principles of faith that they hold one must believe. Because of these divergent goals and views, some hold that one cannot simultaneously be a philosopher and a true adherent of a revealed religion. In this view, all attempts at synthesis ultimately fail.

Others hold that a synthesis between the two is possible. One way to find a synthesis is to use philosophical arguments to prove that one's preset religious principles are true. This is known as apologetics and is a common technique found in the writings of many religious traditions, including Judaism, Christianity and Islam, but is not generally accepted as true philosophy by classical philosophers. Another way to find a synthesis is to abstain from holding as true any religious principles of one's faith at all, unless one independently comes to those conclusions from a philosophical analysis. However, this is not generally accepted as being faithful to one's religion by adherents of that religion. A third, rarer and more difficult path is to apply analytical philosophy to one's own religion. In this case, a religious person would also be a philosopher—by asking questions such as: What is the nature of God? How do we know that God exists? What is the nature of revelation? How do we know that God reveals his will to mankind? Which of our religious traditions must be interpreted literally? Which of our religious traditions must be interpreted allegorically? What must one actually believe to be considered a true adherent of our religion? How can one reconcile the findings of philosophy with religion? How can one reconcile the findings of science with religion?

Some Christian philosophers conceive their task. Others do not conceive the task of Christian philosophy in this way. For instance, some think that proving the existence of God is a meaningless endeavour since God's existence is not put in question by Christian faith, but assumed. A Christian philosophy that does not seek to prove the existence of God but assumes it as an ultimate out of which it forms its specific logic and interest is more apt to address a far different set of tasks in order to reflect on the God-provided creational structures of existence in their diachronic processes of change over time.

Soren Kierkegaard, the father of existentialist philosophy and particularly the school of Christian existentialism, had a major role in the formation of Christian Philosophy. To some readers, Kierkegaard's excruciating analysis of human reactions throws a brilliant light on personal behaviour. In the minds of some, Kierkegaard's Existentialism occupies the place vacated by idealism as the philosophical basis of Christianity.[217] C. S. Lewis was a literary critic of the first order, a mythographer in his children's fantasies, and an apologist for the Christian faith to which he adhered in the latter half of his life. He claimed not to be a philosopher, but his apologetics are foundational to the formation of a Christian worldview for many modern readers. Josef Pieper, a German Roman Catholic philosopher, orientated particularly on Plato and St. Thomas Aquinas. Alvin Plantinga is one of the key figures in the movement of Reformed Epistemology, which synthesises Analytical Philosophy and Christian philosophical concerns. Egbert Schuurman is a leading philosopher of technology who actively espouses a Christian philosophical approach.

Christian and Non-Christian Philosophers

Christian philosophers must enter the domains of philosophy if they have to seriously and honestly face the questions of truth. Christian philosophy was influenced by Greeceo-Western cultural and philosophical trends. There should be considerable interaction between Christian philosophy, Jewish philosophy and Islamic philosophy. Many Christian philosophers are well-read in the works of their Jewish and Islamic counterparts, and arguments developed in one faith often make their way into the arguments of another faith. Medieval Philosophy includes logic and natural science, and medieval theology includes Christian, Jewish and Islamic studies. Coverage extends from the Patristic period through the neo-scholasticism of the seventeenth century.

Reformational philosophy dialogues across acknowledged differences with many other approaches to philosophising with Christian synthetistic views of many kinds, also with some Jewish schools of philosophical thought, as well as some secular philosophies such as Neo-Marxism along with other atheistic philosophical schools; whereas the dialogue with Islamic philosophies is just beginning. It is important to note there is not one single secular philosophy embraced by all philosophers in any of the great religious traditions, not all are dialogical, and atheist-humanist schools are as much in conflict among themselves as are Christian and other self-acknowledged religious schools of philosophising. The problem of philosophy arises for them as something other than a task given by God in Christ to humanity, and so theirs is the problem of reconciling their activity as a deontological imperative insofar as they deny that philosophy is inherent in the creational ensemble as one task-activity among the many given by God. Those Christian philosophies that prioritise creaturely existence with its God-lawed modalities and societal spheres for daily life do not accept the idea of separate fields 'religion' versus 'philosophy' that then must be 'reconciled.' On this alternative view of the Christian philosophical task, philosophy is just one activity among many in a differentiated society, an activity that is entirely appropriate to creaturely human existence, and it may be pursued directly out of the depth of the Christian religion without the mediation of some extraneous reference.

Basic Assumptions of Christian Philosophy

Christian philosophy was a catch-all expression for a two-millennium tradition of rational thought that attempts to fuse the fields of philosophy with the religious teachings of Christianity. The following are the basic assumptions of Christian philosophy.

- Western Philosophy, except such as Greek philosophy, is the philosophy of Christianity or the Christian-influenced philosophy. If a philosopher from any background wants to learn about Western Philosophy, he or she must learn more about Christianity in the West and the relation between the State and the Church in the Medieval Period.

- Medieval philosophy (AD 300-1500) is 'Christian' philosophy, because the philosophy of the medieval period is influenced by Christianity and sometimes 'used' to serve it.

- Most of the classical western philosophers were Christians. It is easy, therefore, for anyone to have comparative study between Christianity and Philosophy.

- A synthesis will be helpful to use philosophical arguments to prove that one's preset religious principles are true. This is known as apologetics. Another way to find a synthesis is to abstain from holding as true religious principles of one's faith at all, unless one independently comes to those conclusions from a philosophical analysis. The next is to apply philosophical questions to one's own religion. In this case, a religious person can also have the role of a philosopher, by asking many questions that are closely related to his faith.

- Religious Philosophy (Philosophy of Religion) itself is the proof that one can relate Philosophy with Christianity. Because Christianity is a religion and the philosophic study of Christian religion is religious philosophy and so known as the 'Christian religious philosophy.' It is also called 'Christian philosophy.'

- Christian philosophies that prioritise creaturely existence with its God-lawed modalities and societal spheres for daily life do not accept the idea of separate fields of theology versus philosophy; rather they must be reconciled and reach in the formation of what is called Christian philosophy.

- On this alternative view of the Christian philosophical task, philosophy is just one activity among many in a differentiated society, an activity that is entirely appropriate to creaturely human existence, and it may be pursued directly out of the depth of the Christian religion without the mediation of some extraneous reference.

- Start with no preconditions for which conclusions they must reach in their investigation, while classical religious believers have a set of religious principles of faith that they hold one must believe. And ultimately they will reach into the world of Christian philosophy.

Role of Christian Philosophers

Search for wisdom is said to be the goal of philosophy. By 'wisdom' one can broadly mean ideas, insights in understanding the world, in its judgments about its truth and their religious and ethical implications, questioning and challenging the presuppositions of these judgments. Philosophers in general and especially Christian philosophers have a major role in this modern world of unsolved issues and uncontrolled situations.

In the early church, there were those such as Justin Martyr and Clement of Alexandria who assured their readers that many a pagan had been led to true religion through philosophy. The Alexandrian fathers Clement and Origen stood firm for classical philosophy. Origen used Platonic ideas to reinterpret the whole range of Christian teaching on God, Christ and salvation. Irenaeus wrote *Against Heresies* to refute Gnosticism. Origen squared off with his pagan counterpart Celsus on numerous occasions. The early Christian philosophers found devising support from philosophy and employed the weapons of the church and the state to defend the orthodox doctrine against all deceptive. They tried to rationalise and harmonise the Christian doctrine with the help of the Greek philosophy, which was in existence. The object of their chief interest was the transcendental world—the word of God, angels and saints; their thought was fixed not so much on things of this phenomenal world.

Apostle Paul frequently exhorted his disciples, especially Timothy and Titus, in the Pastoral epistles that they should differentiate truth from error and to refute the heresies tactfully but directly (1 Tim.6:20-21; 2 Tim. 2:24-26; Tit. 1:9-11). This cannot be done without some knowledge of the teachings of those opposed to sound doctrine, including theoretical and practical implications of the philosophies to be refuted. That is why we have to understand what they are teaching. Paul learned those philosophies and he was well-trained to refute those philosophies in order to prove the doctrines of Christ as a pure Christian philosophy. But the usual evangelical tirade against philosophy based on Paul's statements is normally misunderstandable (Col. 2:8; 1Cor.1:18-25). These are the two references to the anti-intellectual vein of evangelical Christianity. But it must be understood in the context of Paul's refutation against a Gnosticism that crept into the church at Colossae (Col. 2:16-23). Paul is warning the Colossians against a specific heresy that threatened them. Here philosophy is not absolutely condemned; but any philosophy that stands against sound biblical teachings and manifests itself as humanistic and cosmological rather than Christo-centric and theological should be rejected.

We have already seen that a Christian philosopher does not ask what God is, for such a question assumes the existence of God and that God has a knowable nature. Instead, a Christian philosopher asks whether there are sound reasons to think that God does or does not exist. It is the task of the Christian philosopher to interpret the doctrines of scripture that they provide overarching parameters to contemporary Christian philosophy and penetrating insights into detailed specifics. It is the role of the Christian philosopher to attempt to show Christianity's power of interpretation to its followers and well-wishers.

Society of Christian Philosophers
The Society of Christian Philosophers was organised in 1978 in USA to promote fellowship among Christian philosophers and to stimulate study and discussion of the issues that arise from their Christian and philosophical commitments. One of its chief aims is to go beyond the usual philosophy-of-religion sessions to stimulate thinking about the nature and role of Christian commitment in philosophy. Informal discussion among several Christian philosophers led them to believe that it was possible to form a group designed to promote philosophising and fellowship among philosophers who shared a commitment to Christianity. Meetings of the Society are regularly held in conjunction with the American Catholic Philosophical Association, the Eastern, Central and Pacific Divisions of

the American Philosophical Association and the Canadian Philosophical Association at the World Congress of Philosophy.

The primary purpose of the *Canadian Society of Christian Philosophers* is to provide a forum for discussion and exchange on topics in philosophy and religion, especially where these two disciplines meet. The Canadian Society is ecumenical in composition with respect to Christian denomination, theological perspective and philosophical orientation.

Evangelical Philosophical Society was founded in 1974. It (EPS) is an organisation of professional scholars devoted to pursuing philosophical excellence in both the church and the academy. Interested laypersons can join as associates or student members. The EPS journal, *Philosophia Christi*, is a scholarly publication containing discussion of a variety of topics that are of interest to the philosopher and to the philosopher of religion. *Asian Association of Christian Philosophers* is an active Christian philosophical organisation that conducts annual conferences. *The Association of Christian Philosophers of India* (ACPI) was founded in 1976 at Aluva, Kerala, India. The chief activity is the annual meeting, which is held at different places in India, with a topic chosen a year in advance and papers presented largely by the members. Since 2000, the association has begun publishing the proceedings of its annual meetings.

It is the need of the hour that all Christian philosophers should get together and form Christian philosophical associations at regional, national and international levels. The modern world must understand the difference between Christian philosophy and other philosophies. It is also the duty of every committed Christian philosopher to reveal Christian philosophy as the true and pure philosophy. The church in the modern world should reveal pure Christianity through the powerful and emphatic teachings of the Bible. Christian philosophical societies are to be formed in closer connection with the advancement of the ministry of the 'Kingdom of God' here on earth.

Logical Metaphysics (Theory of Knowledge)
Epistemology (Greek *episteme*, 'knowledge, *logos*, theory') is a branch of philosophy that addresses the philosophical problems surrounding the theory of knowledge. Epistemology is concerned with the definition of knowledge and related concepts, the sources and criteria of knowledge, the kinds of knowledge possible and the degree to which each is certain and the exact relation between the one who knows and the object known. Epistemology is the study of the theory of knowledge. Down through the

centuries, many philosophers have presented their philosophical viewpoints. There is no consensus among the philosophers in connection with the theory of knowledge. While some say that reason is the medium of getting knowledge, others say that experience or sense perception is very important. Again, a few of them stand for idealism; others uphold experiment as the way to accumulate knowledge.

It may be said that the theories that have been developed so far are quite convincing but any one of them cannot serve the purpose or stand alone as the theory of knowledge. We can have knowledge through many ways. This epistemology is known as *Logical Metaphysics*. It is also known as the *six-pack Epistemology* because there are six components in this theory of knowledge. There are two main streams under each head; there will be three parts. The two streams are *Logical Theory of Knowledge* and *Metaphysical Theory of Knowledge*. Reason, Experience and Experiment fall under the Logical Theory of Knowledge; Idealism, Faith and Revelation come under Metaphysical Theory of Knowledge.

Logical Theory of Knowledge
Logical theory of knowledge is a system of thought that speaks of the way of acquiring knowledge through logical conclusion, personal experience and objective observation. This system of thought is logically provable. Reason, experience and experiment are the three important sources as the theory of knowledge. Logical theory of knowledge demands some kind of proofs or logical inference in order to reach a conclusion.

Reason
Rationalism is characterised by its stress on the innate or *a priori* ability of human reason to know truth. What is knowable or demonstrable by human reason is true. Reason has precedence over other ways. The author of the book combined all the important prevalant theories of knowledge for the formulation of a new system of epistemology. Lacey said that rationalism is any view appealing to reason as a source of knowledge or justification. In more technical terms, it is a method or a theory in which the criterion of truth is not sensory but intellectual and deductive. In various contexts, the appeal to reason is contrasted with revelation, as in religion, or with emotion and feeling, as in ethics. But reason is possible through natural revelation. Descartes developed a method for attaining truths. These truths are gained 'without any sensory experience.' God exists because the *cogito* reveals that our mind is full of 'innate' ideas among which is the idea of infinite perfection. Leibniz asserted that, *in principle*,

all knowledge, including scientific knowledge, could be gained through the use of reason alone, though they both observed that this was not possible *in practice* for human beings except in specific areas, such as mathematics.

Reason is the philosophical theory of knowledge. It is one of the paths to knowledge. There is a considerable place for reason in Christian philosophy. The apostles reasoned when they defended the gospel among the other religious people groups and especially among the philosophers. But the reason should be subjective and positive in effect. The Holy Bible is the source of wisdom. We know all things related to God are informed to us through the Bible. Therefore, the things that are related to God should not be questioned or reasoned with negative intention. But all other things related to the world can be reasoned. At the same time, our purpose should be justified—that we are for God and His word and not against. For a person, being inquisitive and interested in learning, reasoning all other things related to the world are complementary in Christian philosophy. The objective reason stands against the working of the Holy Spirit. Being always critical with negative spirit will lead the one to blasphemy and backsliding. Liberal theology is the result of such type of reasoning. As a matter of fact, now it became a curse to Christian communities. Liberal theology is a threat to Christian philosophy. The position of pure Christian philosophy is always with the evangelical perspective and just against the liberal perspective. Liberal theology always question the authority of the Bible, the existence of angels, virgin birth of Jesus Christ, salvation through the blood of Jesus Christ, etc. They apply their limited human reason against the infallible word of God and the Creator of the universe. Liberal theologians are always in search of secular wisdom and critical spirit to criticise biblical authority and the spiritual standard of Christianity worldwide.

The Bible supports those who seek wisdom and encourages them to apply wisdom and understanding in their life-situation (Acts 18:4; 21:14; 19:8; 17:17). Therefore, we should distinguish the reason that one may apply in the field of Christian philosophy or in life situation, as whether it is God-accepted and biblical or non-Christian and unbiblical. We do not need to worry about those other than Christians, speaking or writing against God; but those who profess that they are Christians at the same time speaking or writing critically against God is a serious offence in the sight of God. Reason is a God-given gift, which should be properly used by mankind. Reason is the highest level of knowledge, and man should apply it wisely. The Bible gives us commands to seek wisdom and understanding. Also, we are commanded to behave wisely. Reason is the Bible-oriented theory of knowledge, if we apply it to the needy situation for a good purpose.

Experience
Empiricism is a theory of knowledge emphasising the role of experience, especially sensory perception, in the formation of ideas, while discounting the notion of innate ideas. The term "empiricism" comes from the Greek word *empirismos*, the Latin translation of which is *experientia*, from which we derive the word "experience." It holds that all our knowledge is derived from our experience, usually our sense experience, of things and processes in space and time. Hume argued in keeping with the empiricist view that all knowledge derives from sense experience. In particular, he divided all of human knowledge into two categories: relations of ideas and matters of fact. Mathematical and logical propositions are examples of the first, while propositions involving some contingent observation of the world are examples of the second. An 'impression' corresponds roughly with what we call a sensation. Our beliefs are more a result of accumulated habits, developed in response to accumulated sense experiences. Mill's empiricism thus held that knowledge of any kind is not from direct experience but an inductive inference from direct experience.

The Holy Bible supports the empiricist view. 1John 1:1-3 says: "That which was from the beginning, which we have *heard*, which we have *seen* with our eyes, which we have looked upon, and our hands have *handled*, of the Word of life; (For the life was manifested, and we have *seen it*, and bear witness, and shew unto you that eternal life, which was with the Father, and was manifested unto us;) That which we have *seen and heard* declare we unto you, that ye also may have fellowship with us: and truly our fellowship is with the Father, and with his Son Jesus Christ." Here we see that the words "seen, heard, handled" are possible through the sense experience. The Scripture teaches that we can taste or experience the love of God. We can feel the presence of the Living God. When the Lord heals our body, we experience it. Sense perception is the biblically proved theory of knowledge.

Experiments
Experiments emphasise those aspects of scientific knowledge that are closely related to experience, especially as formed through deliberate experimental arrangements. Positivism ascribes absolute prestige to

experiential science; it insists that the scientific methods of experiment, observation, prediction and measurement are ultimately the only methods of accumulating knowledge.[218] Positivists regard philosophy as the servant of science. The term "positive" means "scientific", endowed within five qualities: real, useful, certain, precise and relative.

Comte gave three proofs in favour of the law of the three stages: (a) *Proof by induction*: the historical development of world cultures and civilisation; (b) *Proof by analogy*; and (c) *Proof by demonstration*. Pragmatists contend that one cannot *think* or even *feel* truth, but one can discover it by attempting to *live* it. Truth is not what is *consistent* or what is empirically *adequate* but what is experientially *workable*. Peirce's major contribution was to place inductive reasoning and deductive reasoning as a complementary rather than a competitive mode. To this, Peirce added the concept of adductive reasoning. The combined three forms of reasoning serve as a primary conceptual foundation for the empirically based scientific method today. William James raised a question as to what may precisely be meant by terms such as "agreement" and "reality," when reality is taken as something for our ideas to agree with. The pragmatists are more analytic and painstaking, the intellectualists more unreflective. The popular notion is that a true idea must copy its reality. True ideas are those that we can assimilate, validate, corroborate and verify. Truth happens to an idea. It becomes true and is made true by events. Its verity is in fact an event, a process, the process namely of its verifying itself, its verification. Its validity is the process of its validation.

Metaphysical Theory of Knowledge

Metaphysical theory of knowledge describes theories of the mental or spiritual world, which is closely related to the Divine. These theories are originated as given to man by God and the human understanding of man in God through the supernatural or the mental realm. Man in his understanding of God attempts to grasp the supernaturalness in natural life. These are the unopposed factors and emphatically point out the human experience or any of this same type in acquiring the things of the mental or spiritual world.

Idealism

Idealism is the epistemological doctrine that nothing can be directly known outside the mind of thinking beings. Or, in an alternative stronger form, it is the metaphysical doctrine that nothing exists apart from the mind and the contents of the mind. The first prominent modern Western idealist in the metaphysical sense was George Berkeley. There is no major distinction between mental states, such as feeling pain, and the ideas about the so-called external things that appear to us through the senses. One major theme is that there are fundamental features of reality that escape our direct knowledge because of the natural limits of human faculties. Marcel distinguished three levels of approaches: The first is the sensation level of unconscious involvement or existence passively endured. The second is the reflection level of withdrawal from reality, thought, reason, logic, conceptualisation, objectification and philosophical systemisation into essences. The third is the level of recollection that operates a return to reality, a deeper conscious immersion in life, an ontological participation in being.

Understanding things or matter is possible through the mind. The Hebrew word *yetser* means "form"; figuratively conception (that is, purpose): mind, frame, thing framed, imagination, work, etc. Another Hebrew word is *labe* –form, the heart; also used (figuratively) very widely for the feelings, the will and even the intellect; likewise for the centre of anything. In the Old Testament the word "heart" is used for the mind. The mind is the centre of thoughts, intellect, etc. The Scripture supports the idealistic theory of knowledge. The Greek word for mind is *psyche*. The human mind can have three main types of works:

i. The mind can understand or grasp the things of the world. The Bible fully supports this view in many places.

ii. The mind can imagine. The Bible supports the possibility of human power of imagination. Psalm 55:6 says, "And I said, Oh that I had wings like a dove! For then would I fly away, and be at rest."

iii. The mind can have suppositions and doubts. It has also the Scriptural basis.

Faith

Reason is the discovery of the certainty or probability of such propositions or truths, which the mind arrives at by deduction made from such *ideas*, which it has got by the use of its natural faculties, *viz.* by sensation or reflection. *Faith* is the assent to any proposition not thus made out by the deductions of reason, but upon the credit of the proposer, as coming from God, in some extraordinary way of communication. Belief in God is a personal choice made on the basis of a *passion*, of faith, an observation, or experience. Theistic existentialists can freely choose to believe in God and could, despite one's doubt, have faith that God exists and that God is good. Definitions of human beings are primarily rational. But people actually make decisions based on what has meaning to them rather than what is rational. Faith and reason are mutually exclusive opposites. A statement from the Scripture is worthy of special mention. "I believed and therefore I have spoken" (2 Cor. 4:13). "We having the same spirit of faith, according as it is written I *believed*, and therefore *have I spoken*; we also believe, and therefore speak." 1 Tim.4:3 says, "...... *believe and know the truth.*" Another portion of the Bible that is an important reference in touch with this topic is that we understand through faith. "*Through faith we understand* that the worlds were framed by the word of God, so that things which are seen were not made of things which do appear" (Heb. 11:3). What does it mean? Faith is a way through which we obtain knowledge or we understand.

Faith can be communicated. That means it is a way of acquiring knowledge. "That the communication of thy faith may become effectual by the acknowledging of every good thing which is in you in Christ Jesus" (Phil.6). For therein is the righteousness of God revealed from faith to faith: as it is written, The just shall *live by faith* (Rom.1:17). For we *walk by faith*, not by sight (2 Cor. 5:7). We are advised to live and walk by faith. Apostle Paul said that once faith is come, it will take over all other things. "But after that faith is come, we are no longer under a schoolmaster" (Gal.3:25). That means faith stands on the top of the all other theories of knowledge. On another occasion, Paul said that 'I know whom I believe.' It is only when we encounter the living God in faith that we are in a position to grasp the truth of Christian faith. We cannot believe theological truths for non-theological reasons. Faith is a special revelation. The Bible says, "*Faith* comes by hearing; and hearing by the word of God" (Rom.10:17). That your faith should not stand in the wisdom of men, but in the power of God (1 Cor.2:5). Receiving the Holy Spirit can be done by *the hearing of faith*. "This only would I learn of you, Received ye the Spirit by the works of the law, or by the hearing of faith?" (Gal.3:2). Faith is the way through which we acquire knowledge. And through faith we can communicate to the world, thereby others will get the knowledge of truth.

Revelation
Man's thoughts are caused by a divine illumination. Finite minds alone cannot be a sufficient explanation of the presence of infinite ideas and perfect values. One must conclude that the human mind receives its light from an external source, which must be infinite and perfect: God himself.

Human reason can prove neither the immortality of the soul nor the existence, unity and infinity of God. These truths are known to us by Revelation alone. Special revelation is equivalent to the revelation of God in Jesus Christ. We should understand the relation between faith and revelation. *Faith* is the assent to any proposition not thus made out by the deductions of reason, but upon the credit of the proposer, as coming from God, in some extraordinary way of communication. This way of discovering truths to men we call *Revelation*. Revelation never runs counter to reason, but both poles of the subjective human experience are complementary. But others refuse to offer any sort of bridges between the knowledge of revelation and knowledge of the human world. God is transcendent and immanent. He should be identified directly with anything in the World, such as the words of Scripture. Revelation comes to men in the same way as a vertical line intersects a horizontal plane, or as a tangent touches a circle. Knowledge of God is the result of encounter with God, which in turn is the result of encounter with Christ, for Christ is the revealing Word of God to man (Heb.1:1-3; Rev. 22:18-19; Jn.1;1-2).

The other set of terms which require definition is *a priori* and *posteriori*. *A priori* knowledge is that which was absolutely of all deduction or reason. This contrasts with *posteriori* knowledge, which is empirical knowledge and is possible only through experience. *Posteriori* knowledge—knowledge of people, places and things—depends upon experience. To some extent, these pairs of concepts overlap. Analytic knowledge is also *a priori* knowledge. It is a matter of logical definition of terms and concepts. Synthetic knowledge is *posteriori*. It involves observation and experience through the senses. Knowledge is also both *a priori* and *posteriori*. Knowledge is both *deductive* and *inductive*. We have already gone through the *six-pack Epistemology* or *Logical Metaphysics*, the six components of the theory of knowledge. Also, we have studied that there are two main streams, each of which is subdivided into three parts. The two streams are *Logical Theory of Knowledge* (Reason, Experience and Experiment) and *Metaphysical Theory of Knowledge* (Idealism, Faith and Revelation).

Philosophy: Rational Theory of Knowledge

Origin

Ancient Greek philosophers studied the nature of reasoning. At the two great schools of Greek philosophy in Athens—the Academy, founded by Plato, and the Lyceum, founded by Plato's pupil Aristotle—students learned how to reason in a structured way using logic. The methods taught at these schools included induction, which involves taking particular cases and using them to draw general conclusions, and deduction, the process of correctly inferring new facts from something already known.

Plato's own theory of knowledge is found in the *Republic*, particularly in his discussion of the image of the divided line and the myth of the cave. In the former, Plato distinguishes between two levels of awareness: opinion and knowledge. Claims or assertions about the physical or visible world, including both commonsense observations and the propositions of science, are opinions only. Some of these opinions are well founded and some are not; but none of them counts as genuine knowledge. The higher level of awareness is knowledge, because there reason, rather than sense experience, is involved. Reason, properly used, results in intellectual insights that are certain, and the objects of these rational insights are the abiding universals, the eternal forms or substances that constitute the real world.

Scientific Philosophy
Definitions of scientific method use such concepts as objectivity of approach to and acceptability of the results of scientific study. Objectivity indicates the attempt to observe things as they are, without falsifying observations to accord with some preconceived worldview. Acceptability is judged in terms of the degree to which observations and experimentations can be reproduced. Scientific method also involves the interplay of inductive reasoning (reasoning from specific observations and experiments to more general hypotheses and theories) and deductive reasoning (reasoning from theories to account for specific experimental results). By such reasoning processes, science attempts to develop the broad laws—such as Isaac Newton's law of gravitation—that become part of our understanding of the natural world. One of the early writers on scientific method, the English philosopher and statesman Francis Bacon, wrote in the early 17th century that a tabulation of a sufficiently large number of observations of nature would lead to theories accounting for those operations—the method of inductive reasoning. At about the same time, however, the French mathematician and philosopher Rene Descartes was attempting to account for observed phenomena on the basis of what he called clear and distinct ideas—the method of deductive reasoning.

The ultimate test of the validity of a scientific hypothesis is its consistency with the totality of other aspects of the scientific framework. This inner consistency constitutes the basis for the concept of causality in science, according to which every effect is assumed to be linked with a cause. Scientists, like other human beings, may individually be swayed by some prevailing worldview to look for certain experimental results rather than others, or to 'intuit' some broad theory that they then seek to prove. The scientific community as a whole, however, judges the work of its members by the objectivity and rigour with which that work has been conducted; in this way, the scientific method prevails.

Epistemology for the Wise

Scientific theories are hypotheses from which can be deduced statements testable by observation; if the appropriate experimental observations falsify these statements, the hypothesis is refuted. If a hypothesis survives efforts to falsify it, it may be tentatively accepted. No scientific theory, however, can be conclusively established. Philosophy is the rational theory of knowledge. Philosophy is the epistemology for the wise men. Genuinely speaking, philosophy is not for the common people. Although there is a philosophy known as 'folk philosophy', that itself is very difficult for the common mass to understand. Philosophy is the highest level of wisdom of the world. Therefore, the elite can use philosophy as the rational theory of knowledge. The elite can obtain knowledge through philosophy. Philosophy is the rational medium of obtaining knowledge.

Existence of God

We normally use the word "exist" only in connection with things someone doubts or denies because to say that an object exists is not to give any information about the object. The object's evidence is a pre-condition of our saying anything about it.[219] Belief in God must be the basis of the Christian faith. Many medieval philosophers developed arguments for the existence of God, while attempting to comprehend the precise implications of God's attributes. Reconciling some of those attributes generated important philosophical problems and debates. The seventeenth- and eighteenth-century philosophers erected the framework of theistic belief within which Christian faith and practice seemed to make sense by means of certain arguments, proofs and demonstrations. These arguments are called ontological arguments, cosmological (casual) arguments and teleological arguments (argument from design).

Many arguments for and against the existence of God have been proposed and rejected by philosophers, theologians and other thinkers in the last few centuries. Arguments against the existence of God typically include empirical, deductive and inductive types. Conclusions reached include: 'God exists and this can be proven; 'God exists, but this cannot be proven or disproven'; 'God does not exist' (strong atheism); 'God almost certainly does not exist' (*de facto* atheism); and 'no one knows whether God exists' (agnosticism). There are numerous variations on these positions. Some think that proving the existence of God is a meaningless endeavour since God's existence is not put in question by Christian faith, but assumed. The most recent popular argument for the existence of God is called *intelligent design*, which asserts that certain features of the universe and of living things are best explained by an intelligent cause, not an undirected process such as natural selection. It is a modern form of traditional argument from design, modified to avoid specifying the nature or identity of the designer. We can understand the concept of God better still through experience. Knowledge of God's existence would then be swallowed up in adoration of His nature and love.

Ontological Argument
An ontological argument for the existence of God is one that attempts the method of *a priori* proof, which utilises intuition and reason alone. It was first proposed by the medieval philosopher Anselm of Canterbury in his *Proslogion*, and important variations have been developed by philosophers such as Rene Descartes, Gottfried Leibniz and Charles Hartshorne. The ontological argument has been a controversial topic in philosophy. The argument's different versions arise mainly from using different concepts of God as the starting point. For example, Anselm starts with the notion of God as a 'being than which no greater can be conceived', while Descartes starts with the notion of God as 'being maximally perfect.'

Anselm presented a demonstration in his *Proslogion*; this is his celebrated proof of the existence of God. He broke new ground with the publication of his *Proslogion*, originally called *Faith Seeking Understanding*. God is defined as 'that which nothing greater can be conceived or to put it simply, *the greatest conceivable being.*[220] Anselm's argument proceeds to demonstrate the existence of God as follows: I can think that than which nothing greater can be conceived.' Anselm's philosophy is rationalistic in nature. Anselm was supposedly charged for irrefutable theistic arguments.[221] Anselm presents the ontological argument as part of a prayer directed to God. He starts with a definition of God, or a necessary assumption about the nature of God, or perhaps both. God must exist in reality. The following steps more closely follow Anselm's line of reasoning. God is the entity greater than which no entity can be conceived. Anselm made another *a priori* argument for God, this time based on the idea of necessary existence. God must be necessary. God necessarily exists.

Rene Descartes composed a number of ontological arguments that differed from Anselm's formulation in important ways.[222] Generally speaking, it is less a formal argument than a natural intuition. Many philosophers, including David Hume, Immanuel Kant, Gottlob Frege and Gaunilo of Marmoutiers, have openly criticised the argument. Bertrand Russell noted of the argument: "It is easier to feel convinced that it must be fallacious than to find out precisely where the fallacy lies." David Hume did not believe that an ontological argument was possible. David Hume claimed that nothing could ever be proven to exist through *a priori*, rational argument by arguing as follows: The only way to prove anything *a priori* is through an opposite contradiction. Some argue that ontological arguments began simply with a concept of an absolutely supreme or perfect being. At the same time, ontological argument is widely accepted by theologians.

Cosmological Argument

The cosmological argument avoids the difficulties of the 'series of causes' idea. The cosmos (Gk. *world*) as a whole exists. The existence of the cosmos as a whole is radically contingent. Then, ultimately, there must be a First Cause, a cause that is not itself caused by anything else and this is obviously God. The 'uncaused cause' is the absolutely Supreme Being.[223] If the cosmos needs an efficient cause of its continuing existence, then that cause must be a *supernatural being*. The existence of which is uncaused is the Supreme Being, or God. A merely possible cosmos cannot be an uncaused cosmos. A cosmos that is radically contingent in existence and needs a cause of that existence, needs a supernatural cause, one that exists and acts to exnihilate this merely possible cosmos, thus preventing the realisation of what is always possible for merely a possible cosmos, namely its absolute non-existence or reduction to nothingness. Aristotle first formulated this argument. Aquinas re-formulated the argument as a proof for monotheism, understood the Divine as outside time, viewing all of time, indeed being present in all of time. Aquinas was a staunch advocate of 'cosmological' argument. There is a multiplicity of beings in the world. They are all limited beings. Their existence is not self-existence, but dependent existence.[224] If all the known realities of this world are contingent, there must be a reality, different from them. That is their cause and explanation. Therefore, God exists as the infinite, absolute cause of a finite world. God alone is permanent. Infinite perfection cannot change. [225]In Aristotle's *Metaphysics*, he described the *first cause* as one of the subjects of his investigation. For Aristotle, the *first cause* was the unmoved mover, which has been read as God.

Aquinas formulated the 'argument from contingency.' Thus, according to Aquinas, there must have been a time when nothing existed. If that is so, there would exist nothing that could bring anything into existence. Thus, contingent beings are insufficient to account for the existence of contingent beings, meaning there must exist a *Necessary Being* for which it is impossible not to exist, and from which the existence of all contingent beings were derived. It looks for an ultimate cause of the cosmos. There are five different ways of trying to prove the existence of God; they are really five different arguments or proofs, whether they are varied from one another.[226] In order to evaluate the cosmological arguments, it is necessary to consider the following: The cosmological argument as held by Aquinas does not concern itself with the 'first cause' that starts at the beginning of time. The cosmological argument is posited on the assumption that everything in the experience of our five physical senses is natural and that everything natural is caused, contingent and dependent—subject to cause by the uncaused cause. That includes time.

Several objections to the cosmological argument have been raised. One very simple objection is that *there must be the first cause* leaves open the question of why the First Cause should not require a cause. Another objection is that even if one accepts the argument as a proof of the First Cause, it does not identify this first cause with 'God' in the theistic sense. The claim of the cosmological argument that reason cannot remain content with the contingent world has been challenged. It is not clear that a necessary being is identical with an absolutely perfect being.[227] Although there were some objections, we should accept the fact that there must be a *Being* who created the universe and whose existence is not just a fact that could have been otherwise but is necessarily so. This world is contingent. This contingent world needs a necessary *Being* to produce it. We identify this Being as God.

Teleological Argument
A teleological argument, or argument from design, is an argument for the existence of God or a creator based on perceived evidence of order, purpose, design and direction in nature. The word "teleological" is derived from the Greek word *telos*, meaning *end* or *purpose*. Teleology is the supposition that there is purpose or directive principle in the works and processes of nature. [228] Most of the classic forms of this argument are linked

to monotheism. One can also leave the question of the attributes of a hypothesised 'Designer' completely open, yielding the following simple formulation: Every design has a designer. The universe has a highly complex design. Therefore, the universe has a Designer. Teleology traditionally is contrasted with philosophical naturalism. Teleology depends on the concept of a final cause or purpose inherent in all beings. There are two types of such causes, intrinsic finality and extrinsic finality. Extrinsic finality consists of a being realising a purpose outside that being, for the utility and welfare of other beings. Intrinsic finality consists of a being realising a purpose by means of a natural tendency directed towards the perfection of its own nature.

In *Phaedo*, Plato summarised the argument for teleology as follows, arguing that it is an error to fail to distinguish between the ultimate cause and the mere means by which the ultimate Cause acts: Imagine not being able to distinguish the real cause from that without which the cause would not be able to act as a cause. Aristotle argued that it is an error to attempt to reduce all things to mere necessity, because such thinking neglects the purpose, order and the 'final cause' that causes the apparent necessity. In addition to the final cause, Aristotle's analysis speaks of the material cause, efficient cause and formal cause. Augustine of Hippo presented a classic teleological perspective in his work, *City of God*. Augustine is giving a proposed view of God's teleology. Augustine's perspective follows from and is built upon the *neo-Platonic* views of his era, which in turn have their original roots in Plato's cosmogony. This would set the stage for Aquinas in the thirteenth century, whose arguments were much more thoroughly Aristotelian, *a posteriori* and empirically based than those of his predecessors. Aquinas makes a specific, compact and famous version of the teleological argument, the fifth of his five proofs for the existence of God in his *Summa Theologica*. Colin Brown writes:[229]

> It is true that the Christian belief in God as the Creator means that he is the ultimate cause and designer of the universe. But this article of faith based on an awareness of God over against ourselves – not a rational deduction to be drawn by those capable of following certain arguments. In other words, to claim that we proved the God of Christian faith by using these arguments is a deceptive piece of conjuring. For its effect it depends upon the ambiguity of the word God. Mere use of the word does not mean that we have proved God of the Christian faith.

Historically, teleology may be identified with the philosophical tradition of Aristotelianism. Philo is not satisfied with the teleological argument, however. The rationale of teleology was explored by Immanuel Kant in his *Critique of Judgement* and made central to speculative philosophy by Hegel and the various neo-Hegelian schools, including that of Marx. The empiricist philosopher John Locke, writing in the late 17th century, proposed a new and very influential view wherein the *only* knowledge humans can have is *posteriori* (i.e., based upon sense experience) and that there can be no *a priori* knowledge whatsoever. Berkeley included in his text *Alciphron*, a variant of the teleological argument that held that the order we see in nature is the language or handwriting of God. In the mid-18th century, David Hume presented arguments both for and against the teleological argument. Some of the philosophers say that this world is under chaos and natural calamities. A perfect creator cannot be the author of this imperfect world.[230] However, the world is the proof of God's existence as the teleological argument stresses the importance of a designer in the formation of this universe.

Other Arguments

Inductive arguments argue for their conclusions through inductive reasoning. Taking a hypothesis as a premise, we can deduce certain conclusions. If these conclusions can be tested by experiment and proved to be true, then we should give some evidence for the hypothesis. The more conclusions we can deduce and prove by experiment the more probable it is that the hypothesis is true. The whole process is known as induction.[231] Argument from testimony is another one that relies on the testimony or experience of certain witnesses, possibly embodying the propositions of a specific revealed religion. The witness argument gives credibility to personal witnesses, contemporary and throughout the ages. A variation of this is the argument from miracles that relies on testimony of supernatural events to establish the existence of God. The majority argument argues that the theism of people throughout most of recorded history and in many different places provides *prima facie* demonstration of God's existence. The argument that is grounded in personal experience is another one.

The argument from intuitive knowledge is another argument for the existence of God. Intuition or insight indicates our ability to see directly that a statement is true, as distinct from proving it by a series of logical steps in an argument. There are tests of intuitions such as consistency with other beliefs over a wide range. But to some extent, intuition offers its own guarantee of truth. In his *Emile*, Jean-Jacques Rousseau asserted that when our understanding ponders over the existence of God, it encounters nothing but contradictions; the impulses of our hearts are of more value than the understanding, and these proclaim clearly to us the truths of natural religion, namely the existence of God and the immortality of the soul. The same theory was advocated in Germany by Friedrich Schleiermacher, who assumed an inner religious sense by means of which we feel religious truths. According to Schleiermacher, religion consists solely in this inner perception, and dogmatic doctrines are inessential. Indian logic as represented by the Nyaya School makes intuition the first and most important of the four ways of knowing (sense perception). Rationalistic theism holds that the existence of God can be demonstrated with logical necessity. This is wrong for at least three reasons. First, logic is only a negative test for truth. It can eliminate what is false but cannot establish what must be true. Second, there are no rationally inescapable arguments for the existence of God because it is always logically possible that nothing ever existed. Third, there is no rationally inescapable way of establishing the first principles of reasoning. So, the existence of God cannot be demonstrated with logical necessity.

Pentacle Arguments for the Existence of God

All the above-mentioned arguments, of course, prove the existence of God. Most of them are biblical and acceptable. Although there are criticisms raised by several theologians and philosophers, Christians can understand that all those are Bible-centred. But above all, the author of the book presents a set of five proofs for the existence of God. It is known as the Pentacle Arguments for the existence of God. Pentacle Arguments are arguments such as Textual Argument, Creational Argument, Revelational Argument, Logical Argument and Intuitional Argument. The first three are based on the Bible and the next two are related to reason and the mind.

Textual Argument

The Textual Argument is the best of the proofs of the existence of God. I know God through the Word of God. The Holy Bible is the source of all knowing of God. I know God through biblical text. Therefore, I prove that there is God. Without the Scripture, I do not know about the real God. I have heard of many gods and goddesses. Many made comments on evil powers and occult works. But I know there is a real God through the Holy Bible only. The Bible is a special revelation of God. Jesus Christ, who was manifested in the flesh, can also be described as a special revelation of God. But the people of this generation cannot see Jesus in His physical presence as he lived on earth along with His disciples. People of every generation can get an understanding of the Son of God through the Scripture. The Holy Bible is the authentic document (sacred text), which is the best of all sources for the existence of God. Therefore, the Textual Argument is the best proof of the existence of God.

The Textual Argument cannot be disproved because the Bible says that there is God. The Bible begins with the word 'God' (Gen.1:1). I believe what the Bible says. However, all other above-mentioned arguments do not contradict the Textual Argument. The best is the Textual Argument, because it is deeply rooted in the Scripture. Some may oppose this proof, because everybody does not believe in the Holy Scripture. That is absolutely true. Everybody does not believe in God either. We cannot satisfy the heart that is filled with fury and malevolence. God is clearly pictured in the Scripture. Those who believe that the Bible is the Word of God will get the knowledge of God. Another question that may arise against this view is: Who is the real God, as there are so many religious groups with their gods and goddesses? Here we need to agree that God must be revealed to them through some way, such as teaching or preaching from the Word, evangelism and Bible reading. It is the responsibility of the Church to present Jesus Christ to them. Once they come to know about Christ, they will be able to know God more (John14:7). Jesus Christ said that "he that saw me, has seen my Father" (John14:9). Col.1:19 says that "for in him (Jesus) all the fullness of God was pleased to dwell" (ESV). Moreover, the Scripture says that "faith comes by hearing and hearing by the Word of God" (Rom. 10:17). Therefore, we should say that faith in God will be produced through the hearing of the Word of the Lord. If the text is available, it will be proclaimed—and then faith will be produced. Faith means 'faith in God.'

The Bible says that God exists. It also says: "The fool hath said in his heart, there is no God. They are corrupt, they have done abominable works, there is none that doeth good" (Ps.14:1); the statement is repeated in Psalm 53:1 as well. One may be a scholar, but if one does not believe in God, then one, according to the Bible, is a 'fool.' Human wisdom is nothing in the presence of God.

Creational Argument
The Judeo-Christian creation narrative occurs at the very beginning of the Bible. According to the Bible, the universe was created by God's command. God created the human race 'in His own image.' Genesis 1:1 starts with the word "God." *Elohim* is the first word of the Hebrew text. There was

nothing before God. First, there was God and then all else in the universe. The Bible says that God created the heavens and the earth. Beware of the biblical term "creation", instead of nature. The term "nature" suggests a self-forming and a self-sustaining universe. The biblical term is "creation." Yahweh creates and sustains the heavens and the earth. The Bible announces God as both Creator and Sustainer of the whole universe. Biblical faith has no sympathy with the atheistic notions that the earth and life came into existence through the impersonal impulse of natural laws. Creation is orderly and understandable. It progresses in step-by-step development beginning with the formation of the heavens and the earth and culminating in the creation of humankind. The Creator God is other than the earth; but He is actively and creatively present. Theologians refer to God's otherness, transcendence, presence and immanence. The Bible describes Yahweh as the righteous personal Creator God. Yahweh, the Creator of the universe, invites people into a covenant relationship with himself. He is a covenant God. Yahweh commands His covenant people to worship only Him. Biblical faith is convinced that Yahweh reveals Himself through His acts of creation and His acts in history. The creation event needs no books to describe it. That creation event is self-evident. Even before thousands of years, biblical writers took the responsibility of recording the surprising creative acts of Yahweh in history. The Bible is the record of God's creative events.

We have already seen that ultimately there must be the First Cause, a cause that is not itself caused by anything else—obviously God. Aristotle called the First Cause, the 'Uncaused Cause.' The 'Uncaused Cause' is the absolutely Supreme Being. A merely possible cosmos cannot be an uncaused cosmos. A cosmos that is radically contingent in existence, and needs a cause of that existence, needs a supernatural cause, one that exists and acts to exnihilate this merely possible cosmos, thus preventing the realisation of what is always possible for merely a possible cosmos, namely its absolute non-existence or reduction to nothingness. The creation cannot be the Creator. It is illogical to think that this universe appeared simply from nothing without a creator. The Bible says that "in the beginning, God created the heavens and the earth." Creational argument is the proof of the existence of God, which emphasises the biblical narrative of creation and shows that the creator of the universe is God Himself.

Revelational Argument

Revelation is the self-communication of God; it is God's disclosure of divine being or divine will to humans. Revelation may be in the form of a vision, often accompanied by words, or may consist only of words. In the Old Testament, Moses saw a burning bush and heard God's voice proceeding from it (Exod. 3ch.). General revelation refers to the knowledge of God communicated through the order of nature. Revelation refers to the knowledge of God that comes through specific experiences, such as visions, dreams or events. Christianity teaches that the natural order is revelatory of God, but the emphasis is on the special revelations communicated by the Creator. In Judaism too, the revelations given to Moses and the prophets, as described in the Bible, are fundamental to the faith. In all revelations, the primary element is the encounter with the divine, and the task of religious doctrine and religious tradition is to interpret and convey these revelations.

Jesus Christ spoke on revelation in Matthew 16:17: "And Jesus answered and said unto him, Blessed art thou, Simon Barjona: for flesh and blood hath not revealed *it* unto thee, but my Father which is in heaven." Flesh and blood here means human wisdom. Man cannot reveal the heavenlies; the Heavenly Father can. According to what Jesus said, it is made clear that spiritual truths will be and can be revealed only through God the Father. If man becomes spiritual and has the right relationship with God, divine communication is possible. Those who respect God and obey His commands will be able to have revelation of God and of the spiritual matters. On other occasion, Jesus said, "All things are delivered unto me of my Father: and no man knoweth the Son, but the Father; neither knoweth any man the Father, save the Son, and *he* to whomsoever the Son will reveal *him*" (Matt. 11:27).

Paul had a revelation of Jesus Christ. He was converted to Christianity through a revelation (Acts 9ch.). His important steps were taken by the revelation God gave him (Gal. 2:2). "And I went up by revelation, and communicated unto them that gospel which I preach among the Gentiles, but privately to them which were of reputation, lest by any means I should run, or had run, in vain." In Galatians 1:12, Paul says, "For I neither received it of man, neither was I taught *it*, but by the revelation of Jesus Christ." He got divine education directly from God. He never learned the spiritual truth from men, rather from Lord Jesus Christ. Again Paul says, "To reveal his Son in me, that I might preach him among the heathen; immediately I conferred not with flesh and blood" (Gal.1:16). Paul never asked human dignitaries for direction, rather God revealed to him what to do further. In the same way, we read Apostle John had revelation while he was in the island Patmos and God helped him to write all those things that were revealed to him. Revelation, which was revealed to John, is the last book of the Bible.

Revelation is divine gift given to the devout men by the Lord as a means of communication. 1 Cor.14:26 says that revelation will be given to committed Christians even today, as we gather together, for the edification of the church. This proves the existence of God. When a person has a revelation, it will be his own experience and nobody can reject it. Revelational argument is the argument with the proof of the Holy Scripture (Rom.1:18-32). God reveals Himself and the heavenly related things to his selected people. We have already seen that the Bible is special revelation. We know God and His will through the word of God. The will of God has been demonstrated in the word of God. Jesus Christ is the special revelation through whom we see and know God. John 14:7 says, "If ye had known me, ye should have known my Father also: and from henceforth ye know him, and have seen him." God had been revealed through His Son Jesus Christ. Cosmological and teleological arguments were developed from general revelation, which is the universe. The Scripture speaks of the general revelation (Ps.119:1, 2). Revelational argument is the authoritative proof of the existence of God. God's purpose of revealing Himself in nature is the proof that God exists.

Logical Argument
Logic (Greek *logos*, "word", "speech", "reason"), deals with the principles of valid reasoning and argument. Traditionally, logic is studied as a branch of philosophy. Philosophical logic has a much greater concern with the connection between natural language and logic. As a result, logical philosophers have contributed a great deal to the development of non-standard logics as well as various extensions of classical logic, and non-standard semantics for such logics. The study of logic is the effort to determine the conditions under which one is justified in passing from given statements called premises to a conclusion that is claimed to follow. Logical validity is a relationship between the premises and the conclusion such that if the premises are true then the conclusion is also true.

Logically, it is provable that God exists. There is no name for a person, thing or concept that does not exist. This is the premise. The Creator of the universe or the Uncaused Cause has a name—'God.' Therefore, God exists. It is the logical conclusion. We call that Uncaused Cause, the Cause of the universe, God Almighty. It is illogical to say that there is no God or that God does not exist.

Intuitional Argument
Intuition is the understanding of self-evident principles about which no doubts are possible; it is instinctive knowledge. It is the knowledge of being aware of or knowing something without having to discover or perceive it or the ability to do it. Intuition is something known or believed instinctively without actual evidence for it. Philosophically, intuition is the immediate knowledge of something. The philosophical perspective of the intuitive perception is the doctrine that asserts that a perceived object is intuitively known to be real. Intuition in the ethical perspective is the doctrine that knowledge of goodness or obligation and the principles governing them can be discerned by themselves. It is made clear that the intuitive knowledge is known directly and instinctively without being discovered or consciously perceived. The reality of perceived objects is known by intuition. Man has inherent moral consciousness through being made in God's image. Paul writes that conscience also bears witness; thoughts accuse and try to defend. (Rom.2:15). It is the inherent apprehension we are concerned here.

Intuitional argument is that all human beings have an idea of the super power over the entire universe. We call that super power "God, Creator, Sustainer" etc. Normally, people fear the Creator, or they revere Him. Without having any teaching or direction, even the aborigines in dense forests worship their deities. It is of course true that they do not know who the real God is; because of that they worship the Sun, Moon, lightening, hills, trees, etc. They too believe that God exists. There is an intuitive knowledge in all human beings about a God who controls the universe. Intuitional argument is the general revelation that God has given to everyone in the world.

Conclusion
The five proofs, Pentacle arguments, of the existence of God are the real and irrefutable proofs of God's existence. There are many other proofs that have been described earlier by many other philosophers. All those philosophical arguments cannot be disproved easily, though a few criticisms have been raised. God exists. The existence of God is a reality. All proofs, especially Pentacle arguments, are strong proofs of God's existence in the universe.

Kingdom of God

The term "kingdom of God" is unforgettable for the blood-washed saints because it is unavoidable for the descriptive history of biblical Christianity. Even today, we frequently use the phrase in our preaching and in our prayers. 'The kingdom of God' are the main words of the Bible. The manifestation of God's kingdom here on earth is the sum total of God, not of man, but manifested in a historically developed idea, nor firstly used by a theologian; rather it is mostly seen in the ever-remembered teachings of Jesus Christ.

Terminology

The word "kingdom" is derived from the Greek word *basileia*, which is the same as *Malkuth* in the Hebrew language. *Basileia* is the abstract or dynamic idea of reign, rule or dominion rather than the concrete idea in the Old Testament. But the word *malkuth* can be both reign and realm in which He reigns.[232] An increasing number of scholars widely recognise the above-mentioned meaning of the root words. *Malkuth* is God's sovereignty; it describes the rule of God.

The kingdom of God is the absolute purpose of God accomplished in the human history. God was, is and will be supreme in God's kingdom. The kingdom is not the work prepared by man for God, rather it is the masterpiece of God for man; it is not the result of human effort, nor the outcome of man's intellectual development. The kingdom of God is not simply a matter of outward words or signs. The central message of the kingdom is neither theology nor political action. It is as spiritual kingdom that we all need to receive.[233] We can easily find the term "kingdom of God" in the Holy Bible, which has several meanings and represents many dispensational periods. A sincere attempt has been made to isolate four distinct uses of the phrase.[234]

i. In a few places, the "kingdom of God" bears clearly the abstract meaning of reign or rule. In RSV, we read *basileia* by kingly power in Luke's Gospel (19:11, 15; 23:42) and by kingship in John 18:36.

ii. It refers to the kingdom as a future apocalyptic order into which the righteous will enter at the end of the age. Thus the "kingdom of God" is interchangeable with the age to come (Mark 10:23; Matt. 18:10; Luke 13:28).

iii. The "kingdom of God" is something present among men; man is supposed to receive it. It is the responsibility of man to seek the kingdom. God's kingdom is present within or among men (Matt. 6:33; Mark 10:15; Luke 12:31, 17:21).

iv. The "kingdom of God" is represented as a realm or sphere into which men are now entering (Matt.11:11; Luke16:16).

Jesus and the Kingdom
"The kingdom of God" is the key term of the Bible. The Kingdom is the absolute purpose of God accomplished in the human history. God was, is and will be supreme in God's kingdom. We look at Jesus to whom the Kingdom is basically a society upon earth where God's will is as perfectly done as it is in heaven. The passport to the Kingdom as Jesus saw it consists of child-like spirit, forgiving spirit and serving spirit. To introduce Jesus Christ, the centre of salvation and victory, into the world is an important purpose of the Kingdom. People of deep spiritual perception and reality can easily find out the lines of prophesies and their fulfillment in the Old Testament as well as the New Testament in touch with the Kingdom. The central message of the Kingdom is about Jesus Christ, the all-glorious head. Therefore, preachers of the Kingdom must hold the redemptive message of Jesus Christ as the purpose of the proclamation of the kingdom of God. The very foundation of the Kingdom is laid in the gospel of Christ's accomplished redemption. The purpose of the Kingdom is the proclamation of the gospel.

The works of God's kingdom were manifested through Jesus' ministry too. He proclaimed it, acted upon it (Matt. 12:28), told disciples to preach it, explained it in parables and disputed its meaning with others. The ministry of Jesus is of the Kingdom. The concept of God's Kingdom occupies the central position in Jesus preaching. Jesus' preaching of the Kingdom is a revelation concerning the messiah. Kingdom of God and the Son of man are co-related in Jesus' preaching. The coming of the Son of man is synonymous with the coming of the kingdom of God (Matt. 16:19; Mark 9:1).

Kingdom of God in the New Testament
God the Father established His everlasting Kingdom here on earth through nobody else but His only Son Jesus Christ. If we want to understand the kingdom of God, all we need to do is to see what Jesus said and did throughout His ministry. The good news of the Kingdom becomes Jesus Himself. He lived, taught and worked with the thoughts of the kingdom of God. His ministry was started with the proclamation of God's Kingdom.

The kingdom of God in the Scripture is called the Kingdom of His Son. He is the perfect revelation and demonstration of the Kingdom. There are five ways through which Jesus reveals Kingdom realities: (1) His teaching, (2) His life, (3) His death, (4) His risen life and (5) His teaching through the church. It is a five-fold revelation, confirmation and re-affirmation of Kingdom-living.

The kingdom of God was Jesus' central theme (Mark 1:15-4:17). We read about it in the introductory summary of Mark. It is the task of Jesus Christ (Luke 4:43). Evangelists echo his words (Matt.4:23; 9:35; Luke 8:1). He appointed his disciples to proclaim the Kingdom (Luke 9:2; 10:9). He proclaimed it and acted upon it (Matt.12:28; Luke 11:20). The scriptures seem to indicate that the kingdom of God existed in the time of Jesus since He seemed very desirous to cause His followers to seek the Kingdom. It is God's will that we definitely participate in or receive His Kingdom here on earth. Christians ought to know and be certain that they can walk in the power and presence of the kingdom of God today. We should know that we belong to the family of God; therefore, we are part of the Kingdom. The power of God's kingdom entered into human history through the ministry of His disciples.

Among all the New Testament books, the gospels play an important role in 'the kingdom.' The word "kingdom" is found 55 times in Matthew, 20 times in Mark, 46 times in Luke and 5 times in John. "Kingdom of heaven" and "the kingdom of the Son of Man" are the other important terms in Matthew. The word "God" was not in common use among the Jews. Because Matthew wrote the gospel for the Jews, he did not use the term "the kingdom of God", but that of heaven (Matt.13:43, 41, 16:28). The kingdom of God is described in three ways: (1) Jesus declares that kingdom of God is at hand (Mark 1:14, 15; 4:11); (2) entering or receiving the kingdom (Mark 9:47, 10:14, 15, 23); and (3) Jesus looks forward to the day when God's kingdom will appear in Glory and perfection (Matt. 25:31-46; Mark 9:1).

The kingdom of God was manifested in human history through the ministry of Jesus' disciples and other followers. The description of that history is seen in the Book of Acts. We read in the Acts of the Apostles that the Kingdom was manifested in history. After the resurrection, Jesus spoke about the kingdom of God over a period of forty days (Acts 1:3). Philip preached the good news of the Kingdom (Acts 8:12). We must go through many hardships to enter the kingdom of God (Acts 19:8). The kingdom of God was preached among the people (Acts 20:25). Apostle Paul persuasively argued about the Kingdom of God (Acts 19:8). Paul explained and declared to them, the kingdom of God and tried to convince them about it (Acts 28:23).

Heirs of the Kingdom

The Kingdom is something that is to be received here and now (Mark 10:15). What must be received is not a realm, present or future, but the reign and blessings that accompany it. To receive the kingdom of God is to accept God's rule, the yoke of God's sovereignty. The Kingdom is working quietly among men. It does not force itself upon them. It must be willingly received. The word of the Kingdom, which is practically identical with the Kingdom itself, brings forth much fruit. We understand that the Kingdom is to be received as children receive gifts (Mark 10:15; Luke18:16, 17). In this rule of God's kingdom, trustfulness and receptivity are required of the sons of the Kingdom (Matt. 19:14); Kingdom of God is a present possession of the childlike. The door to be knocked at is the door that gives entrance into the kingdom of God.

Jesus speaks about the kingdom of God in terms of the need to enter the Kingdom like a child (Mark10:15). The only condition is that we should repent and believe and receive this good news (Matt.18:3). Becoming a child means to come into a condition of complete dependence on God, to be ready to let God work. Acceptance of the Kingdom in Rabbinic terms was the way of the 'wise and prudent.' But Jesus swept away this legalistic learning and taught that God's reign may be accepted by the simple and the child like; and one must submit to God's reign in complete childlike obedience and trustful receptiveness. God's will alone is the principle of the Kingdom. All that is required of the child is submission.

The presence of the Kingdom demands a radical conduct. Men cannot passively await the coming of the eschatological Kingdom. On the contrary, the Kingdom has come to them and they are actively, aggressively and forcefully to seize it. The Greek word *biastai* is used for the term "violence." The kingdom of God does not belong to sleepers and sluggards; the man of force seizes it. This is the only good force, to force God, and seize life from God. Since Jesus used radical metaphors involving physical violence to describe the reaction of men to the Kingdom, it is consistent with this teaching to interpret *biastai* in terms of the radical reaction of those who receive the Kingdom. The kingdom of God exercises its 'force' or 'makes its way powerful' in the world. This rendering of the verb is most consistent with the dynamic view of the kingdom of God. The kingdom of God acts powerfully and requires a powerful reaction. The acts of violence are required from those who would enter the Kingdom (Matt.11:12). Jesus demanded violent conduct of those who would be his disciples (Luke 14:26). A man should be willing to surrender to the kingdom (Matt. 13:44-f). He told a rich man that he must rid himself of all his earthly possessions to enter into the kingdom (Mark 10:23). The age of fulfillment is present, but the time of consummation still awaits the age to come. Entrance into the Kingdom is totally dependent upon grace and not upon any kind of status or merit. But there are requisites. One must be born again by accepting the free gift of salvation that he alone provides, learn from him and put his principles into practice. Entrance into the kingdom would be possible by (a) new birth (John 3: 1-8); (b) Granted (Luke 22:29); (c) Diving call (1 Thess. 2:12); (d) Repentance (Matt. 3:2); (e) Salvation (2 Tim. 4:18); (f) Suffering (Acts. 14:22).

Who are the citizens of the Kingdom? Those who seek the Kingdom first suffer persecution for the sake of God's kingdom (Matt.6:33; Acts 14:22). Citizen of the Kingdom understand the mysteries that our Lord revealed. Our Lord meant to hide from others the very truths that the people of the Kingdom are privileged to discover. A man whose heart pursues the spiritual commodities of communion with God, life, truth and righteousness is certain to be a citizen of God's kingdom. The righteousness of the Kingdom can be experienced only by the man who has submitted to the reign of God, which has been manifested in Jesus and, therefore, who has experienced the power of God's kingdom. Those who do the will of God and the poor in spirit will inherit the Kingdom (Matt.5:3; 7:21). Jesus said that the tax collectors and the prostitutes who believed and repented will enter the kingdom of God (Matt.21:31). Also, those who will be on the right side of the king will enter the kingdom of God (Matt.25:34). God has been pleased to give 'little flock', 'the kingdom' (Luke 12:32). Abraham, Isaac, Jacob and all the prophets will be in the kingdom of God (Luke13:28-29).

Two Stages of the Kingdom

The words of Jesus are manifestation of the kingdom of God as 'two-age' terminology: present and future. The Kingdom has come into history in the person and mission of Jesus, and in the same way, the Kingdom will continue to work in the world until the hour of its eschatological manifestation. The Kingdom is not just a future gift; it is also a present gift to those who will renounce all else and throw themselves unreservedly upon the grace of God; the Kingdom is imminent and present. The presence of the Kingdom is to be understood from the nature of God's present activity and the future of the Kingdom is the redemptive manifestation of his kingly rule at the end of the age. The present and future stages of the Kingdom are discussed below. The Kingdom in this age is called 'Moral Kingdom' and that in the age to come is called 'Spiritual Kingdom.'

Moral Kingdom
As we have seen, the kingdom of God exists now here. It operates in a specified manner. The kingdom of God is the actualisation in history of God's power and wisdom as the secret of all true human welfare. The Kingdom is the supreme spiritual reality present in the experience of believers. The Kingdom in its essence is the reign of God in the experience of the individual soul. The kingdom of God is where God's will is done on earth. The sayings about the presence of the Kingdom mean that the process of the coming of the Kingdom is already under way. Before the eyes of John's messengers, Jesus cured many diseases and plagues and evil spirits, and on many that were blind, he bestowed sight (Luke 7:19-23; Matt. 11:2-6). In his curing of the sick and the possessed and his preaching to the poor, having been engaged in a holy war, Jesus was invading the realm of evil and releasing its prisoners. When we pray with laying our hands for the sick, we may see the manifestation of God's kingdom which is here at hand now. Christianity is a manifestation of God's kingdom on earth. It is a new way of living. The sentence, 'the kingdom is in the midst of you' stands for the moral kingdom. Matt. 24:14 is proof for the end of the moral kingdom. Also, Satan must be absolutely defeated.

Like all other kingdoms, the kingdom of God established principles or laws that we must understand to enjoy full kingdom-blessing. He stated principles of the Kingdom that he would shortly extend by the outpouring of his spirit and that would be understood and become the laws of life for those born of the spirit, especially those baptised or immersed in the spirit. The character or the constitution of the kingdom of God is generally known as the Sermon on the Mount (Matt. 5-7 ch). Moral law is the objective expression of God's will for man as it necessarily emerges from his own moral perfection. Love to God is the heart of moral law. Moral law shows us the way to perfect love. To manifest the kingdom is to be a manifestation of God's peace, joy, faith, etc., through our submission (Matt.5:19), righteousness (Matt. 5:20), resolute determination to overcome temptation (Mark 9:47), forgiveness to others (Matt. 18:23) and the primacy of heart's love (Mark 12:31-34). We read again in the Gospel of Matthew as God's Kingdom would be manifested through spiritual beggars (5:3), the intercessors (5:4), a matter of control (5:5), a work of the spirit-righteousness (5:6), the flow of mercy (5:7), the ultimate happiness (5:8), the way of inheritance (5:9) and persecution (5:10, 11). The three cardinal virtues in the kingdom of God are faith, hope and love. Pat Robertson writes about the laws of the Kingdom as such: (1) The law of reciprocity (Luke 6:38), (2) the law of use (Matt. 25:14), (3) the law of perseverance (Matt. 7:7-11), (4) the law of responsibility (Luke 12:48), (5) the law of greatness (Matt. 18:2-4), (6) the law of unity (Matt. 6:10), (7) the law of miracles (John 14:2; Matt. 8:11) and (8) the law of Domination (Matt. 16:18-19).

The ethics of Jesus is the ideal standard of conduct that is valid for the moral kingdom. The beatitudes, the golden rule and the parable of the good Samaritan are among the choicest selections of the world's ethical literature. The kingdom has this constitution, a system of fundamental principles and virtues to determine the quality and conduct of life. The ethics of Jesus is the Kingdom ethics, the ethics of the reign of God. They are relevant only for those who have experienced the reign of God.

Spiritual Kingdom

The second stage of the kingdom of God is spiritual kingdom. We read the scriptural evidence of the beginning of stages in Luke 21:29-31. Spiritual kingdom is the eternal kingdom of God in which God will reign literally and will defeat his enemies, the satanic dominion. It is an ever-lasting kingdom; it will never be defeated. The kingdom of God is made after the plan of God. God is spirit. Therefore, the kingdom of God must basically be a spiritual dimension. The spiritual kingdom covers the period of eternity order above history where God's rule is always present; it would bring the death of the present order. The kingdom is not primarily physical—material to be seen with our eyes. The expectation of the future bears a universal and realistic character and it is not permissible somehow to sublimate this eschatology of the kingdom of God. The coming of the Kingdom is the consummation of history, not in the sense of the end of the natural development, but in that of fulfillment of the time appointed for it by God (Mark 1:15).

When will the kingdom of God be set up? (a) At the return of the King from glory (Matt. 25:31-46; Rev. 17:14). (b) When Jerusalem is surrounded by armies (Zech. 14 ch). (c) After the church is raptured (1 Cor. 15:51-58). (d) After the future tribulation (Matt. 24:15-31; Zeb. 14:1-21). (e) After the great apostasy and the revelation of antichrist (2 Tim.1:12; Rev.19:11-21). (f) At the time, Antichrist is destroyed and Satan is bound for 1000 years (Rev. 5:10; 22:12-17). (g) After the first resurrection (Rev. 5:9, 10; 20:1-6). (h) When Ezekiel's temple is built (Ezek. 40:1-43:7). (h) After Israel is gathered back from all countries (Ezek. 20:33-36). (i) When Israel is repentant (Zech. 12:10-14; 13:1-9). (j) When Jews will be delivered from the enemies (Acts. 15:13-18). (k) In the days of the kings' end (Rev. 17:8-18; Dan. 2:40). (l) At the end of the time of the gentiles (Luke 21:20-24; Acts 15:13-17). (m) After all of revelation is fulfilled (ch 4-19). The kingdom of God will come down from above and effect a marvelous transformation of the world. God will create the new heaven and new earth where there will be untroubled joy, prosperity, peace and righteousness. The final visitation of God will mean the redemption of the world for a redeemed earth.

In short, the kingdom of God is the historical fulfillment of the messianic prophecy. It is the realisation of God's power and wisdom in the history of the virtue and welfare of the people. God is the Lord of history. He works in history and will establish the kingdom at the end. The kingdom is defined as the scope of history and the hope of redemption.

Philosophy of the Church
God's church is a witnessing community. The message of Christ shall have to be communicated within our cultural context. Our words must relate to the actual world, where people are meant to reach. Christians must be seen as salt of the earth and light of the nation, imparting kingdom values to people. Our message needs to be heard from our lives touched by Christ and rooted within our cultural context. The church must bring glory to our God the Father. Human beings are gregarious with a need for social relations and companionship. The Bible continually speaks not only of the importance of the family, but also of the individual's responsibility to a wider community. This community is called in Greek *ecclesia*. In the New Testament, the concept is given a fuller meaning as seen in the writings of the Apostle Paul about the nature of the church. The church is portrayed not merely as a collection of individuals, but as an inter-related organism—a body. *Ecclesia* is not merely a human association or a gathering of like-minded individuals; rather it is a divinely-created affair.[235]

Practical Community
The church shall not better be signified as the New Testament church, because the church is only in the New Testament. It is clearly understood in the term itself. There was no church in the Old Testament. God had a people in the Old Testament, through whom God wanted to reveal His purpose in the whole world. The response of the Israelites to the fulfillment of God's plan remained unsuccessful. That is why God intently made His people 'the church' in the New Testament period in order to reveal His will to His universe. The church is destined to be a model in the world according to the pattern given to them through the Holy Scriptures. The church is the divine agent of God in the universe. The Lord of the universe deals with the universe through the church only. The demonstration of God's love is clearly visible in the living model of the church. The universal purpose of God is being fulfilled in and through the church as a testimony to the world. The uniqueness of the church is a concrete demonstration as well as representation of universal salvation. Church is a practical community through which people may see the works of God in society. The practical application of Christ's teaching is more important than the theoretical implication. The world's expectation of the Christian community is nothing but Christian practicality. The church as a practical community must exhibit the love of God in action in the non-Christian world of darkness. Scripture presents the church as the people of God, the community and body of Christ and the fellowship of the Holy Spirit. The church is a Messianic Community that confesses that Jesus is the Lord. As ruler of the universe and Lord of the Church, He sends disciples to gather the nations. His saving rule constitutes, governs and protects the Church as the Community of the Kingdom.[236]

'Love your neighbour' does not simply mean that we may show a smiling face or say a few loving words to our neighbour, rather it is meant that we should be practice-oriented. Our love for our neighbour precedes our action. It is an easy task for Christians to show their love to their neighbour through their words, but here the deeds of Christians are very much prioritised. The permanent stay of a Christian in a particular place is a clear indication that his or her actions are clearly visible to his or her neighbour. A Christian is not an alien in his or her society. Love in action is strictly demanded as it is an unavoidable factor of Christianity.

Neighbour-People
When we talk of the people beyond the level of a committed Christian, the term 'non-Christian' is not up to the mark. It will lead us to think and

work against those who are not in Christ. This very word separates us from our duties to this world. Jesus Christ taught us to think of those who are yet to come to Him shall be considered as our 'neighbour.' 'Love your neighbour as yourself' is the golden rule of Christianity (Matt.19:19; 22:39; Mark12:31-33; Luke10:27-29).This life-changing principle of Jesus' teaching demands the solemn responsibility of each Christian to the neighbour of his world. They may be regarded as 'neighbours' or 'neighbour-people.' We are commanded to love them as we love ourselves. Those who are not in the cosmic church of Christ are our neighbours only. That means they are not very far from us; rather they are really very close to the Christ of the Church. Jesus once said the same thing that 'he is not very far from the Kingdom of God', referring to a person other than a disciple or follower of Jesus. This sound teaching of Jesus Christ helps us to love and render our service to them that are very near to us.

The people in the Old Testament apart from the Israelites were far from God. They were considered alien. But in the New Testament, the wall of separation was broken down through the cross of Christ's death; people in the world were 'the distant-society' in the Old Testament. But from the New Testament perspective, God has made the distant-society very near to God, a neighbour-people. Now the message of the gospel is applicable to everyone who comes to him. We are commanded by Christ to consider them as our 'neighbour.' Those who belong to other religions and isms shall be considered our neighbour. It is the gospel that makes it possible; but at the same time this neighbour-people should believe in Lord Jesus Christ as their Lord and Saviour in order to enter the Kingdom of God. Thus the neighbour-people will be the members of the church, a 'Practical Community.'

Baptism

The sacrament of baptism has the outward sign of washing. Sacrament does not come from the water, but from the act of pouring the water, in the form of washing. The outward reality is in the washing with water, while the sacramental sign in the inward justification; this is the reality, or inward reality of the sacrament. The inward reality is a seal and a safeguarding. The power of Baptism was initiated when Christ was baptised. The proper way to baptise is "Baptizing in the name of the Father, the Son and the Holy Ghost." This comes from Matthew 28:19: 'Going... teach all nations, baptizing them in the name of the Father, and of the Son, and of the Holy Spirit." Ephesians 5:26 also gives the implication of the same: "Cleansing the world by the cleaning laver of the water."

Jesus Christ authorised His disciples or followers to perform baptism. It is the Holy Spirit who takes an active part in the ministry of baptism. God the father accepts this through His Son Jesus Christ. We see here the power of baptism from which when a man comes forth, the gates of the heavenly kingdom are opened to him. Baptism has an equal effect in all. Ephesians 4:5 speaks of 'one Faith, one Baptism.' After one has reached the age of reason, it is necessary to receive baptism with sincerity. According to Augustine, if the Sacrament is received in bad faith, then one has a change of heart; the effects of baptism are salutary.

Eternal Life

Death and After-life

Christian anthropology has implications for beliefs about death and afterlife. The Christian church has traditionally taught that the soul of each individual separates from the body at death, to be reunited at the resurrection. This is closely related to the doctrine of the immortality of the soul. For example, the Westminster Confession (chapter XXXII) states: "The bodies of men, after death, return to dust, and see corruption: but their souls, which neither die nor sleep, having an immortal subsistence, immediately return to God who gave them." God is holy and as such must judge and punish that which is not perfect. At death, men are judged by God and are transformed to enter an existence with God or be forever separated from Him. These existences are generally known as heaven and hell.

Intermediate State

Where exactly does the disembodied soul 'go' at death? Christian philosophers refer to this subject as the intermediate state. The Old Testament speaks of a place called *sheol*, where the spirits of the dead reside. In the New Testament, *hades*, the classical Greek realm of the dead, takes the place of *sheol*. In particular, Jesus teaches in Luke 16:19-31 that *hades* consists of two separate 'sections', one for the righteous and one for the unrighteous. His teaching is consistent with intertestamental Jewish thought on the subject.

Roman Catholicism teaches a third possible location: Purgatory; it is denied by Protestants. Some Christian groups that stress a monistic anthropology deny that the soul can exist consciously apart from the body. For example, the Seventh-day Adventists teach that the intermediate state is an unconscious sleep; this teaching is informally known as 'soul sleep.'

Fully developed Christian theology goes a step further; on the basis of such texts as Luke 23:43 and Philippians 1:23, it has traditionally been taught that the souls of the dead are received immediately either into heaven or hell, where they will experience a foretaste of their eternal destiny prior to the resurrection. "The souls of the righteous, being then made perfect in holiness are received into the highest heavens, where they behold the face of God, in light and glory, waiting for the full redemption of their bodies. And the souls of the wicked are cast into hell, where they remain in torments and utter darkness, reserved to the judgment of the great day."[237]

Final State
Some Old Testament writers suggest that there will be eventually some final change when the wicked will be destroyed and the righteous will prosper (Ps.9:18; Jer.31:17). Many scholars draw our attention to two forms of hope, which are expressed in the Old Testament: The *prophetic hope and the apocalyptic hope*. The former is closely related to the coming events in the history of Israel and the latter is based on the belief that God will intervene in history by establishing his rule of righteousness (Isa. 47:1-5; Dan. 7:1-14).

   i. The biblical expectation of the future can be envisaged in two ways with regard to the change of this world: *The transformation of the present world* (Amos 9:13-f; Ezek. 47:12; 34:22; Isa. 65:17,20; Zech. 8:4) and *the establishment of a righteous community* (Zech. 8:7-9; 8:22; Isa. 66:18; 27:12-13).

   ii. The fulfilment of this expectation could be seen in two ways in connection with the works of God: *The Day of the Lord* (Isa. 24; 14; 2:3, 4; 12:5; Mic.4: 6,7; Joel 2:32; Hab. 2:14) and *the one who will come* (Duet.18:15-19; 34:10; Isa. 9:6-7; 11-1-5; Mic. 5:2-4; Zech.9:9-15).

In Christian belief, both the righteous and the unrighteous will be resurrected at the last judgment. The righteous will receive incorruptible, immortal bodies (1Cor. 15), while the unrighteous will be sent to hell. Traditionally, Christians have believed that hell will be a place of eternal, physical and psychological punishment. The terminology for hell is a lake of fire. Hell is an awful place of judgement. There are two types of people—either walk in the light and have eternal life or walk in the darkness and experience eternal death. Christians everywhere are motivated to share the good news of the Kingdom of God with all peoples everywhere.

Christian philosophy teaches the urgency of entering the Kingdom of God so that men and women are not lost, rather they are saved. Those who had been guaranteed with eternal salvation will enter the eternal Kingdom of God and dwell in the heaven with God forever.

Conclusion

Christian philosophy is a systematic enquiry of God with His relation to man and His universe. It is an outlook on life and a way to live. The centre of Christian philosophy is Christ and His cross. It is of course a stumbling block to the Jews and an outright foolishness to the Greeks. It is clearly revealed when we look at the dominant philosophies of the first century—Epicureanism and Stoicism, which always stood against pure Christian philosophy.

Religious philosophy itself is proof that one can relate philosophy with Christianity. Christianity is a religion and the philosophic study of Christian religion is religious philosophy. It is also called 'Christian philosophy.' It is the task of the Christian philosopher to so interpret the doctrines of scripture that they provide overarching parameters to contemporary Christian philosophy and penetrating insights into detailed specifics. It is the role of the Christian philosopher to attempt to show Christianity's power of interpretation to its followers and well-wishers.

We have already studied that there is a set of five proofs for the existence of God, It is known as the Pentacle Arguments for the existence of God. Pentacle Arguments consist of Textual Argument, Creational Argument, Revelational Argument, Logical Argument and Intuitional Argument. The first three are based on the Bible and the other two are related to reason and the mind. It is also understood that classical Christian philosophy is theological philosophy.

Jesus actually died on the cross and was buried in Joseph's tomb. Jesus bodily rose from the dead. On the basis of the historical reliability of the New Testament, we can be sure that we possess the essence of the teachings of Christ about himself. Also, we have seen that God was, is and will be supreme in God's Kingdom. We look at Jesus to whom the kingdom is a society upon earth where God's will is as perfectly done as it is in heaven. The presence of the Kingdom is to be understood from the nature of God's present activity and the future of Kingdom is the redemptive manifestation of his kingly rule at the end of the age. In this age, the Kingdom is known as 'Moral kingdom.' In the age to come, it is known as 'Spiritual kingdom.'

Helpful Questions

1. What is Christian philosophy? Describe its nature and basic assumptions.

2. What is the role of the Christian philosopher?

3. What do you know about Logical Metaphysics?

4. Write notes on Cosmological arguments, Pentacle arguments and Practical Community.

Conclusion

We were able to pass through various fields of philosophy in order to grasp true Christian philosophy by way of making a comparative study of secular philosophy and religious philosophy. Although much material was presented in connection with philosophy, the author personally has the belief in the full Gospel and always supports the evangelical perspective, not the liberal perspective of philosophy. The author fully accepts what the Bible says and always stands for full gospel truths. Different viewpoints of various philosophers are dealt with in this book. Secular philosophy utterly fails to make sense of man, the world, history and personal experience as a whole by refusing to accept anything but what its rationalistic premises will allow. On the other hand, the belief system presented by the Bible does make good sense. This is nothing but 'Christian Philosophy.'

The trend towards secularisation has continued with increasing momentum down to the present day. In the Middle Ages, Aquinas' scheme of thought left room for revelation, but by the Age of Enlightenment, the supernatural was banished from rational thought. 'Rationalism was now well developed and entrenched', and there was no concept of revelation in any area. Consequently, the problem was now defined, not in terms of 'nature and grace', but of 'nature and freedom' In Kant's deterministic universe, freedom is not a rational concept, but an idea posited by ethics. Rousseau sought freedom in the irrational. Already in their mechanistic world 'freedom makes no sense, and thus autonomous freedom and the autonomous machine stand facing each other.' The nineteenth century closed with a remarkable number of rival philosophies vying for the attention of modern man. Liberals tended to latch on to some form of Hegelianism or Kantianism. Both were in principle sub-Christian and even anti–Christian. Roman Catholics were officially encouraged to espouse Thomism as an antidote for skepticism. Conservative Protestants did great work in the field of biblical scholarship, but few, if any, saw the need for a positive approach to philosophy relating it to their biblical faith. The history of philosophy in the twentieth century shows painfully in what way the Christian church has inherited the legacy of the nineteenth century.

The Christian view of Revelation of God is revealing Himself in history and personal experience through events. Bible stories are all right and meant for the ignorant masses. They present a graphic way of teaching morality. But in the first analysis it is universal human reason, which is the supremely commanding principle. The Christian view of grace and salvation is replaced by an unbending religion of self-help. Knowledge of God arises out of encounter with God. It is mediated by the Son. But according to the New Testament, there can be no knowledge of God without the illuminating work of the Holy Spirit. Moreover, to make progress in the knowledge of God, it is not a matter of intellectual acuteness. The knowledge of God operates, as it were, on a different plane. What matters more is faith, love, humility and prayer. The knowledge of God is not something separate from the gospel of Jesus Christ. It is not something that man can arrive at just as he wishes by following certain subtle philosophical arguments. Knowledge of God is the result of encounter with God, which in turn is the result of encounter with Christ. Christ is the revealing Word of God to man.

God, who revealed Himself, is not an object of time and space. He is one who is 'Wholly Other', and therefore, strictly speaking, indescribable. And if this is really the case, there is nothing more to be said. God has revealed himself through scripture not only as the creator but also as the redeemer in Christ. In Scripture, God had spoken to man and revealed Himself in a special way, a way significant for all ages. The scheme of thought referred here is that of theism that defines as belief in 'a supreme Person, a self-existent subject of infinite goodness and power, who enters into a relationship with us comparable with that of one human personality with another.'

Man is shown as a sinner who has turned his back on God and who is blind to Him. It is not in man's power to know God as and when he pleases. Knowledge of God is a gift of God that comes through Christ. Man can do nothing to deserve it. He can only receive it in simple faith. These insights were not new. They have been shared by Christians down through the ages, especially those in Reformed, evangelical traditions. The Christian can never agree for a moment to a non-theistic interpretation of reality, and the naturalistic unbeliever of our generation finds it intellectually impossible to comprehend the supernatural and transcendent dimension of reality. This gap will grow wider until a Christian philosopher takes a step further to convince him through the effective presentation of the Christian philosophical teaching in the simplest form in the light of the word of God. When the light of the gospel enters the heart of people of other faiths, the true understanding of the teachings of Christianity will be made possible and the distance between the true God and the unbeliever will disappear.

The task of Christian philosophers is not to try to discover some neutral, common ground on which the believer and the unbeliever may both stand. The believer and the unbeliever are already aware of God's existence and his own responsibility before God. The task is to force him to face up to this and to show that there are no legitimate escape-routes. In other words, it is to lay bare the presuppositions of our thinking. In their attempts to grapple with the problems presented by *being*, the ways of a philosopher and the theologian tend to part at three points: (1) Whereas the philosopher tries to be detached as he looks at a structure of *being*, the theologian is 'existential'. He looks at *being* as one who is desperately involved—'with his self-contradictions and his despair, with the healing forces in him and his social situation. (2)There is also a difference of sources. The philosopher is concerned with the structure of reality as a whole; he seeks to grasp the *logos* or reason that permeates all being. The theologian looks not at *logos* in general, but at the *logos* who becomes flesh and is manifested in the life of the church. (3) Whereas the philosopher deals with the structures of *being* in general (time and space, etc.), the theologian is concerned with the human aspect of *being*, the personal problems of life.

As we saw when we were looking at theological trends in the nineteenth century, Evangelicals made great contributions to evangelism and even to biblical scholarship, but they contributed little or nothing to the philosophical defense of their faith. Few Evangelicals seem to have considered the philosophical implications of the faith-based upon God's revelation of him self and their significance for apologetics. Christianity is true, not because the evangelists and apostles taught it. On the contrary, they taught it because it is always true.

Conclusion

Philosophers have returned to many of the traditional claims of orthodox Christianity and have begun to apply the tools of contemporary philosophy in ways that are somewhat more eclectic than those described in the Thomistic model. In keeping with the recent academic trend, contemporary philosophers of religion have been unwilling to maintain hard and fast distinctions between the two disciplines. As a result, it is often difficult in reading recent work to distinguish what the philosophers are doing from what the theologians of past centuries regarded as strictly within the theological domain. However, like theologians of the medieval period, much recent work in philosophy of religion seems to fall into one of two categories. The first category includes attempts to demonstrate the truth of religious claims by appeal to evidence available apart from purported divine revelations. The second category includes attempts to demonstrate the consistency and plausibility of theological claims using philosophical techniques.

The centre of the Christian philosophy is Christ and His cross—stumbling blocks to the Jews and an outright foolishness to the Greeks. This is the very point of 1 Cor. 1:18-25. Why the gospel is foolishness to the Greek mind can be better understood by looking at the dominant philosophies of the first century. The philosophers with Paul on Mars Hill in Acts 17:18 is an example for this fact. The scripture does not support secular philosophy. The passage in Colossians (Col.2:8) is closely related to the rejection of Gnostic philosophy. Philosophy that begins only with temporal horizons and self-deduced wisdom can never know the eternal and infinite God (1Cor. 1:21). In regard to assumptions and content, Christianity is anti-philosophy as this verse makes abundantly clear or it is against secular philosophy. However, there is a Christian philosophy, an outlook on life and a way to live. This outlook is not discovered by man, but given to man. It is God-initiated through historical and propositional revelation, culminating in the revelation or uncovering of God Himself in Jesus Christ.

Some of the writers of the Bible knew or learned very well the then available philosophic teachings. Philosophy is usually defined as an examination of basic concepts, a system of thought, or a set of beliefs. The scripture gives us the impact of the revelation on the fallible minds and hearts of those who respond to or receive the revelation. Their utterances cannot be regarded as infallible. Theology is religious philosophy. Therefore, we can say that the Christian theologian is the religious philosopher. A philosopher is always trying to answer consistently the questions of everyday life. Theologians deal with Christian theology. Christian theology is religious philosophy. Therefore, a theologian is a philosopher. We have to develop a Christian philosophy that must support biblical teaching and stand contradictory to the unsound teachings of the heretics and secular philosophy. Secular philosophy or philosophy in general cannot be accepted as it is. It is the role of the Christian philosopher to reveal pure Christianity and stand against the non-Christian teachings of philosophy. The Christian philosopher has the responsibility to distinguish between Christ-centred philosophy and other philosophies. Christian philosophy is the philosophy that reveals pure Christianity to the non-Christian world. The Bible is the primary source book for Christian philosophy. A proper understanding of God's Word as it relates to our socio-cultural context is imperative. The Bible is the divine norm for both our God-ward and man-ward relationships. It can be best addressed as the 'Book of Philosophy.'

Endnotes

[1] Anand Amaldass, *The Role of the Philosopher Today*, p.8.
[2] Gregory D' Souza, *Culture, Inculture and Interculture*, p. 89.
[3] James Richmond, *Faith and Philosophy*, p. 11.
[4] *Ibid*, p. 11.
[5] S. Radhakrishnan, *Indian Philosophy*, p. 771.
[6] Josh McDowell, *Concise Guide to Today's Religions*, p.12
[7] *Religions*, ISPCK, p.2.
[8] Y. Masih, *Introduction to Religious Philosophy*, pp. 1-2.
[9] Sinclair B. Ferguson (Ed.), *New Dictionary of Theology*, p. 50.
[10] *Ibid*, p. 512.
[11] *Ibid*, p. 510.
[12] *Ibid.*, p. 28.
[13] Sinclair B. Ferguson, *New Dictionary of Theology*, p. 513.
[14] Webster, *New Collegiate Dictionary*.
[15] Gregory D' Souza, *Culture, Inculture and Interculture*, p. 232.
[16] Daya Krishna, *The Nature of Philosophy*, p. 4.
[17] W. J. Marshall, *Philosophy and Christian Faith*, p. 10.
[18] *Op. cit.*, p. 95.
[19] Daya Krishna, *The Nature of Philosophy*, p. 72.
[20] *Op.cit.*, p. 76.
[21] Sinclair B. Ferguson, *New Dictionary of Theology*, p. 8.
[22] Daya Krishna, *The Nature of Philosaphy*, p. 8.
[23] Anand Amaladass, *The Role of the Philosopher Today*, p. 34.
[24] *Op.cit.*, p. 101.

[25] W. J. Marshal, *Philosophy and the Christian Faith*, p. 2.
[26] *Ibid.*
[27] Ronald B. Mayers, *Balanced Apologetics*, p. 214.
[28] W. J. Marshall, *Philosophy and Christian Faith*, p. 8.
[29] Daya Krishna, *The Nature of Philosophy*, p. 3.
[30] Archana Banerjee, *Models of Metaphilosophy*, p. 75.
[31] *Ibid.*, p. 76.
[32] *Ibid.*, p. 78.
[33] Tony Lane, p. 76.
[34] Daya Krishna, *The Nature of Philosophy*, p. 235.
[35] Bimal Matilal , *Logical and Ethical Issues*, p. 54.
[36] Andand Amaladass, *The Role of the Philospher Today*, p. xviii.
[37] W. J. Marshal, *Philosophy and Christian Faith*, p. 6.
[38] Daya Krishna, *The Nature of Philosophy*, p. 323.
[39] James Richmond, *Faith and Philosophy*, p. 12.
[40] Anand Amaladas, *The Role of the Philosopher Today*, p. xiii.
[41] *Ibid.*, p. 13.
[42] *Ibid.*, p. 5.
[43] *Ibid.*, p. 12.
[44] Jean L. Mercier, *From Socrates to Wittgenstein*, p. 9.
[45] Daya Krishna, *The Nature of Philosophy*, p. 33.
[46] Jean L. Mercier, p. 10.
[47] *Ibid.*, p. 11.
[48] Daya Krishna, *The Nature of Philosophy*, p. 33.
[49] *Ibid.*, p. 13.
[50] *Ibid.*, pp. 14-15.
[51] *Ibid.*, pp. 17-20.
[52] Daya Krishna, *The Nature of Philosophy*, p .62.
[53] *Ibid.*, p. 61.
[54] Daya Krishna, *The Nature of Philosophy*, p. 73.
[55] Tony Lane, *The Lion Book of Christian Thought*, p. 11.
[56] *Ibid.*, p. 21.
[57] *Ibid.*, pp. 21-24.
[58] Ronald B. Mayers, *Balanced Apologetics*, p. 11.
[59] Jean L. Mercier, pp. 27-28.

60 Jean L. Mercier, p. 30.
61 Jean L. Mercier, pp. 29-31.
62 Tony Lane, *The Lion Book of Christian Thought*, p. 11.
63 *New Dictionary of Theology*, p. 43.
64 Israel Selvanayagam, *Biblical Insights on Inter-Faith Dialogue*, p. 18.
65 Ronald B. Mayers, *Balanced Apologetics*, p. 78.
66 *Ibid.*, p. 139.
67 Tony Lane, *The Lion Book of Christian Thought*, p. 10.
68 *Op.cit.*, p. 186.
69 *Op.cit.*, p.14.
70 Jean L. Mercier, *From Socrates to Wittgenstein*, p. 34.
71 *Op.cit.*, p. 15.
72 *Ibid.*, p. 15.
73 Ronald B. Mayers, *Balanced Apologetics*, p. 193.
74 Tony Lane, *A Lion Book of Christian Thought*, p. 16.
75 *New Dictionary of Theology*, p. 148.
76 *Op.cit.*, p. 20.
77 *Ibid.*, p. 21.
78 Jean L. Mercier, *From Socrates to Wittgenstein*, p. 34.
79 Tony Lane, *op.cit.*, p. 21.
80 *Ibid.*, p. 22.
81 Leornado, Fernando, *Christian Faith Meets Other Faiths*, p. 238.
82 Jean L. Mercier, *From Socrates to Wittgenstein*, p. 33.
83 *Op.cit.*, p. 15.
84 Tony Lane, *A Lion Book of Christian Thought*, p. 41.
85 Jean L. Mercier, *From Socrates to Wittgenstein*, p. 35.
86 *Ibid.*, p. 38.
87 *Ibid.*, p. 37.
88 Jean L. Mercier, *From Socrates to Wittgenstein*, p. 37.
89 Tony Lane, *A Lion Book of Christian Thought*, p. 41.
90 *Op.cit.*, p. 38.
91 *Op.cit.*, p. 87.
92 Colin Brown, *Philosophy and the Christian Faith*, p. 20.
93 *New Dictionary of Theology*, p. 27.
94 Colin Brown, *Philosophy and the Christian Faith*, p. 24.

95 *Ibid.*
96 Tony Lane, *A Lion Book of Christian Thought*, p. 100.
97 Jeans Mercier, *From Socrates to Wittgenstein*, pp. 40-41.
98 Tony Lane, *A Lion Book of Christian Thought*, p. 101.
99 *Ibid.*, p. 101.
100 Tony Lane, *A Lion Book of Christian Thought*, p. 101.
101 Jean L. Mercier, *From Socrates to Wittgenstein*, p. 42.
102 Tony Lane, *A Lion Book of Christian Thought*, p. 103.
103 Jean L. Mercier, *From Socrates to Wittgenstein*, p. 45.
104 Tony Lane, *The Lion Book of Christian Thought*, p. 104.
105 *Op. cit.*, p. 105.
106 *Ibid.*
107 *Op. cit.*, p.106.
108 *Ibid.*
109 Tony Lane, *A Lion Book of Christian Thought*, p. 124.
110 *Ibid.*, p. 126.
111 *Ibid.*, p. 127.
112 Collin Brown, *Philosophy and Christian Faith*, p. 40.
113 *Ibid.*, p. 43.
114 Radhakrishnan, *Eastern Religions and Western Thought*, p. 15.
115 Collin Brown, *Philosophy and Christian Faith*, p. 41.
116 Tony Lane, *The Lion Book of Christian Thought*, pp. 137-139.
117 Colin Brown, *Philosophy and the Christian Faith*, p. 41.
118 *Ibid.*, p. 43.
119 *New Dictionary of Theology*, p. 120.
120 *Ibid.*, p. 124.
121 Sinclair B. Ferguson, *New Dictionary of Theology*, p. 206.
122 Tony Lane, p. 121.
123 Colin Brown, *Philosophy and the Christian Faith*, p. 48.
124 *Ibid.*
125 *New Dictionary of Theology*, p. 193.
126 Jean L. Mercier, *From Socrates to Wittgenstein*, p. 48.
127 *New Dictionary of Theology*, p. 193.
128 Colin Brown, p. 52.
129 *Ibid.*, p. 50.

130 Norman L. Geisler, p. 41.
131 Daya Krishna, *The Nature of Philosophy*, p. 62.
132 James Richmond, *Faith and Philosophy*, p. 47.
133 Colin Brown, p. 60.
134 *Ibid.*, p. 63.
135 Colin Brown, *Philosophy and the Christian Faith*, p. 64.
136 Debiprasad Chattopadhyaya, *Philosophy from Bacon to Marx*, p. 95.
137 *Ibid.*, p. 117.
138 Debiprasad Chattopadhyaya, *Philosophy from Bacon to Marx*, p. 103.
139 Colin Brown, *Philosophy and the Christian Faith*, p. 102.
140 James Richmond, *Faith and Philosophy*, p. 41.
141 Daya Krishna, *The Nature of Philosophy*, p. 47.
142 Colin Brown, *Philosophy and the Christian Faith*, p. 91.
143 Colin Brown, *Philosophy and the Christian Faith*, p. 95.
144 *Ibid.*, p. 119.
145 S. P. Banerjee, p. 1.
146 Daya Krishna, *The Nature of Philosophy*, p. 43.
147 Jean Mercier, p. 71.
148 Colin Brown, *Philosophy and the Christian Faith*, p. 181.
149 *Ibid.*, p. 125.
150 Jean Mercier, p. 131.
151 James Richmond, *Faith and Philosophy*, p. 163.
152 Young-Ho Chun, *Tillich and Religion*, p. 14.
153 Jean Mercier, p. 104.
154 Colin Brown, *Philosophy and the Christian Faith*, p. 145.
155 Banerjee, S.P., *Philosophy in Europe After Hegel*, p. 51.
156 Jean Mercier, p. 87.
157 Collin Brown, *Philosophy and Christian Faith*, p. 145.
158 *Ibid.*, p. 146.
159 Norman L. Geisler, p. 112.
160 *Ibid.*, p. 113.
161 Daya Krishna, *The Nature of Philosophy*, p.73.
162 Colin Brown, *Philosophy and the Christian Faith*, p. 227.
163 Archana Banerjee, *Models of Metaphilosophy*, p.113.
164 *Ibid.*, p. 222.

[165] Archana Banerjee, *Models of Metaphilosophy*, p. 95.
[166] Jean Mercier, pp. 117-123.
[167] Tony Lane, *The Lion Book of Christian Thought*, p. 238.
[168] *Ibid*.
[169] *Ibid*, p. 239.
[170] Ken Ganakan, *Proclaiming Christ in a Pluralistic Context*, p. 35.
[171] Martin Goldsmith, *What about Other Faiths?* p. 123.
[172] Kaiser, Robert Blair, *Catholic New Time*, July 1, 2001.
[173] Aloysius Pieris, *An Asian Theology of Liberation*, p. 52.
[174] James Richmond, *Faith and Philosophy*, p. 55.
[175] Tony Lane, *The Lion Book of Christian Thought*, p. 183.
[176] Colin Brown, *Philosophy and the Christian Faith*, p. 111.
[177] *Ibid.*, p. 114.
[178] *Ibid.*, p. 185.
[179] *Ibid.*, p. 186.
[180] Ken, Gnanakan (Ed.), *Salvation—Some Asian Perspectives*, p. 25.
[181] Sunand Sumithra: *Revolution as Revelation: A Study of M. M. Thomas' Theology*.
[182] John Mbiti, *African Religions and Philosophy*, p. 10.
[183] *Op.cit*, p. 247.
[184] *Ibid.*, p. 138.
[185] Sinclair B. Ferguson (Ed.), *New Dictionary of Theology*, p. 76.
[186] *Ibid.*, p. 252.
[187] Sinclair B. Ferguson (Ed.), *New Dictionary of Theology*, p. 77.
[188] *Op.cit.*, p. 253.
[189] Sinclair B. Ferguson (Ed.), *New Dictionary of Theology*, p. 76.
[190] Collin Brown, *Philosophy and Christian Faith*, p. 303.
[191] Tony Lane, *A Lion Book of Christian Thought*, p. 207.
[192] Sinclair B. Ferguson, *New Dictionary of Theology*, p. 108.
[193] *Ibid.*, p. 209.
[194] *Ibid.*, p. 191.
[195] *Ibid.*, p. 192.
[196] Collin Brown, *Philosophy and Christian Faith*, p. 260.
[197] *Ibid.*, p. 262.
[198] Ken, Gnanakan, *Salvation—Some Asian Perspectives*, pp. 17-18.

[199] Bong Rin Ro, *The Bible and Theology in Asian Contexts*, p. 74.
[200] *Ibid.*
[201] Ken, Gnanakan, *Salvation—Some Asian Perspectives*, p. 17.
[202] Gregory D, Souza, *Culture, Inculture and Interculture*, p. 54.
[203] Sinclair B. Ferguson, *New Dictionary of Theology*, p. 517.
[204] *Ibid.*, p. 517.
[205] Ken Gnanakan, *Proclaiming Christ in a Pluralistic Context*, p. 21.
[206] Ken Gnanakan, *Proclaiming Christ in a Pluralistic Context*, p. 8.
[207] *Ibid.*, p. 41.
[208] *Ibid.*, p. 55.
[209] *Ibid.*, p. 48.
[210] Ken Gnanakan, *Kingdom Concern*, p. 63.
[211] *Ibid.*, p. 74.
[212] *Ibid.*, pp.177-180.
[213] Jean L. Mercier, *From Socrates to Wittgenstein*, p. 33.
[214] Colin Brown, *Philosophy and the Christian Faith*, p. 19.
[215] *Ibid.*, p. 13.
[216] Colin Brown, *Philosophy and the Christian Faith*, p. 35.
[217] *Ibid.*, p. 125.
[218] James Richmond, *Faith and Philosophy*, p. 47.
[219] W. J. Marshall, *Philosophy and Christian Faith*, p. 13.
[220] Tony Lane, *The Lion Book of Christian Thought*, p. 88.
[221] Ronald B. Mayers, *Balanced Apologetics*, p. 16.
[222] W. J. Marshall, *Philosophy and Christian Faith*, p. 21.
[223] *Ibid.*, p. 23.
[224] Jean L. Mercier, *From Socrates to Wittgenstein*, p. 42.
[225] Ronald Mayers, *Balanced Apologetics*, p. 16.
[226] Colin Brown, *Philosophy and the Christian Faith*, p. 26.
[227] W. J. Marshall, *Philosophy and Christian Faith*, pp. 25-26
[228] *Ibid.*, p. 26.
[229] Colin Brown, p. 28.
[230] W. J. Marshall, *Philosophy and the Christian Faith*, p. 27.
[231] *Ibid.*, p. 29.
[232] Bouvert Regulas, *The Kingdom of God*, p. 5.
[233] *Ibid.*

[234] *Ibid.*, p. 119.
[235] David Burnett, *Clash of Worlds*, p. 216.
[236] Sinclair B. Ferguson (Ed.), New Dictionary of Theology, p.141.
[237] *Westminster Confession.*

Bibliography

Books

Amaldass, Anand (Ed.): *The Role of Philosopher Today* (Madras, T. R. Publications, 1994).

Anderson, Sir Norman: *Christianity and World Religions* (Illinois, Intervarsity Press, 1984).

Ango, Samuel Peni (Ed.): *Principles and Dynamics of Integrated Christian Teaching and Learning* (Bangalore, Theological Book Trust, 2011).

Banarjee, Archana: *Models of Metaphilosophy* (India, Minerva, 1989).

Banerjee, S. P.: *Philosophy in Europe After Hegel* (Bangalore, Navakarnataka, 1991)

Belvakar, S. K. & R. D. Rande: *History of Indian Philosophy* (New Delhi, Munshiram Manoharlal Publishers, 1997).

Bhattacharya, Gopinath: *Essays in Analytical Philosophy* (Calcutta, Sanskrit Pustak Bandar, 1989).

Bhattacharya D. P.: *Philosophy of Science, Phenomenology and Other Essays.*

Bilimoria, Purushotthama: *Contemporary Philosophy and J. L. Shaw* (Kolkota, Punthi Pustak, 2006).

Boyd, Robin: *Indian Christian Theology* (Delhi, ISPCK, 1991).

Brown, Colin: *Philosophy and the Christian Faith* (Illinois, Intervarsity Press, 1968).

Brown, David: *The Divine Trinity* (LaSalle, Illinois: Open Court, 1985).

Burnett, David: *Clash of Worlds* (Eastbourne, MARC, 1990).

Chattopadhyaya, Debiprasad: *Indian Philosophy* (New Delhi, People's Publishing House, 1986).

Chattopadhyaya, Debiprasad: *Philosophy From Bacon to Marx* (Navakarnataka, Bangalore, 1991).

Chattopadhyaya, D.P.: *Philosophy of Science, Phenomenology and Other Essays* (New Delhi, Indian Council of Philosophical Research, 2003).

Chun, Young-Ho: *Tillich and Religion* (1998).

D'Souza, Gregaory: *Interculturality of Philosophy and Religion* (Bangalore, NBCL Centre, 1996).

Durant, Will: *The Story of Philosophy* (Washington Square Press, New York, 1953).

Dutta R.: *Philosophy in Ancient Greece* (Bangalore, Navakaranataka Publications, 1990).

Ferguson, Sinclair B. (Ed.): *New Dictionary of Theology* (England, Intervarsity Press, 1988).

Fernando, Leornado: *Christian Faith Meets Other Faiths* (Delhi, ISPCK, 1998).

Geisler, Norman N.: *Christian Apologetics* (Secunderabad, OM Books, 2002).

Gnanakan, Ken: *The Pluralistic Predicament,* (Bangalore, Theological Book Trust, 1992).

Gannakan, Ken: *Proclaiming Christ in a Pluralistic Context* (Bangalore, Theological Book trust, 2000).

Gnanakan, Ken: *Kingdom Concerns* (Bangalore, TBT, 1989).

Gnanakan, Ken (Ed.): *Salvation—Some Asian Perspectives* (Bangalore, ATA, 1992).

Goldsmith, Martin: *What About Other Faiths?* (London, Hodder & Saoughton,1989).

Hegel, G.W.F.: *The Philosophy of History.*

Hiriyanna, M.: *Outlines of Indian Philosophy,* (Motilal Banarsidass Publishers, Delhi, 1994).

Jevons, Frank Byron: *The History of Religion* (Orient Publications, Delhi,1985).

Krishna, Daya: *The Nature of Philosophy* (Delhi, Indian Council of Philosophical Research, 2009).

Lane, Tony: *The Lion Book of Christian Thought* (England, A Lion Paperback, 1992).

Marshall, W.J.: *Philosophy and the Christian Faith* (Madras, C. L. S., 1972).

Masih, Y: *Introduction to Religious Philosophy* (Delhi, Motilal Banarsidass Publishers, 1991).

Matilal, Bimal Krishna: *Logical and Ethical Issues* (New Delhi, Chronicle Books, 2004).

Mayers, Ronald B.: *Balanced Apologetics* (Secunderabad, OM Books, 2000).

McDowell, Josh: *Evidence that Demands a Verdict* (Nashville, Thomas Nelson Publishers, 1979).

McDowell, Josh & Don Stewart: *Concise Guide to Today's Religions* (England, Scripture Press, 1990).

Mercier, Jean L.: *From Socrates to Wittgenstein* (India, Asian Trading Corporation, 2002).

Mondin, Battista: *Philosophical Anthropology* (Bangalore, Theological Publications in India, 2004).

Murthi, K. Satchidananda: *Philosophy in India* (New Delhi, Indian Council of Research, 1985).

Newbigin, Lesslie: *The Gospel in a Pluralist Society* (William B. Eerdmans Publishing Company, Michigan, 1989).

Nihinlola, Emiola: *Integrating Theology and Pastoral Ministry in Africa* (Bangalore, Theological Book Trust, 2011).

Passmore, John: *A Hundred Years of Philosophy* (England, Penguin Books, 1966).

Pieris, Aloysius: *An Asian Theology of Liberation.*

Pirouet, Louise: *Christianity Worldwide* (Delhi, ISPCK, 1989).

Radhakrishnan, S.: *Eastern Religions and Western Thought* (New York, Oxford University Press, 1993).

Puthanangadi, Paul: *Popular Devotions in India* (Bangalore, NBCLC, 1986).

Radhakrishnan, S.: *Indian Philosophy* (New York, Oxford University Press, 1999).

Rajasekhar, VT: *Dalits: The Black Untouchables of India.*

Regulas, Bouvert: *The Kingdom of God*, (Kerala, India, Regulas Publications, 1992).

Richmond, James: *Faith and Philosophy* (London, Hoddon and Stoughton, 1966).

Ro, Bong Rin: *The Bible and Theology in Asian Contexts* (Bangalore, ATA, 1884).

Selvanayagam, Israel: *Biblical Insights on Inter-faith Dialogue* (Bangalore, BTESSC).

Shah, Ashwin J: *Glimpses of World Religions* (Jaico Publishing House, 1957).

Sharma, Chandradhar: *Indian Philosophy—A Critical Survey* (London, Barnes and Nobles, Inc., 1962).

Sumithra, Sunand: *Doing Theology in Context* (Bangalore, Theological Book Trust, 1992).

Tenney, Merrill C., *Pictorial Bible Dictionary* (Michigan, Zondervan Publishing House, 1967).

Periodicals

Bowers, Paul: "Evangelical Theology in Africa: Byang Kato's Legacy", *Trinity Journal*-1 (1980).

Eleonore, Stump, *Truth Journal*, "Modern Biblical Scholarship, Philosophy of Religion and Traditional Christianity".

Kaiser, Robert Blair: *East Meets West: The Journey of Aloysius Pieris*, (Catholic New Time, July 01, 2001).

Mukharjee, Satis Chandra: *The Dawn-Vol.3* (Bengal, National Council of Education, 1899).

Unpublished Documents

Baldwin, John T: *The Bible and the Philosophy of Science* (Silver Spring, USA, 2000).

Basu, Ananyo: *Essay* (University of Massachusetts, Boston).

Bowers, Paul: *Byang Kato's Evangelical Theology in Africa.*

Evans, Robert: *An evangelical world-view philosophy.*

Kato, Byang: *Theological Pitfalls in Africa* (1975).

Kuhn, Thomas: *The Structure of Scientific Revolutions.*

Oruka, Odera H: *The future of philosophical research in Africa* (Nairobi University1996).

Sumithra, Sunand: *Revolution as Revelation: A Study of M. M. Thomas's Theology* (New Delhi: T.R.C.I., 1984).